CU00684116

The Locomotive
Pioneers

'There has sprung into existence in a few years, a piece of human workmanship of the most stupendous kind; which, when considered with respect to its scientific character, magnitude, and mechanical contrivance, eclipses all former works of art. Compared to it, how shabby a structure would be the celebrated Roman wall, or even the more extensive one of the Chinese; as for the Egyptian pyramids, they, so far from being fit to be mentioned in comparison with the railway, are merely the uncouth monuments of the ignorance and superstition of their founders.'

Guide to the London & Birmingham Railway 1840

The Locomotive Pioneers

Anthony Burton

PEN & SWORD
TRANSPORT

First published in Great Britain in 2017 by
Pen & Sword Transport
an imprint of
Pen & Sword Books Ltd
47 Church Street
Barnsley
South Yorkshire
S70 2AS

ISBN 978 1 47384 368 4

Typeset in Ehrhardt by
Mac Style Ltd, Bridlington, East Yorkshire
Printed and bound by Replika Press

Pen & Sword Books Ltd incorporates the imprints of Pen & Sword Archaeology,
Atlas, Aviation, Battleground, Discovery, Family History, History, Maritime,
Military, Naval, Politics, Railways, Select, Transport, True Crime, and Fiction,
Frontline Books, Leo Cooper, Praetorian Press, Seaforth Publishing and Wharncliffe.

For a complete list of Pen & Sword titles please contact
PEN & SWORD BOOKS LIMITED
47 Church Street, Barnsley, South Yorkshire, S70 2AS, England
E-mail: enquiries@pen-and-sword.co.uk
Website: www.pen-and-sword.co.uk

Contents

Acknowledgements

The author would like to thank Michael Bailey for permission to quote from his article on the Planet replica and the following for permission to use illustrations. Where no acknowledgement is given the illustrations are either from the author's own collection or taken from out of copyright documents and books.

Baltimore & Ohio Railroad Museum, 131; Best friend of Charleston Museum, 94; Ben Brookshaw, 111; Birmingham Museum & Art Gallery, 8; Canterbury Heritage Museum, CFV3V Mariemborg, 98, 100; Cité du Train, 139, 144; City & Council of Swansea, Museum Collection, 39; Darlington Railway Museum, 53; DB Museum von Verkhermuseum, Nurmberg, 104, 147; Ffestiniog Railway, 153; Gil Scott, 14; Franklin Institute, Philadelphia, 129; John Minnis, 17; Mansell Collection, 34; Martin Bell, 67; Museo Nationale Ferroviano, 138; Museum of Science & Industry, Chicago, 85; Museum of Science & Industry, Manchester, 80; North of England Open Air Museum, Beamish, 26, 48; Nova Scotia Museum of Industry, 96; Science & Society, 65, 66, 107, 161, 182; Simon Cook, 21; Smithsonian Institute, 179; Steam Museum, Straffan, 10; Steam, Swindon, 162, 172 (bottom); Swindon Borough Council, 159; Trevithick Society, 11; Trustees of the National Museum of Scotland, 27; University of Atacama, 130.

Preface

My interest in early locomotives, as opposed to railway history in general, was first aroused when I was invited to write and present the BBC TV series *The Past at Work*. Although the series was about the remains of the Industrial Revolution and we had set ourselves a terminal date of 1825, it did provide an opportunity to look at two iconic railways: the Middleton Colliery, the world's first successful commercial line and the Stockton & Darlington. Shortly afterwards I was again working with BBC TV, this time on *The Rainhill Story*, in which we followed the construction of the replicas of the three engines that took part in the original trials. I can vividly remember the excitement of being present when a fire was lit in a boiler for the first time, and the splendid replica steamed off or – in the case of *Novelty* – tottered off. My next major involvement came when I decided to write a biography of Richard Trevithick and once again became involved with seeing working replicas come to life. There was an exciting, if bone-shaking ride on the 1801 road locomotive and a rather more dignified journey in the astonishing London road carriage, where I shared the experience with Frank Trevithick Okuno, a direct descendant of the great man. Best moment of all came when I was invited onto the footplate of the replica of the 1803 engine at the Ironbridge Gorge Open Air Museum and was invited to drive, though, to be honest, I did nothing more than open and close the regulator but that made it none the less thrilling.

These varied experiences gave me a new appreciation of just how inventive the early engineers were, who had to devise these engines for themselves with no precedents to work on. It also showed me how well they had done their work, for each of these engines from Trevithick's first attempt right up to *Rocket* a quarter of a century later, impressed by their mechanical ingenuity and by their performance. So when I was invited to write this book, there was no hesitation. I am grateful to John Scott Morgan for issuing the invitation and for his help and encouragement, not least for his assistance in providing many of the illustrations. Needless to say, any errors that readers find are entirely my own. I should also like to say a special thank you to Michael Bailey, firstly for allowing me to quote him at length on the working of the *Planet* replica. His own book *Loco Motion* appeared shortly after I started my research, and it proved invaluable for the technical details it listed on early, surviving locomotives.

Finally, a word about units: I have used the units in use at the time, rather than their modern equivalents. A British engineer, for example, would never have designed a locomotive with a 38.1 cm diameter cylinder, but he would have taken a great deal of care to make sure it was manufactured as close to 15 inches as possible.

Chapter One

Before the Railways Came

The work of the men who designed and built the world's first locomotives represents a quite extraordinary achievement. To understand just how significant it really was, one has to look at the transport situation in Britain at the dawn of the railway age. The latter part of the eighteenth century had seen a revolution in transport, with the development of the canal system. It was, at the time, the most efficient and cheapest way of moving goods from place to place. Experiments carried out by two of the leading engineers of the day, John Smeaton and Thomas Telford, compared the loads that could be moved by a single horse. The best results for a waggon on one of the new, surfaced roads was two tons, whereas on a canal the horse could pull a load of fifty tons – though in practice, the narrow boats in use on much of the system could only hold around twenty-five tons. It is easy to see why the canal engineers felt that they had achieved a massive improvement in the transport of goods and saw no reason to look for other solutions. Telford was to go so far as to argue that the only point of railways was to bring goods down to canals and rivers. Canals, however, had very little impact on passenger travel, which still relied almost entirely on stage-coaches. Thanks to road improvements, journey times had been cut drastically from those of the mid-eighteenth century. Telford had overseen the reconstruction of the London-Holyhead road, work that included the building of the two great suspension bridges at Conway and the Menai Straits. As a result, the fast mail service on the 261 mile route was set at 26 hours and 55 minutes and that included 27 stops to change horses and just one 40-minute meal break. It was the ultimate in travel by horse-drawn vehicles. It represented, however, only the very best that stage-coach travel could offer: ordinary stage-coaches moved at a more leisurely pace. The experience of stage-coach travel was to be undergone rather than enjoyed. Travellers could either pay top fares to sit inside or travel more cheaply on top, out in the open with no protection from the weather. Even inside travel was rarely comfortable. In the more cramped carriages, passengers sat bolt upright, three to a seat, elbows jostling and knees almost touching the three sets of knees opposite. Doctor William Kitchiner, writing as late as 1827 in his book *The Traveller's Oracle* gave this advice to outside passengers:

'If circumstances compel you to ride on the outside of a Coach, put on Two Shirts and Two Pairs of Stockings, turn up the collar of your Great Coat and tie an handkerchief round it, and have plenty of dry Straw to set your feet on.'

This was probably sound advice that had not been taken by two outside passengers on the London to Bath coach in 1812 who, when the coach stopped at Chippenham, were found to have frozen to death. We have become used to seeing jolly scenes on Christmas cards of merry travellers at coaching inns keenly looking forward to the excitement of the journey. Reality was a good deal less romantic. At the peak of the coaching age, there were some 4,000 coaches in regular service in Britain. Considering that the largest coaches could only carry six inside passengers and ten outside, it is obvious that travel was strictly limited by both the high cost and the number of vehicles. But just to keep this service running required 150,000 horses, and it is difficult to see how major changes could ever occur – there was simply not enough capacity to keep and feed more animals. It was a system that would either stagnate or be transformed by a totally different transport system. There was, however, a hint of a new solution in those experiments by Smeaton and Telford mentioned earlier. The largest load that could be drawn by a single horse on land was only possible if the waggon ran on iron rails, when it rose from two tons on an ordinary road to eight tons. It was a system widely used on the tramways that acted as feeders for canals and rivers. These were designed to be worked by horses, and to allow space for the animals to walk, the cast iron rails were mounted on square, stone sleeper blocks. Steam engines were in use on some, but these were massive stationary engines, used for haulage up and down steep inclines. It was on just such a tramway that the very first railway locomotives were to run, as we shall see in the next chapter.

By the end of the eighteenth century Britain was already well into that great technological upheaval known as the Industrial Revolution. This was the new technological age, in which work that had once been carried out in homes and small workshops had moved to factories

Typical coal waggons or chaldrons of the north eastern tramways at the Beamish Open Air Museum.

and mills thanks to the development of machines. Yet very little that had been achieved was due to the work of academically trained scientists and engineers. Compared with other countries, particularly France, Britain had virtually nothing to offer in the way of formal training in any branch of technology. James Sims expressed the situation perfectly in his book, *The Mining Almanack for 1849*:

> 'Amongst all the heroes and all the statesmen that have ever yet lived none have ever accomplished anything of such vast importance to the world as large as have been realised by a few simple mechanics.'

This was initially true to a certain extent of the men who designed and built the first locomotives. None of them came from an academic background nor had they any scientific education – but then neither did most 'educated' gentlemen in Britain. The first engineers were practical men dealing with practical problems on a day-to-day basis. They had few

Stage coach travel has always had a rather romantic image, but as this illustration by the eighteenth century artist W. H. Pyne shows it was far from comfortable for many passengers, and four horses were needed to move fewer than a dozen people.

specialist tools to rely on and knew little, if anything, of theory. Yet in just a few years they transformed the world of transport. This book tells the story of these men, some of whom have become famous and others, who made vital contributions, have been largely forgotten. And although it is customary to speak of such-and-such an engineer as having built a particular locomotive, that does not, of course, mean that they personally machined the parts and assembled them. That was the job of some highly skilled mechanics who should also be honoured among the list of locomotive pioneers; as should those who designed the increasingly sophisticated machine tools that made the whole process possible.

The story of the birth and development of the railway locomotive is also the tale of the lingering demise of the stage-coach, and an anonymous Victorian author wrote this obituary:

'Died after a long and protracted existence, the near leader of the "Red Rover", the last of the London and Southampton coaches. The symptoms of decay, which ended in the event we now record, set in on the day the South Western Railway opened, the severe grief produced by which brought on an affection of the heart, which upon a frame not of the strongest, induced the calamity, so much deplored by the inconsolable proprietors'

Chapter Two

Steam on the Move

The first practical steam engines were developed to pump water from mines, and the most successful of these was the machine invented by Thomas Newcomen at the beginning of the eighteenth century. It was a beam engine, in which the pump rods were attached to one end of an overhead beam and their weight automatically dragged that end down. What was needed was a force that could be applied to the opposite end of the beam to pull that end down and thus raise up the pump rods. In Newcomen's engine this was achieved by means of passing steam into a cylinder fitted with a piston attached to the beam by a chain, then spraying the cylinder with cold water to condense the steam. This created a partial vacuum and air pressure would force the piston down. It did the job but was very inefficient. It was James Watt who recognised that the problem was caused by the constant repetition of heating and cooling the cylinder. His solution was to condense the steam in a separate vessel, so that the cylinder could be kept permanently hot. There was still a difficulty with heat loss from the open topped cylinder, and he dealt with this by closing the top and replacing air pressure with steam pressure. The atmospheric engine had become a genuine steam engine.

The first engines built by the company formed by Watt and the Birmingham industrialist Matthew Boulton, were single acting. As the connection between piston and beam was still by means of a chain, the piston could only pull down, not push up. It was Boulton who urged Watt to find some means of making a double-acting engine that could be used for a far greater variety of tasks. The difficulty was caused by the fact that the piston needed to go straight up and down in the cylinder, but a straight connection to the end of a beam moving through the arc of a circle made this impossible. Watt came up with what he always referred to as his greatest invention: the parallel motion. In effect, the piston was now suspended from a parallelogram of shifting rods. The device was first produced in 1784 and was soon being applied to produce rotative engines that could be used to turn the wheels and shafts that would power the machinery in mills and factories.

Watt had a patent that lasted until the end of the eighteenth century and effectively prevented anyone else from experimenting with steam engines, at least in theory, though a number of 'steam pirates' tried to get away with inventing new engines of their own. It was not just the all-embracing patent that discouraged innovation, but Watt himself had very firm views on how a steam engine should be operated. To him, high-pressure steam was anathema: if you wanted more power then you simply built a bigger engine. That was fine in some respects, but it ruled out any possibility of using the engine in the world of transport. There was no way a massive beam engine, weighing several tons and standing twenty feet or more high, was about to go trundling off down the road. But Watt's writ did not run in France, and there a former army officer had different ideas.

Nicolas Joseph Cugnot had fought throughout the Seven Years War and when he retired from the army in 1763 he began to think of how steam power could be used in warfare. Moving artillery had always required a team of horses and skilled handlers and he felt that the job would be more efficiently performed using a steam tractor. He built a prototype in 1769 and followed it up with a more refined version a year later, and the original machine is still preserved in the Musée des Arts et Métiers in Paris. It was a cumbersome affair, mounted on three wheels with a massive copper boiler overhanging the single front wheel, supplying steam to two cylinders mounted to either side. It was successful in that it proved capable of towing a load of five tonnes at a brisk walking pace, but it could not keep going: it had to be stopped at regular intervals and allowed to cool down so that the boiler could be refilled. It had no brakes and proved difficult to steer, hardly surprising since the steering was through the front wheel, overhung by the heavy boiler. A probably apocryphal story has it that on one of the inaugural runs it got out of control and demolished a brick wall, at which point the authorities banned it from the streets. It was never developed; the project was simply abandoned and it is doubtful if many people outside French military circles ever heard about it. It certainly seems unlikely that the news ever reached England where the next development of steam power on the road was to take place.

The Boulton & Watt steam engine had been a great success in the tin and copper mines of Cornwall. The powerful pumps enabled miners to go to ever-greater depths to recover valuable ore deposits, and the improved efficiency over the previous Newcomen engines was of huge significance in a region where coal had to be imported from other areas such as South Wales. But the Cornish mine engineers were a very independent minded body of men. They were used to making their own decisions and working on their own new developments. They had earlier found ways of improving the efficiency of the atmospheric engines, but now they were prevented by the patent from even considering improvements to the Boulton & Watt engines. This rankled and several local men began working on new ideas. Among them was a young engineer called Richard Trevithick. Born in 1771, he was fascinated by steam from an early age – and his father, Richard Trevithick Snr., was one of those who had improved early engines. The son followed the same career as his father, becoming a mine captain, the chief engineer at the mine, while still in his twenties.

Even as a child he showed his impetuous nature; when he was told off by his teacher for not showing how he had arrived at the answer to the sums he'd been told to do, he simply pointed out that he didn't need to and could do six sums while his teacher did one. It might have been true, but hardly endeared him to the school, which might explain the school report that described him, among other things, as 'inattentive' and 'frequently absent'. The absence was easily explained – he was more interested in spending his time around the machinery at the local mine, puzzling out how everything worked. The report also mentioned his obstinacy, which was certainly a trait of his character which, combined with a rather short temper, was to be a factor in many of his dealings with others. This was exemplified later in his career, when he had devised a new way of salvaging sunken vessels, by attaching iron tanks that were then pumped full of air. He used it successfully to lift a vessel at Margate, but when it was raised the owners demanded that he also had it towed to harbour before they would pay.

Trevithick pointed out that he had only been contracted to raise the vessel and he'd need an extra payment for arranging the tow; the owners refused. Trevithick ordered his men to cut off the tanks and the vessel subsided back to the seabed. It was a typically quixotic gesture, which made a point, but lost him his fee. He was not always able to see where his own best interests lay. And from the first, he was always one to go his own way, regardless of opposition.

The family had several legal tussles with Boulton & Watt. In particular, Trevithick had worked with another engineer, Edward Bull, in developing a pumping engine that was worked on a different principle, being inverted over the shaft to work directly. Boulton and Watt won a court case against Bull and got an injunction against his continuing to work with his experiments, but Trevithick was not included in the injunction. There was a famous story at the time of a bailiff being sent to serve a paper on the engineer, but being picked up and suspended over an open mine shaft before agreeing that, on the whole, he would like to go home, taking his papers with him. Trevithick eventually became over confident and actually visited Birmingham, where the manufacturers had their base; he was recognised and served with the injunction.

The legal battles left a bitter legacy of enmity between the two camps, and Boulton and Watt were never to lose the opportunity to disparage anything Trevithick might aspire to do. But by the 1790s young Richard was already entertaining some new and very revolutionary ideas. He was starting to think about using high-pressure steam. He began to wonder if it was actually necessary to use a condenser at all, but whether he could simply allow the exhaust steam to blow out into the atmosphere. He was a practical man with no scientific training, but he had a friend, Davies Gilbert, who was ready and willing to advise him. 'What', asked Trevithick, 'would be the loss of power in working an Engine by the force of Steam raised to the Pressure of several Atmospheres, but instead of condensing it let the steam escape?' Gilbert was able to assure the engineer that the only power that would be lost could never exceed one atmosphere or, in other words, it would never be more than 14.7 pounds per square inch (psi) – 100 kilopascals in today's units. Trevithick was understandably delighted and set to work, and he was more than able to compensate for the loss of one atmosphere by having engines working at a boiler pressure of 60psi. He began to think not just of manufacturing compact engines, small enough to be transported to where they were needed, but also considered engines that could move themselves. He began by making a simple model that was given a first outing on the kitchen table in his own home, where the boiler was simply, in his own words, 'a strong iron kettle'. It worked and he was able to build little models that ran around the table. The third model he built is preserved in Dublin, and is the first four-wheel locomotive. It is a very different concept from Cugnot's tractor. The boiler acts as the main frame, with the single, vertical steam cylinder let into the top. The drive is taken via a cross head above the piston head, via connecting rods to cranks on the outside of one pair of wheels. There is no means of steering. It is the first such engine that looks recognisable as any type of steam locomotive. Trevithick, however, was not the only one thinking along these lines and considering ways of designing steam carriages.

William Murdoch was Boulton & Watt's representative in Cornwall, overseeing the construction and operation of their mine engines. He began his experiments in the 1780s, and one of his fellow engineers, Thomas Wilson, wrote to Watt on the subject on 7 March 1784:

> 'He has mentioned to me a new scheme which you may be assured he is very intent upon, but which he is afraid of mentioning to you for fear of your laughing at him, it is no less than drawing carriages along the road with steam engines'

Watt was inclined to humour him at first, but when he found that Murdoch was actually serious and had built a working model, he was adamant. Murdoch had a choice; continue as a well-paid and respected member of the Boulton & Watt team or leave and continue the experiments on his own. Murdoch, not unreasonably, opted for the latter. It is not certain how far Trevithick was influenced by Murdoch's work or even how much he knew about it. They were neighbours at the time, but Murdoch was very secretive about what he was doing and carried out his experiments at night. There is a well-known story, that one night he set his little engine trundling down a quiet lane near the church when the vicar was just on his way home. The startled clergyman was convinced he had met a fiery demon from hell.

William Murdoch's model for a road locomotive, which was never developed to a full scale trial due to the opposition of his employers, Boulton & Watt.

Murdoch's model is very different from Trevithick's. The driving force is a form of beam engine, usually referred to as a 'grasshopper', in which the beam, instead of pivoting about its centre, is attached to a vertical post at one end. The cylinder at the opposite end is set behind the axle of the driving wheels, and a vertical connecting rod descends from the beam, close to the piston to transmit the drive to the wheels. Because this was a genuine prototype for a road vehicle it had to be steered and this was accomplished by means of a simple tiller to single front wheel. The little engine contained several interesting and good ideas, including an early version of a slide valve, but it was never developed. It was Trevithick who would have the honour of creating the first locomotive to steam along the roads of Britain.

By the beginning of the nineteenth century Trevithick had already successfully developed his high-pressure steam engine for work in the local mines as a whim engine, hauling men and material up and down the shaft. They became known as 'puffers' because of the way the exhaust steam puffed noisily out at each stroke. In a trial against a traditional Boulton & Watt engine to measure their relative efficiency, the Trevithick engine came out the clear winner, which did nothing to improve relations between the two camps. Now Trevithick began working on a puffer that would not merely turn a wheel above a shaft, but would move itself too. His first question was one that we would not even consider today; could a vehicle be moved simply by turning the wheels round, relying on the effect of friction between the wheels and the ground? He settled that matter with a simple experiment by taking an ordinary cart, and, instead of pulling it, simply turned the wheels by hand; it moved. He was now ready to build a prototype. The engine was assembled from a variety of sources; the boiler and cylinder were cast at the works of the Cornish engine manufacturer, Harvey's of Hayle, an obvious choice as Trevithick had married Henry Harvey's sister, Jane. The ironwork was prepared by the Camborne blacksmith Jonathan Tyack. Some of the more intricate work was entrusted to Trevithick's cousin and friend Andrew Vivian, who had his own workshop and lathe. According to an eyewitness, 'There was a great deal of trouble in getting everything to fit together'.

The first trial run was held in Camborne and in Francis Trevithick's biography of his father there is a graphic account by someone, only known to us as 'old Stephen Williams':

'In the year 1801, upon Christmas-eve, coming on evening, Captain Dick got up steam, out in the high-road, just outside the shop at the Weith. When we get see'd that Captain Dick was agoing to turn on steam, we jumped up as many as could; maybe seven or eight of us. 'Twas a stiffish hill going from the Weith up to Camborne Beacon, but she went off like a little bird.

'When she had gone about a quarter of a mile, there was a roughish piece of road covered with loose stones; she didn't go quite so fast, and as it was a flood of rain, and we were very squeezed together, I jumped off. She was going faster than I could walk and went on up the hill about a quarter or half a mile farther, when they turned her and came back again to the shop.'

This is a remarkable achievement for a prototype, coping with a steep road made slippery with rain and we are fortunate to have this account of the day. What we do not have is any detailed

Richard Trevithick began his experiments on steam locomotives with tabletop models: this is the third version, completed in 1797.

The replica of the Trevithick experimental steam road locomotive was built to celebrate the bicentenary of the original, which was given its trial in Camborne in 1801. The photograph gives an idea of the effort required to steer the machine.

A replica of Trevithick's London carriage brought back to the capital for the unveiling of a plaque to mark the site of William Felton of Leather Lane, Clerkenwell where the original coach was constructed. The original steam mechanism was built in Cornwall.

description of the engine itself. Francis Trevithick produced what he considered to be the most accurate account available, based on what he heard from those who had been involved. At the heart of the little engine was the boiler, with a return flue. The firebox was next to the chimney, and the hot gases passed through a U-tube immersed in the water. In the drawing in his biography of his father, Francis Trevithick shows a bellows arrangement, worked by a rod from the engine to increase the blast to the fire. The single cylinder is encased in the boiler, with crossheads to connecting rods to either side, providing drive to the rear wheels, as in the little tabletop model. The steam was admitted to the cylinder and exhausted by means of a simple four-way cock. Turned in one direction, it opened a valve to let steam into one end of the cylinder and at the same time allowed an opening at the other end to allow exhaust steam to escape. Turned through ninety degrees, it reversed the process, steam coming in at the opposite end of the cylinder. One outstanding feature was the way in which the exhaust steam was passed into the chimney, increasing the blast to the fire. This arrangement was then apparently forgotten or ignored until revived over a quarter of a century later by Robert

A closer view of the London carriage, showing the simple firebox and gearing; the water gauge has been added to meet modern safety requirements, but had not yet been invented when the original was built.

Stephenson. Steering isn't shown in Trevithick's drawing but was said to be by means of a pole to guide the front wheels, in other words some sort of tiller mechanism.

Following the successful trial, Trevithick agreed on a partnership with Andrew Vivian to carry out further development. One of the most important local families was the Dedunstanvilles, recently elevated to the peerage and owners of several large mines. They had supported Trevithick's experiments and it had been Lady Dedunstanville who had been given the honour of opening the valve to let steam into the very first model on the Trevithick kitchen table. It seemed only right and proper that Trevithick should now steam across to their home, Tehidy House. Everything was going well until a wheel caught in an open watercourse, the tiller was jerked out of Vivian's hand and the carriage turned over. It was unfortunate, but what happened next turned a mishap into a disaster. Trevithick and Vivian managed to get the vehicle into a shed and then decided to go and have a meal at the local inn. Unfortunately, they forgot to dowse the fire, the water evaporated, the boiler became red hot, the wooden parts caught fire and the engine was completely destroyed. Its working life had lasted just two days.

The Trevithick Society built a replica of this engine, but without the unnecessary bellows, to celebrate the bicentenary. Anyone who has had the good fortune to travel on it will know just how difficult it is to steer. When cornering, the tiller has to be held in place against a peg set in one of a series of holes in a board. It is not difficult to see how the accident occurred. It was not, however, a catastrophe. This was always an experimental vehicle built to prove the theory that a steam carriage was a viable proposition. It was now time to turn the prototype into a genuine steam passenger coach.

The new carriage was to be built for display, not in Cornwall, but on the streets of the capital. The design was entirely different. The coach itself, built in London, looked exactly like a stage-coach of the period. The most obvious difference from the outside was that instead of four wheels it had three; two immense eight-foot diameter drive wheels at the rear and a much smaller wheel at the front, controlled by a tiller. It was, quite literally, a 'horseless carriage'. The engine was unlike the Camborne one, in that the cylinder, though still set inside the boiler, was now horizontal. The piston rod was forked to allow for the movement of the crankshaft that turned the rear axle. There was also a simple gear arrangement. Steering, however, proved as problematic on the steam coach as it had on the original road engine. John Vivian gave a hair-raising account of a trip that started off in Tottenham Court Road one day and on which he estimated that they reached speeds of 'eight or nine miles an hour'.

'I was steering, and Captain Trevithick and some one else were attending to the engine. Captain Dick came alongside of me and said 'She is going all right.' "Yes," said I, "I think we had better go on to Cornwall". She was going along five or six miles an hour and Captain Dick called out, "Put the helm down John!" and before I could tell what was up, Captain Dick's foot was upon the steering-wheel handle, and we were tearing down six or seven yards of railing from a garden wall. A person put his head from a window, and called out, "What the devil are you doing there! What the devil is that thing!"'

Steering was not the only problem; on rough roads the fire bars often worked loose, dropping the fire down into the ash pan. Nevertheless, it seems the engine aroused great excitement. When a special trial was arranged in Oxford Street all the shops were closed, huge crowds gathered and all the windows of the upper storeys were crowded with spectators. It must have been an extraordinary sight over two centuries ago, and when the full-scale replica was brought back to London for the unveiling of a plaque at the site of the coach building works of William Felton in Leather Lane, Clerkenwell, it proved to be just as eye catching. Afterwards it was taken to Regent's Park and run round the Outer Circle, the memorable day in which I rode in the carriage with Frank Trevithick Okuno. The ride was actually extremely smooth and one felt as if one was making a royal progress as everyone stopped to stare. The original carriage may have attracted huge interest, but it did not appeal to the one group who Trevithick had hoped to impress. No investors came forward to back the project. The whole scheme was abandoned and he gave up any further idea of developing steam road vehicles.

The next stage of the story of steam on the move is only sketchily documented. In 1802, Trevithick went up to the famous Darby ironworks at Coalbrookdale to install one of his puffer engines. The letter he wrote from there is remarkable in showing how far he had pushed high-pressure steam in a short time. One has to remember that Watt considered a pressure of 10psi to be more than adequate, but here he was describing an engine working up to 145psi. In a long letter describing the working of this engine he added this intriguing postscript: 'The Dale Co. have begun a carriage at their own cost for the real-roads (sic) and is forcing it with all expedition.' The railroad referred to would probably have been one of the tramways linking the works to a wharf on the Severn, along which goods would have been hauled down railed tracks by horses. Some commentators have suggested that the experimental railway locomotive was never built, but there is some evidence that it was completed. The man in charge at Coalbrookdale at that time was William Reynolds and his nephew, W.A. Reynolds, described being given 'a beautifully executed wooden model of this locomotive' when he was a boy. He broke it up to make a model of his own – 'an act which I now repent of as if it had been a sin'. He also recalls the boiler being used as a water tank and seeing other parts of the engine in the yard at a nearby ironworks. A visitor to Coalbrookdale in 1884 also recorded being shown a cylinder, preserved as a relic of the locomotive. None of these relics have survived, but a drawing does exist, dated 1803, simply labelled as the 'tram engine', which shows a locomotive fitted with a 4¾-inch diameter cylinder with a 3-foot stroke. For a long time this was thought to be a drawing for the 1804 engine described below, but it now seems more likely to have been for the Coalbrookdale locomotive. So it seems more than probable that an engine was indeed built at Coalbrookdale and if so it can claim to be the world's very first railway locomotive. The drawing was used as the basis for the replica that now runs at the Blists Hill Museum site

The replica of the Coalbrookdale locomotive, based on the best available evidence of how the original would have been constructed, is regularly steamed at the Ironbridge Gorge Museum.

near Coalbrookdale. It is possible to see that the drawing could equally well apply to the next engine, and more details will be given below.

If this really was a world first, it seems reasonable to ask why it wasn't more widely known. One answer might be found in a disaster that happened in Greenwich just as work would have been going forward on the Coalbrookdale engine. A Trevithick high-pressure boiler exploded, killing three men and seriously injuring a fourth. The engineer rushed to the scene and to give a sense of the scale of the explosion recorded discovering a piece of iron weighing an estimated 500lb buried in the ground 100 yards away from the site of the explosion. The cause of the explosion was soon determined. The boy in charge had gone fishing and left a labourer in charge. The man, thinking the engine was working too fast, shut it down, but failed to notice that the safety valve had been jammed shut by a spanner. Steam pressure continued building with the inevitable result. Trevithick realised that this would be seized on by the critics of high-pressure steam, as he explained in a letter to Davies Gilbert:

> 'I believe that Mr. B & Watt is abt to do mee every engurey in their power for the have done their outemost to repoart the exploseion both in the newspapers and private letters very different to what it really is.'

Potential customers for high-pressure engines were undoubtedly now rather nervous. It was bad enough having a potentially explosive device situated on a specific site; it would have seemed even more dangerous to have it trundling through the countryside. If we do not know quite why the Coalbrookdale locomotive was not publicised, we are equally uncertain about what it looked like and how it performed. Happily, we have very much more information about the next engine.

In 1803 Trevithick was asked to visit Samuel Homfray of the Penydarren iron works at Merthyr Tydfil to discuss the use of high-pressure engines. Penydarren was one of four great iron works in the region and the leading iron masters had got together to promote a canal to link Merthyr to the port of Cardiff. With forty-nine locks in just twenty-four miles, the Glamorgan Canal soon became very congested and matters were made worse when the major shareholder, Richard Crawshay of the Cyfarthfa ironworks, insisted that his boats be given precedence. The remaining shareholders decided to get round this difficulty by bypassing the worst of the blockages by means of a tramway from Merthyr to join the canal at Abercynon nine and a half miles away. It was a typical tramway with L-shaped rails set on stone blocks, designed to take waggons with plain wheels, not the flanged wheels of later railways. The rails were just 3ft long and were set to a 4ft 4in gauge. There are no actual records of the first meeting between Homfray and Trevithick, but we do know that as a result of it, Homfray decided to commission a steam locomotive to replace the horses on the Penydarren tramway.

News of the proposal reached Richard Crawshay. There was no love lost between him and Homfray and he scoffed at the whole notion, arguing that smooth wheels would be unable to get a grip on iron rails and wagered 500 guineas that the engine would not work. This was an enormous sum of money equivalent to something like £20,000 at today's prices. The terms of the bet were that the engine should be able to haul 10 tons of iron from the works

The Penydarren tramway, along which Trevithick's pioneering locomotive was given its trial, was still in use in the 1860s when this photograph was taken and was still using horses for haulage. The viaduct under construction was being widened as part of the improvement programme for the Taff Vale Railway.

to Abercynon and return with the empty waggons. This engine was very different from the first road locomotive. Once again, the boiler had a return flue with the cylinder set inside the boiler but this time, however, the cylinder was horizontal, so that the cross head projected in front of the locomotive and the connecting rods moved backwards and forwards like the slide of some giant trombone. As the driver's position was next to the chimney, the moving parts were all right next to him, which tended to make the experience of travelling on the footplate quite interesting as I, having had the opportunity of travelling on the replica of the earlier Coalbrookdale engine, can testify. Steam was again controlled via a four-way cock; a simple mechanism allowed the timing of the cock to be reversed to send the engine also into reverse, which was also the method used to stop it in the absence of brakes. Unlike the Camborne engine, the drive was not transmitted directly, but went via a crank to a small, toothed wheel, set in the centre of a huge flywheel that engaged with a larger wheel that in turn meshed with cogs on one end of each of the two axles. In modern terms this was a 0-4-0 locomotive,

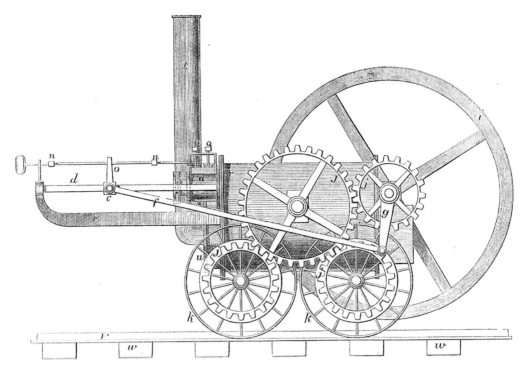

This drawing of the Penydarren locomotive was specially prepared from the best available evidence by Richard Trevithick's son Francis for use in his biography of his father. It was used as the basis for constructing a working replica.

though having all the drive on just one side of the locomotive was far from ideal. The flywheel was necessary with an engine having just one cylinder, but it also hints at another feature of the engine; it was not intended merely to work as a locomotive but could also be used as a stationary engine, driving machinery at the works. Trevithick wrote at the time:

> 'I am now preparing a pump to lift water. A Barrel to wind a Ball up & down – with any other matter I may think you would like to see it do – & move it about from place to place.'

In other words, the little engine was intended as a cross between a locomotive and a versatile puffer. It was expected to be used for working machinery at the ironworks as well as hauling trucks on the tramway.

Trevithick wrote many letters to Davies Gilbert during the trials for the new engine. Among other points he raised was the significant one in terms of future development that 'the fire burns much brighter when the steam goes up the Chimney than what it do when the engine is Idle'. On 22 February 1804 he was able to write in triumph:

> 'The Gentleman who bet Five Hundd Guineas against it rid the whole of the journey with us and is satisfyde that he has lost the bet. We shall continue to work on the road,

and shall take forty tons the next journey. The publick until now call'd mee a schemeing fellow but now their tone is much altered.'

The triumph, however, was far from complete. The problem was that the heavy locomotive broke the brittle cast iron rails and it was a major one. William Menelaus, who had been works manager at the big Dowlais ironworks at Merthyr Tydfil, took it upon himself to investigate exactly what had happened to the Penydarren engine after the bet had been won. He was able to track down an eyewitness and produced this account:

'When the engine was finished she was used for bringing metal from the furnaces to the old forge. She worked very well, but frequently from her weight broke the tram-plates, and also the hooks between the trams. After working for some time in this way, she took a journey of iron from Penydarren down the Basin Road, upon which road she was intended to work. On the journey she broke a great many tram-plates; and before reaching the Basin she ran off the road, and was brought back by horses. The engine was never used as a locomotive after this; she was used as a stationary engine, and worked this way for several years.'

It is quite clear from this account that the problem was not with the engine itself but with the track. There was one order for a locomotive from Christopher Blackett of the Wylam colliery on Tyneside. Many of the collieries of the region had tramways linking them to the Tyne, and the Wylam line differed from the Penydarren in that it had edge rails instead of plates. The locomotive was fundamentally the same as the Welsh engine, but Trevithick did make a few changes. One that would have been welcomed by the driver was the setting of the cylinder at the opposite end of the boiler to the chimney, so that there was more freedom of movement on the footplate. The boiler and flue were manufactured from wrought iron instead of the cast iron of the earlier engine. The wheels were set a little further apart, allowing for a steadier ride, and were flanged to run on the new rails. As the gauge at Wylam was 4ft 10in, the engine had to be built slightly bigger. But the same problem of heavy engine and weak rails meant that the experiment was rapidly abandoned. It was a major disappointment for Trevithick but he determined to make one more effort to interest major investors in developing the locomotive. He was about to go back to London.

He worked on a new locomotive, which reverted to something closer to the original road engine, but was more directly derived from a small engine that he had recently built to work a dredger on the Thames. It had the cylinder again set vertically in the boiler and did away with the complex gearing system, driving the rear wheels through a simple connecting rod and crank. The engine was built at the Hazeldine iron works under the supervision of John Urpeth Raistrick. The wager between Homfray and Crawshay had attracted a great deal of interest and Trevithick reasoned that if that was what was needed to get people interested in his invention then he would use the idea again. Adverts started to appear in the press representing a new challenge; the engineer offered to bring his locomotive to Newmarket and race it against any of the best horses. It certainly aroused a great deal of interest and, as *The*

Trevithick's final attempt to interest the world in steam locomotives was made in London, near the site of the present Euston station. The illustration shows *Catch-me-who-can* running on its circular track; the very first example of passengers paying to travel on a steam railway.

Times of 8 July 1808 reported, the idea 'created admiration in the minds of every scientific man'. The race never happened – perhaps it was no more than a public relations gimmick, but Trevithick did arrange to have his engine put on public display. The site he selected was quite close to the present Euston Station, where he built a circular track. An open carriage was coupled to the engine and the public were invited to take rides at a shilling a go. To encourage people to come along, Davies Gilbert's sister, Mrs. Guilmard, came up with a suitably exciting name for the locomotive – *Catch-me-who-can*.

Among those who came to see the engine was another engineer, Isaac Hawkins, who arrived armed with a watch. He would later describe the experience in the *Mechanics Magazine* in 1847, where he reported that he had timed the engine at twelve miles an hour, but had been assured by Trevithick that on a straight track it was capable of twenty miles an hour. But once again, it was not the engine that let him down but the track. The ground was soft, a rail gave way and the engine flew off and overturned. Hawkins recorded the sad result:

'Mr Trevithick having expended all his means in erecting the works and inclosure, and the shillings not having come in fast enough to pay current expenses, the engine was not set again on the rails.'

The engine was sold off and found a new and rather exotic home, installed in a grand barge for the Lord Mayor of London. But for Trevithick it was yet another bitter disappointment.

He had tried everything he could think of to persuade the world at large that steam locomotives represented the future for transport and the world had not listened. Time and again the failure had not been due to his own engines but to the tracks on which they ran. After the debacle of *Catch-me-who-can* he turned away from locomotive development forever.

Trevithick was not a man to brood over his failures. Having decided to abandon steam locomotives he threw himself into new projects, continuing to work on many other steam engine developments over the next few years, but a decisive event in his life was the arrival of a man from Peru, Francisco Uvillé, who wanted the engineer to provide high-pressure engines for silver mines high in the Andes. Trevithick was happy to oblige and sent out engines with a team of men to supervise them. Things did not go well and in 1816 he felt obliged to travel to South America himself to sort things out. It was supposed to be a short visit; in the event he was away for eleven years. During those years, the whole world of steam locomotion was transformed, but he was to put in one more appearance in this story, as we shall see later.

Trevithick's importance in the development of the steam locomotive was played down after his death, largely because of the growing

Richard Trevithick is remembered in his native Cornwall by this statue in Camborne, showing him holding a model of the 1801 road engine.

reputation of George Stephenson. The obituary in the *Civil Engineers' and Architects' Journal* of 1833 was sadly all too typical:

'Trevithick began better than Stephenson; he had friends in Cornwall and London, and he ought not to have left Stephenson to work out the locomotive engine and the railway. Trevithick was always unhappy and unlucky; always beginning something new, and never ending what he had in hand. The world was ever wrong with him, he said, but in truth he was always wrong with the world. The world would have done enough for him, had he chosen to make a right use of any one thing. He found a partner for his high-pressure engine; he built a locomotive, he had orders for others; he sent one to Wylam, which like most things in which he had a hand was so wretchedly made that it was put to other uses.'

Hopefully, enough has already been written about Trevithick's contribution to make it clear how far these comments are from an accurate assessment of his work. For the first decade of the nineteenth century, Trevithick was the only man working on the development of the locomotive and the failures were not due to mechanical problems with the engines but with the only available tracks on which they could be run. To suggest that Trevithick had enormous advantages and Stephenson none is a travesty. Trevithick largely worked on his own initiative, while the latter's forays into engine construction were entirely financed by colliery owners. As for the idea that it was left to Stephenson to work out the steam locomotive, the accuracy of that statement will soon be tested. The statement that the Wylam engine was badly made can be simply refuted. Blackett later tried to order a second engine from Trevithick, so he could hardly have been dissatisfied with the first, but by then Trevithick had abandoned the idea of working on locomotives for good. Perhaps the last word should be left with the engineer himself, writing to his old friend Davies Gilbert:

'I have been branded with folly and madness for attempting what the world calls impossibilities, and even from that great engineer, Mr. James Watt, who said to an eminent scientific character still living, that I deserved hanging for bringing into use the high-pressure engine. This so far has been my reward from the public; but should this be all, I shall be satisfied by the great secret pleasure and laudable pride that I feel in my own breast from having been the instrument of bringing forward and maturing new principles and new arrangements of boundless value to my country.'

Chapter Three

The Colliery Years

Once Trevithick had abandoned locomotive construction, there was no one else prepared to take on the development work for a number of years. The renewal of interest came thanks to the wars with France that caused a steep rise in the price of fodder. This was bad news for colliery owners, who relied on horses to haul the trains on their tramways, so it seemed a logical step to see if it was possible to replace them with steam engines. After all, the one thing all collieries had was access to cheap coal. Middleton Colliery lay just south of Leeds and was connected to the navigable River Aire by its own tramway. The colliery was just one of several owned by Charles Brandling, all of which were managed by his agent John Blenkinsop, who was entrusted with the job of designing a steam system. He would have been well aware of the problem of breaking rails, so Blenkinsop began to consider ways in which a comparatively light engine could haul a heavy load. To do so it would have to use some method for increasing the traction while reducing the weight of the locomotive, and the solution he came up with was a rack and pinion. A rotating cog on the locomotive would engage with a toothed rail; a system that would later be revived for mountain railways. To design the engine, he turned to Matthew Murray of the engine-building firm Fenton, Murray and Wood in Leeds.

Although rather roughly drawn, this gives the clearest indication of any of the contemporary illustrations of how the Blenkinsop-Murray locomotive for the Middleton Colliery Railway might have looked. It shows the gear and cog arrangement and also the exhaust steam puffing up from the pipe above the boiler.

Blenkinsop could not have gone to a better man. Not a great deal is known about Murray's early life, other than that he was trained as a mechanic in Stockton-on-Tees. His fortunes changed when in 1789, at the age of 24, he was employed by the manufacturer John Marshall to work on improving flax-spinning machinery for the linen industry. In 1793, Marshall purchased a Boulton & Watt engine for his mill. Murray was put in charge and at once began making his own improvements, which was, of course, in breach of Watt's patent. On this occasion the company did nothing, convinced that Murray would make a hash of things anyway. They were to prove mistaken. He was so successful and made so many improvements in flax working machinery that he was able to set up in business with a partner, David Wood, as machinery manufacturers. Later they were joined by a third partner, James Fenton. By now, Murray had decided to concentrate on steam engines and he built a splendid factory in Leeds, the Round Foundry, eighty-one feet in diameter and four storeys high. In an attempt to heal the rift with Boulton & Watt, he invited Matthew Boulton to visit him. Boulton came, but the result was not at all what Murray had hoped for. When he asked if, in return, he might come and see the Soho Works in Birmingham, Boulton refused. He had seen enough to recognise Murray as a serious rival, and word was going around that he was able to produce castings for engine parts superior to anything being turned out in Birmingham. Boulton hatched a plot to prevent him expanding his business. He sent his agent up to Leeds, who managed to buy up all the available land adjacent to the Round Foundry, to stop him adding extra buildings and workshops. It cost Boulton £1,000 but had little effect on Murray's continuing success.

Among the customers for whom he built engines was Richard Trevithick, and in 1811 the two men worked together on designing a high-pressure engine for a steamboat. So, when Blenkinsop wanted a locomotive, Murray knew just what was required. He bought the rights to Trevithick's patent – which unfortunately for the latter had earlier been sold to a third party – and in 1812 set to work on the design. The resulting engine was in some ways an improvement on all the earlier versions. It had two cylinders instead of one, both set vertically into the boiler. This gave a smoother ride than was possible with a single cylinder engine. There were vertical connecting rods from each cylinder, connected by a pair of gears to a third gear on a central shaft. This rotating shaft held the larger rack wheel. Ideally, rack and pinion railways work using a central toothed rail, to provide a balanced ride, but this was impossible here, as the centre of the track had to be kept clear for the horses that were still at work on the line. An alternative efficient solution would have been to have rack rails at both sides, but this idea was rejected because of the cost, so the arrangement was entirely one sided. The engine was built with a single straight flue in the boiler unlike Trevithick's return flue. The reason is not clear. It meant that less steam could be raised as there was a smaller heating surface in contact with the water, but as fuel economy was not an issue, the engineer may simply have decided to go for the simpler option. Unlike Trevithick's engines, the exhaust steam did not go up the chimney but simply blew out into the atmosphere through vertical pipes. This would have been very wasteful on a long run, but the Middleton railway was only 3½miles. Murray made one very important improvement over Trevithick's engines. Instead of the four-way cock that made no allowance for steam to expand in the cylinder, he introduced the slide valve. This type of valve is operated by an eccentric gear that transforms the circular motion of the crankshaft to the backward and forward motion of the slide, which is surrounded by high-pressure steam from the boiler and mounted on the steam chest.

The steam chest of the valve has three openings: the two outer ones admit steam and lead to either end of the cylinder, and the larger central one allows the steam to exhaust. The different openings are covered and uncovered by a D-shaped slide, moving backwards and forwards across the face of the openings. For this type of valve to operate efficiently, there has to be a very tight fit between the slide and the steam chest to prevent steam escaping. Murray was an engineer who not only invented machines, he also developed and made his own machine tools. He had already designed a very efficient planer, originally used for making machinery for the flax industry, but which was now developed to provide appropriately smooth, machined surfaces for these slide valves. Murray's contribution to locomotive development has been largely played down, simply because the rack and pinion system proved to be a dead-end as far as immediate development was concerned. But he showed himself to be capable of making genuine improvements, not least in developing the machine tools without which progress would have been hampered, if not impossible.

Unlike the simple four-way cock, the slide valve allows for the use of the expansive power of steam, though it is unclear whether Murray either knew this or made use of the valve in this way. In later locomotives this was to prove an essential feature for efficient running, with the use of what became known as variable cut-off. The sequence of events starts with the admission of steam to a point where the admission port is completely closed and steam to the cylinder is cut off. The steam now continues to expand in the cylinder, followed by a period of release of used steam. Then, with the valves closed there is a period of compression. By this time, the piston has completed its travel from one end of the cylinder to the other and there is now a brief period of admission of live steam, before the piston begins to return in the opposite direction. The diagram (page 119), reproduced from the British Transport Commission's *Handbook for Railway Steam Locomotive Enginemen* (1957) shows the different positions for the valve, the piston and the cylinder and the crank on the driving wheel during one revolution. As engines developed so too did the mechanism for using the valve gear, and using it efficiently became the mark of a good driver. In his book *Locomotive Engine Driving* published in 1904, Michael Reynolds wrote:

'A driver may be able to work his engine with creditable economy, keep time and all that kind of thing; but so long as he is a comparative stranger to the action of the valves he feels within himself that one thing is needful. Such thoughts frequently occupy the minds of young enginemen.'

Blenkinsop and Murray were sufficiently confident to start not with one experimental engine but with two, *Prince Regent* and *Salamanca*, that were at once put into service. The experiment was an immediate success, and two more engines were ordered. The 5-ton engines proved capable of hauling 95 tons at a walking pace, which was said to be the equivalent of the work done by 16 horses. They were to remain in service for thirty years. A nineteenth century

This more general view of the Middleton Colliery Railway shows a train of typical coal waggons of the period crossing the viaduct by Leeds Parish Church.

illustration does exist, showing one of the locomotives hauling a passenger coach, but there seem to be no records of any such event ever having taken place.

The railway attracted far more interest than Trevithick's attempts to excite the London investors had ever done. It was not too surprising. Trevithick had hoped to suggest a new form of passenger system, but the Londoners simply regarded it as an amusing novelty. Here in the north of England, things were very different. Other collieries were facing precisely the same problem of rising feed costs and recognised that here was a potential answer. But it was not only the locals who came to look and wonder. Grand Duke Nicholas of Russia, soon to be Czar Nicholas I, also made the trip to Leeds. He must have been impressed, as when he came to power he helped to make Russia into one of the first countries apart from Britain to have a steam railway.

Blenkinsop was understandably proud of what had been achieved, and was always eager to promote the sale of his idea to other mine managers. In 1813, he sent a detailed estimate of costs and savings to the manager of Oxledge colliery. He declared that the average cost of haulage had originally been £9,653 13/- per annum, the major part of which had been feed for the eighty-one horses at £50 per annum each. The men to tend the horses came somewhat cheaper at just £40 a year. The cost could be reduced by selling the manure for £200. Using what he called 'steam carriages' the annual cost had been reduced to £1,468 4/-, an impressive saving. Blenkinsop then gave the cost of converting the system to a rack rail as £6,247, of which £4,465 could be recouped by selling off seventy-seven of the horses. It seemed a very attractive proposition, with the initial costs of track conversion being rapidly wiped out. There was, however, no mention of the cost of locomotives. There is one curious factor here. He claimed that he could sell off nearly all the horses and replace them with the locomotives. If he was no longer planning to use horses on the tramway, then he could have opted for the more efficient central rail. Perhaps he was not quite that confident of success when he started after all. Murray was to supply two engines to another line near Newcastle in 1813, and two more were built under licence at the Royal Iron Foundry in Berlin.

Blenkinsop and Murray were not the only ones looking to find ingenious solutions to the problem of producing locomotives with enough power to do useful work without demolishing the track in the process. One of the early histories of railway development was Nicholas Wood's *Treatise on Rail-Roads*, first published in 1825. In it he gave a description of a system invented by William and Edward Chapman. A chain was laid down the centre of the track and held above ground on forked supports set at eight to ten yard intervals. Wood described in some detail how the system worked:

> 'This chain was made to wind partly round, or to pass over, a grooved wheel, turned by the engine, of such a form that the wheel could not turn round without causing the chain to pass along with it.'

In other words, the engine dragged itself along the chain. The system was patented in 1812 but trials were not a success. The Chapmans went on to produce a second engine, which spread the load over two four-wheeled bogies. There was apparently some form of gearing to drive the wheels but the central chain wheel was still included in the arrangement, though this was only intended for use on steep inclines. There is no record of this engine being any more successful than the first, though the idea of increasing the number of wheels to spread the load was to be taken up very shortly afterwards by another engineer.

The next attempt to find an alternative to the conventional locomotive was far stranger. William Brunton worked at the Butterley ironworks in Derbyshire, a company founded by the engineers William Jessop and Benjamin Outram and which had become a major supplier of rails for tramways. The actual engine was conventional enough, consisting of a single flue boiler with a horizontal cylinder above the firebox, the whole mounted on four wheels. Brunton decided that as there was a problem with wheels not supplying sufficient traction, his machine would walk. There was a complex mechanism that operated a pair of legs, each of which had metal feet attached by flexible 'ankles'. At each stroke of the piston, one leg was moved forward and the other back to create the walking action. It was a very lightweight machine, weighing in at just over two tons, and was able to move at the very modest speed of 2½mph. It suffered from one great disadvantage, apart from the obvious fact that it was complex, clumsy and incapable of further development – it had no reversing mechanism. To be of any use it would have had to work on a line with either a loop for it to walk round or a turntable. In the event it would never be put to use. At the trials in 1815 the engine blew up, killing the crew and several spectators. The experiment was abandoned.

Events followed an altogether more rational course with the work of our next engineer, William Hedley. He was born in 1779 and instead of following his father into the grocery

A working replica of Chapman's 'Steam Elephant', originally built in 1815 for the Wallsend Colliery. It is standing outside the building recreated to represent part of Hackworth's works at Shildon and incorporates ironwork from Robert Stephenson & Co. Newcastle works.

business took a job at a local colliery. When he was just 22 he was appointed to the responsible position of viewer at the Walbottle colliery. He later took a similar post at the Wylam colliery close to the Tyne. It had a waggon-way that connected to the staithes at Lemington on the outskirts of Newcastle, where the coal was loaded into boats on the Tyne. Parts of the waggon-way survive as a public footpath alongside the river. Like other engineers from the north-eastern mining community he was impressed by the results at Middleton, but was unconvinced of the need for a rack and pinion system. He decided that, before he could set out to build a locomotive of his own, he needed more information on traction. As no one could supply facts and figure he set up experiments of his own. He built a waggon, which could be moved along the track by men turning a crank. He increased the load by adding weights and was able to calculate tractive effort. He could then extrapolate the figures for manpower to the steam power of an engine.

His first attempt at an engine was given trials in February 1813, but was not a great success. It had a single flue and just the one cylinder and a flywheel. He worked on the design and the next engine was built in May of that year and turned out to be a great improvement. Three other engines to the same design were constructed, two of which have survived: *Puffing Billy* and *Wylam Dilly*. Unlike Murray's engines, the boiler was fitted with a return flue,

The *Wylam Dilly*, built by William Hedley for the Wylam colliery in 1813, survived long enough to be photographed half a century later, with Hedley's two sons. One can see how the drive mechanism is derived from the stationary beam engines of the previous century.

an obvious and sensible decision, and was able to raise steam at 50psi – the same pressure as was applied to Trevithick's pioneering puffers. There were two cylinders, set outside the boiler, and where the earlier engine had allowed the exhaust steam to simply blow noisily into the atmosphere, Hadley passed the steam first through a silencer box. This was still not altogether satisfactory and, in a later adaptation he arranged for the steam to pass up the chimney, discovering as Trevithick had discovered before him, that it pulled air through the firebox, greatly improving its performance.

The system for transferring the drive from the pistons to the wheels was complex. In effect, each cylinder worked through something like the old beam engine. The beam itself pivoted from one end that was attached to a vertical support behind the chimney. The opposite end was connected to the piston that drove upwards from the vertical cylinder. Connecting rods from the centres of the two beams transmitted the drive to a single central shaft with gears transferring the power to the two wheel axles. The arrangement is something like a hybrid between the 'grasshopper' type arrangement used by Murdoch, and the gear system used in the Murray engines, except that in the latter each cylinder drove a separate shaft and the drive was only applied to one side of the engine. In spite of the experiments, however, the

Puffing Billy was Hedley's other locomotive of 1813 and basically the same as *Wylam Dilly*. It was later converted to an 8-wheeled version as shown in the illustration on p.31. It is the oldest preserved steam locomotive in the world.

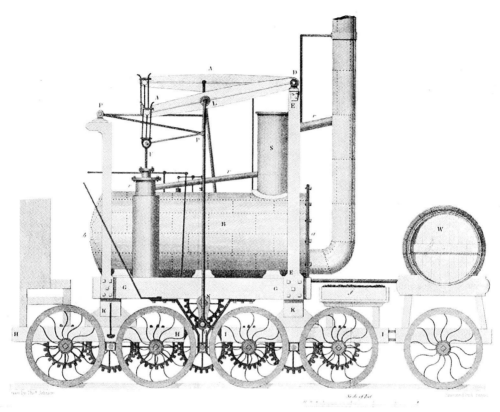

Hedley's locomotive on eight wheels from Nicholas Wood's *Treatise on Railways* of 1825. All the axles are connected by gearing, although the wheels are mounted on two bogies, making this the first 0-8-0 locomotive.

engine was found to be too heavy for the tracks, so Hedley borrowed the idea first used by the Chapmans. He mounted the engine on two four-wheel bogies, with an attached section on another two wheels to carry the water barrel. The only evidence for the wheel arrangement is an illustration in Wood's treatise so that it is impossible to tell whether or not the bogies could swivel; it might not have been important on the very straight Wylam line. Over the years, there were modifications to the engines. In 1830, the plateway was replaced by edged rails and the beam mechanism was altered so that the pivotal movement of the beam was controlled by a system closely related to Watt's parallel linkage and the engines reverted to the conventional four-wheel arrangement. In spite of the fact that Hedley's locomotives were slow and lumbering, speed was not important on a line that was only five miles long, and the sturdy engines worked on into the 1860s.

Hedley was to make one other contribution to the use of steam. In 1808 he set up in business as a ship owner, one of the many running vessels to carry coal from Newcastle. The coal was carried to the staithes, where it was dropped down chutes into special barges known as keels to be carried to the waiting ships. In 1822, there was a strike of keelmen so Hedley took one of his engines into a boat, attached it to paddle wheels and used it as a steam tug to haul the keels to and from the staithes.

One name has so far been notably absent from the roster of engine designers and builders – George Stephenson. The reason is very simple; he had not yet built his first locomotive. While it is certainly reasonable to grant Stephenson the title 'Father of the Railways' he was certainly not 'Father of the Locomotive'. In a list of pioneer engine builders he does not even make the first three. Nevertheless his contribution to railway development was so massive that it is necessary to look at his life and what he did do in some detail.

Stephenson was born at Wylam in 1781, in a cottage right next to the waggonway, which had been built in 1748 with wooden rails, later replaced by iron – the line on which Hedley had conducted his experiments. He was the son of a miner and although as a boy he followed his father to the colliery he was not destined to work underground. Very early on he showed an aptitude for all things mechanical and in 1798, while still only in his teens, he was put in charge of a pumping engine and by 1801 he had moved to the position of 'bankman'. He was in charge of a whim engine, controlling the movement of men and materials in the shaft. This was a very responsible job; the safety of the men depended on his skill and diligence. The following year he married, and in 1803 his son Robert was born. At the same time he got a

The Stephenson family cottage, where George was born, stands beside the track bed of the former Wylam waggonway. It is now in the care of the National Trust.

new job. A steam engine had been recently installed by the Tyne to work an inclined plane, a steeply sloping railed track along which trucks of coal were lowered to waiting boats and the empty trucks were hauled back up again. Stephenson was put in charge; he was moving up in the world. His character was very different from that of his predecessor Trevithick. Where the latter was mercurial, constantly moving from one project to another, Stephenson was diligent, a man who set his mind to something and stayed with it to the end. Trevithick never retired, but in his later years Stephenson did. He became an enthusiastic gardener, filling hothouses with exotic fruit and devoting his inventive mind to the problem of how to grow straight cucumbers; he succeeded.

Stephenson was very conscious that he had never had the opportunity to receive more than the most elementary education. His wife Fanny died as did his only other child, a baby girl. He now concentrated all his efforts on doing the best he could for his only surviving child, Robert. He paid for the boy to go to school and in the evenings father and son would go over subjects such as mathematics, the schoolboy becoming the father's tutor. Meanwhile, George was continuing to advance through the colliery world. In 1811 the Grand Allies, the largest pit owning group in the north-east were opening up a new mine, High Pit. To drain it they were using a, by then, very old-fashioned Newcomen engine and it was performing badly. George looked it over and recognised the problem but kept his views to himself. Instead, he went to the managers and suggested that if he was given the opportunity he might be able to solve the problem. He had worked out that the steam was not being properly condensed for two reasons: the cold water tank was too low to give a good head of pressure, and the valve controlling the spray was too small. It was a simple matter to make the corrections, but the result was so successful that the managers offered him a new job shortly afterwards. He was appointed engine-wright for the Killingworth colliery and had overall responsibility for all the steam engines in the group. It was a major step forward but only moved him upwards as a result of his work within an existing system. The next major event in his life came about literally by accident.

On the morning of 25 May 1812, just as the shifts were changing, there was an explosion at the Felling Colliery near Gateshead. It was a major disaster in which 92 men and boys lost their lives and it was generally agreed that the cause was all too obvious. Methane gas

George Stephenson's portrait from Samuel Smiles' *Lives of the Engineers.*

had seeped out of the seams and been ignited by a naked flame. It might seem absurd to use naked flames in a notoriously gaseous mine, but there were few alternatives available – suggested safe lighting methods included using the luminescence from putrefying fish, hardly a practical or acceptable idea. A local clergyman, Rev. John Hodgson, led a campaign to find a safe lamp for use in mines, and a substantial reward was offered to anyone who could find the solution to the problem. The winner of the prize was, as everyone knows, Sir Humphry Davy, and the committee awarded him £2,000 and his safety lamp was to remain in use in mines throughout the country right up to the present day. What is less well known is that Stephenson also designed a safety lamp, generally known as the Geordie lamp that was also successful and it too went into general use, particularly in the north-east. The committee considered it not quite as good as Davy's and awarded him a hundred guineas, but local people felt that this was a slight on their man and raised a further £1,000 by

The Hetton colliery railway: the upper illustration shows a typical line of the period, with the train steaming away from the staithes and the vessels on the river, waiting to be loaded with coal. The lower section shows a Stephenson locomotive of the period, with the chain drive clearly visible.

subscription. Davy was incensed. To him it was inconceivable that an illiterate pitman could achieve a result using mere common sense when he had applied his considerable scientific expertise to the task. He wrote to the benefactors asking them to withdraw the address of thanks to Stephenson 'which every Man of Science in the Kingdom knows to be as false in substance as it is absurd in expression'. The men of the north-east stood firmly behind their man but Davy's tirade had a profound effect on Stephenson. It bred in him a deep distrust of self-professed experts and especially those who came from the south of England. It was an attitude that was to colour many of his later actions.

The Grand Allies were, like other mine owners of the region, intrigued by the Middleton Colliery Railway, so they sent their engine man, Stephenson, to Leeds to take a look. He was obviously impressed by what he saw and borrowed many of the ideas from the locomotives he saw at work there. His first locomotive, *Blucher*, had its inaugural run in July 1814. Like the Middleton engine, it had a single flue boiler, an arrangement that Stephenson stuck with for a surprisingly long time, but then all his first engines were intended for short colliery lines where saving fuel was of little interest. He also followed the earlier design in allowing steam to exhaust straight into the atmosphere. Once again, the drive was through a complex system of gears. There was one difference from earlier engines; the Killingworth tramway was laid with edge rails, so the locomotive had to be fitted with flanged wheels.

The early engine has not survived and once again Nicholas Wood supplies much of the information on the locomotive and its successors. He described Stephenson as being dissatisfied with the way his engine worked: 'the communication of the pressure upon the cogwheels produced great noise, and in some parts of the stroke considerable jerks, and when the teeth became all worn caused a rattling noise'. It also seems to have been somewhat unreliable. There is an entertaining anecdote, quoted in L. T. C. Rolt's admirable biography of George and Robert Stephenson describing an incident involving George's elder brother James, the first driver of *Blucher*. Apparently the locomotive was struggling with a load of thirty-six tons when it simply packed up, unfortunately with the train stuck at just the point where the line crossed the main turnpike road, entirely blocking the way. It was, however, close to James' house and he called for his wife, Jinnie, to come out and apply her shoulder to the engine. She must have been a powerful young lady for she got the engine going again. It was also said that she used to get up at four every morning to light the fire in the boiler.

Stephenson worked with the head viewer at the colliery at the colliery, Ralph Dodds, to work on improvements to the drive. Eventually, they were so satisfied with the new arrangement that they took out a patent for direct drive, without the use of gears. The patent, number 3887, was taken out in both their names on 28 February 1815. It described two basic methods. In the first the wheels were driven directly by connecting rods, each of which was attached to 'a pin fixed to one of the spokes of each of the travelling wheels; which connecting rods are joined at both ends by ball and socket joints, to give way to the rise and fall of the road.' The two pistons worked alternately, and the drive was to be transmitted, in theory, by means of cranked axles and coupling rods between the frames. Producing the cranked axle proved well beyond the capabilities of the only available forge, that of the colliery blacksmith. The second method involved chains connecting the two sets of wheels. With either arrangement

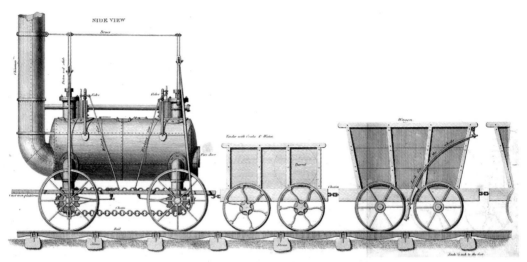

This more detailed drawing from Nicholas Wood's *Treatise on Railways* shows a typical Stephenson, chain-driven engine in some detail. The 'steam springs' can be seen immediately above the wheels, fed by steam pipes from the boiler.

an engine was said to be capable of hauling sixty tons on an iron road. If the load was any greater, extra traction could be obtained by a third set of wheels, supporting the water barrel, also linked by a chain. In the event, the chain drive was the system that was put into practice on the next locomotive. Having named his first engine after Field Marshal Blücher, who had led the Prussian army against Napoleon, he named his next after Britain's own military hero, *Wellington*. It sounds a cumbersome system but it worked and remained in use for several years.

The patent mentioned the use of ball and socket joints to try and overcome the effects of a rough ride. Stephenson set about looking for a better system. Locomotives up to this time had no springs, mainly because the technology for providing a sufficiently robust material was not yet available, so Stephenson devised a form of 'steam spring'. Each axle was solidly attached to a piston, working in a cylinder enclosed in the boiler, with the top of the cylinder open to the steam. As steam pressure increased, the piston was forced down and the steam in the cylinder provided a cushioning effect, helping to absorb the bumps. The effect was much as one saw more than a century later in the Citroen DS, which when not in use, sat down on its frame, but when the engine was turned on, rose up using a hydraulic system. Like the chain drive, the steam springs remained in use until the early 1820s. A more conventional system was adopted using laminated springs when appropriate materials became available.

It was Nicholas Wood who suggested a major improvement to the Killingworth locomotives. He introduced eccentrics to operate the valves. The eccentrics were, as the name suggests, mounted so that they did not have a centre coinciding with the centre of the wheel. Consequently, as the wheel turned, the eccentric followed an elliptical rather than a circular path. By attaching this via a crank and connecting rod to a slide valve, the valve could be made to move backwards and forwards. This also enabled the valve to be adjusted to allow steam to expand in the cylinder, as described above. There was one disadvantage to the system; it was difficult to reverse the engine. To change direction, everything had to be in the correct position. Consider the simplest case, in which the piston of a vertical cylinder provides the drive through a connecting rod. If on the downward stroke of the piston, it pushes with the crank on the forward side of the wheel, the wheel will turn clockwise; if at the rear it will go anticlockwise. By adjusting the system accordingly, the driver can decide whether the engine goes forward or into reverse. In effect this is what happened on early Stephenson locomotives, which entailed allowing the engine to begin moving in one direction and then disengaging the connecting rods and adjusting the valves by hand.

All the early engineers struggling to design working engines were trying to overcome the same basic problem; how to get power without increasing the weight of the engine to the point where it smashed the track. Now engineers and scientists began to consider ways of solving the difficulty from the opposite direction; make the problem disappear by improving the rails. The patent for the steam spring appeared under the name of both Stephenson and William Losh. The latter was the senior partner in Losh, Wilson & Bell, who manufactured chemicals at their works near Newcastle. Losh had already shown himself to be a man on the lookout for new ideas and had been the first to introduce the Leblanc process for making

This old photograph of a Stephenson locomotive for the Hetton colliery was taken in the appropriate setting of a colliery engine house – part of the ending gear can be seen in the background. This is the improved version in which the rather clumsy chain drive has given way to the more efficient connecting rods.

alkali into Britain from France. He also had an interest in the Walker ironworks. He had been one of those who had supported Stephenson's cause in the argument over the safety lamp and in 1815 he invited the engineer to come for two days a week to Walker to work on new ideas. He was to receive a salary of £100 per annum and would have a share in the profits made from any invention. The steam spring had been the first profitable venture, but now the two men turned their attention to rails.

The old tramways had stone sleepers, set in chairs sat square on top of stone blocks. The rails simply butted end-to-end, so if the stone block shifted, the chair canted, taking the rail with it. The Stephenson-Losh system used rails that met in lap joins, that is where the two ends overlapped. They were also sat in slightly curved chairs, so that if the stone block shifted it did not automatically move the rails as well, which would simply slide down to the lowest point of the curve. The system was so successful that the whole of the Killingworth system was relaid with the new rails.

Stephenson continued building Killingworth type locomotives, including one for Scotland. The Kilmarnock & Troon Railway was incorporated in 1808 and opened in 1812, operated by horses. There had already been a number of waggonways in Scotland serving industrial areas, mainly coalfields, but the Kilmarnock & Troon was rather different. Although it was promoted by the Duke of Portland, who owned collieries in Kilmarnock and held over eighty per cent of the shares, it was a public carrier and had a profitable passenger business as well. In 1817, Stephenson built a locomotive for the 9¾-mile long, 4ft gauge track. Unlike his previous engines, the locomotive was carried on six wheels, all joined by chain drive, making it a 0-6-0 locomotive. It was not, it seems, a great success.

The Kilmarnock & Troon was not the only horse-operated line to carry passengers, nor even the first to do so. The Swansea and Oystermouth Railway was incorporated in 1804 and originally intended merely as a conventional tramway serving stone quarries. But in 1807 a local man, Benjamin French, paid the company a fee of £20 per annum for the privilege of running a passenger service. At the time, Swansea had been developed as a smoky town of copper smelting works, and the locals soon found that the little railway provided an ideal chance to escape the industrial town, not yet a city, for the clean air and sea breezes of Mumbles Head. It proved to be immensely popular, but reports on the quality of the ride varied dramatically. A Miss Spencer recorded of her trip made in 1808 that she 'had never spent an afternoon with more delight'. Richard Ayrton, who wrote an account of his voyage round Britain in 1813, was less impressed. He described the sixteen-seat carriage as being made of iron with iron wheels and he travelled along the track to the accompaniment of 'the noise of twenty sledge hammers in full play'. The passengers, he declared, got off at the end of the ride 'in a state of dizziness and confusion of the sense that it is well if he recovers from in a week'. Perhaps the lady was made of sterner stuff.

The Kilmarnock & Troon and Swansea & Oystermouth lines had demonstrated that there was a demand for passenger services on railways, but neither used steam haulage in the early years. There were those who advocated steam passenger services, such as Thomas Gray in his *Observations on a General Iron Rail-way* published in 1820, in which he cheerfully prophesied that soon one steam engine would be able to pull the equivalent of three stage-coaches full

The Swansea & Mumbles Railway was carrying passengers as early as 1807, but originally drawn by horses. The photograph is in poor condition, but it shows a very heavily laden coach at Oystermouth. The line would later be converted to take steam locomotives.

of passengers from London to Edinburgh in 30 hours, where the journey then required 300 horses and took 50 hours. As he considered it essential to build the imagined line using the Blenkinsop–Murray rack and pinion system, this was more than trifle optimistic, as it would require an average speed of more than 10mph, a speed the Middleton locomotives never even got near to achieving. Contemporaries, as noted by a later writer, considered him 'a whimsical crochet' and 'he was voted an intolerable bore'. Gray was, of course, ahead of his time. There may have been a growing interest in passenger traffic on railways, but in the early 1820s all efforts were based on supplying locomotives for industrial use. There was no great incentive to improve on speed. The distance travelled by steam locomotives on the journey from colliery to customer was only a small percentage of the whole. On the Middleton line, for example, the coal would have been unloaded into horse-drawn barges on the river. And as without exception the railways were serving collieries there was little interest in working towards greater fuel economy, where coal was inevitably cheap and plentiful. These were privately owned concerns, built to meet the requirements of the owners, who had no need to consider anyone else. That was about to change.

Chapter Four

The Stockton & Darlington Railway

The Stockton & Darlington Railway has become famous in history, simply because it was the first to receive an Act of Parliament as a public railway to contain the vital clause that it could be worked using 'loco-motive or moveable engines'. It was not notable in its beginnings for any great advance in locomotive design, but it was to have a profound effect on all later developments. It did not start off in a hurry.

The reasons for promoting the line in the first place were exactly the same as those for promoting tramways further north in Northumberland; the necessity to provide an efficient transport route from the coalfields to the navigable River Tees. Not surprisingly, in the Canal Age of the eighteenth century, various waterways were proposed instead of tramways, but nothing happened. Then, on 18 September 1810, a public meeting was held in the town hall at Stockton-on-Tees and the Recorder, Leonard Raisbeck, put forward the motion 'that a Committee should be appointed to inquire into the practicability and advantage of a railway or canal from Stockton, Darlington and Winston for the more expeditious carriage of coals, lead etc.' A canal was still a possibility, but it had second billing. Two years went past and eventually the committee reached a decision to ask one of the leading civil engineers of the day, John Rennie, to survey a possible line. He showed no more sense of urgency than the committee and by the time he produced his report three years later, there had been a dramatic reversal of fortune in the area. Several banks had collapsed and no one was in the mood for investment.

It was 1818 before public confidence had been restored to the point where the locals felt ready to restart the process. A letter was despatched to Rennie asking him for a new survey, this time working in partnership with another engineer, Robert Stevenson, possibly with a view to injecting a little more urgency into proceedings. Rennie was not impressed. He replied in a very huffy letter, writing:

> 'I have been accustomed to think for myself in the numerous Publick Works in which I have been engaged, many of them of infinitely greater magnitude and importance than the Darlington railway.'

With this insult to their cherished scheme, the locals bid goodbye to Rennie and turned to another notable engineer, George Overton, the man who had been responsible for the Penydarren tramway. More or less from that moment onwards, all talk of canal construction ended, though it is unlikely that Overton made any efforts to promote locomotives. He had seen quite enough of the damage caused to tramways by steam locomotives.

Things should now have moved forward rather more rapidly, but as so often happens when committees are formed, factions began to develop. The Stockton group wanted a route that took a direct line to the coalfields, which would have involved missing out Darlington altogether, an idea which the Darlington interest, not surprisingly, rejected. In the event, Overton's proposed line through Darlington was accepted and formed the basis for the plans that went to Parliament for approval. The Act, passed in April 1821, authorised the construction of 'a Railway or Tramroad', with a total length of almost thirty-seven miles. The long period of eleven years that it took to agree on what was to be built is significant. It shows that the idea of railway construction was still not fully accepted. We tend to think that once the steam locomotive had appeared and shown its worth, canal construction would have come to an end. But Canal Acts were still being passed in the 1820s and the leading civil engineer of the day, Thomas Telford, still maintained his very firm ideas about the value of railways; their only purpose should be to bring goods down to navigable waterways. That is what all the railways constructed so far had been doing, usually down very short lines.

Most of the coal from the Durham and Northumberland coalfields was carried along rivers and on coastal vessels; the different tramways were quite short. This is where the Stockton & Darlington differed from its predecessors, in being that much longer. No locomotives up to that date had been required to go that far in a single journey. But it was still, in its essentials, a long colliery line. In the official Act it was actually described as running from 'the River Tees, at Stockton, to Witton Park Colliery, with several Branches therefrom'. In spite of the company's name, Darlington itself was only reached by a branch off the main line. And there was still a question to be answered; how was the line to be worked? At this point, Stephenson comes into the story.

At about the same time as the Act was passed, George Stephenson called on Edward Pease, one of the main promoters of the railway. Pease was an industrialist and merchant based in Darlington. As a Quaker he was faced with restrictions that prevented him taking any sort of public office, so he threw his time and energy into schemes that would promote industry and commerce. He was to prove a good and reliable friend to George Stephenson.

Samuel Smiles, who wrote biographies of all the early engineering pioneers, including Stephenson, loved a good story, and he was particularly fond of any that promoted his main theme – that progress was not being made by academics and theorists but by ordinary men with practical skills. In his version of the meeting, Stephenson walked as a barefoot pitman, who appeared on Pease's doorstep, modestly announcing himself as 'only the engine-wright at Killingworth'. He then talked his way into the house to try and persuade Pease that the new line should be run by steam locomotives. The truth is rather less romantic. Even ignoring the fact that Stephenson was, thanks to the safety lamp, one of the best-known men in north-east England, he actually arrived by appointment. Nicholas Wood, an eloquent advocate of steam locomotives, went with Stephenson to the meeting. He described how they took the coach from Newcastle to Stockton. It is true that they then walked to Darlington, but that was along the proposed line of the railway to get a clearer idea of the lie of the land. At this point the two stories do converge. Stephenson and Wood were able to convince Pease that the line could be worked more efficiently by steam power than by using horses, and that the line should be constructed with edge rails, not the tram plates proposed by Overton. Pease was convinced and he used his considerable influence to ensure that Stephenson was appointed to carry out a new survey of the proposed line

Stephenson began his own survey of the line with a young assistant, his eighteen-year-old son, Robert. Officially, Robert was still apprenticed to Nicholas Wood, but he suffered from poor health and, to his father's great relief, he was released from colliery work to enjoy a far healthier lifestyle, striding out across the line of the new railway. The partnership that was to develop between father and son had its ups and downs but in the event both were to make major contributions to the development of all aspects of the railway world and would be accepted as two of the most influential of all the pioneers.

The Stephenson route differed quite considerably from the Overton plan, but it was far from revolutionary. The surveying and construction techniques that had been used on the canals were used again on the early railway. Canal engineers had, by the beginning of the nineteenth century, moved away from the ideas of the first generation of constructors, who had tried to avoid changes in level by following the natural contours of the land. Now they were taking a bolder approach, carving through hills in cuttings and tunnels and crossing valleys on high embankments, the spoil from the former often being used to build up the latter, a technique known as 'cut and fill'. Exactly the same technology could now be used on the railways. But there were still places on the canals where they had to overcome changes in level by building locks. Stephenson followed the same pattern, following contours in places, creating cuttings and building embankments and where canal engineers would have used

One of the few survivors of the Stratford & Moreton line is the bridge across the Avon at Stratford: the promoter William James had always planned it to be used by locomotives, but it didn't happen.

locks, he planned to use inclined planes. Trains would be hauled up and down the slopes by stationary steam engines. He had no confidence in the ability of a locomotive to cope with anything but the most gentle of slopes.

Stephenson explained his ideas to one of the earliest of the railway pioneers, William James. The latter was a great enthusiast for both railways and steam locomotives and was the promoter behind the Stratford & Moreton Railway, a line that was planned to run from Stratford-on-Avon to Moreton-in-the-Marsh, a route that James saw as a start in building a greater Midland rail network. James was born at Henley-in-Arden, not far from Stratford. He was heir to a considerable fortune and ran one of the biggest land agency businesses in the country. His interest in transport began with canals and river navigations, and he supervised much of the work on the Stratford Canal and improvements to the River Avon. Then, when he heard what was happening on the railways of the north, he became a zealous convert, writing pamphlets in praise of the new systems and he began to consider how to use locomotives on the Stratford & Moreton. He wrote to Stephenson to ask about exactly what his locomotives could manage and received a very detailed reply that goes a long way to explaining the use of cable haulage on the Stockton & Darlington.

Stephenson gave figures for speeds that might be obtained on different gradients for a locomotive hauling twelve loaded waggons with a total weight of fifty tons. This varied from 4–8mph on the flat, but dropped to as little as 2½mph on a slope of 1:144. After setting out the figures, he added this note:

> 'I would not recommend my locomotive engine to travel on a line that ascends or descends more than 3/16 in. [per yard or 1 in 192] where there is a load both ways, but if the load was always passing on a descending line the engines would return with empty waggons up an ascent of 2 in per yard [1 in 72] or in a short distance from 5/8 to 6/8 ascent per yard [1 in 57 to 1 in 48].'

James was convinced that locomotives were the answer for his line, but he failed to move the other directors. They argued that it would be more expensive to construct a line that would need to carry locomotives, which was certainly true; that there was no cost saving, that locomotives could not be used when there was snow on the line or in very wet weather, which was also at that time probably true as well. They ended by the old arguments: 'the frightening appearance of locomotives in action' and 'the danger of explosions'. The line was built, but was worked by horses. Part of it survives, in a bridge over the Avon at Stratford.

The plans for the Stockton & Darlington had to be resubmitted to Parliament, because of the many changes that Stephenson had proposed. The new Act, passed in 1824, contained the historic Clause No.8: 'The Company is empowered to erect as many locomotive engines as they think proper and employ the same on the railways … for the conveyance and carriage of goods and passengers'. It was the very first Act to authorise a railway to be worked by locomotives for both goods and passengers. But, with its inclines and lingering doubts on how everything should be moved, it was not yet the first true modern railway. It was still, in effect, a colliery line that differed from its predecessors only in the scale of its operations.

As the engineer in charge of civil engineering, Stephenson had the ideal opportunity to make a personal profit by laying the track with the rails he had developed with Losh, but he had already heard of a new type of rail that had been developed by John Birkinshaw. Stephenson was impressed. As early as June 1821 he was enthusing over the invention: 'I think in a short time they will do away with the cast-iron railways.' What was it about the new system that made it so attractive?

Metallurgy was not so much a science in its infancy as an unborn child, but the properties of different kinds of iron were known, even if little was understood about why one variety differed from another. The earliest foundries had been based on the charcoal furnace that produced a very pure form of the metal, wrought iron. They had faced real problems in that they used vast quantities of wood to make the essential fuel. Early in the eighteenth century, Abraham Darby had succeeded in making iron in a furnace fired by coke, but in the process a certain amount of carbon was incorporated into the metal and the end product was cast iron. We know, thanks to modern microscopy, that wrought iron has a fibrous structure that makes it weak in compression but strong in tension, while cast iron has a crystalline structure with exactly the opposite characteristics. As a result, when the heavy engine went over a cast-iron rail, the metal had no give in it, so if it was unable to take the weight it would simply fracture. There is a third form of iron, with a carbon content in between the other two forms, steel, but in the early nineteenth century this could only be made in quite small quantities.

Later in the eighteenth century, Henry Cort, the owner of an iron works in Hampshire, developed a new technology that was able to convert cast iron from the coke furnaces into wrought iron. It was his process that Birkinshaw had developed. He used a technique already used by Cort of working the white hot metal by squeezing it through rollers. Birkinshaw improved on this system by using grooved rollers that could give the iron an appropriate cross section. These rails were 'I' shaped in cross section and could be rolled in fifteen-foot lengths. He later developed his rails into what was known as the fish-bellied type, in which the underside curved downwards to give a greater depth to the centre of the rail, where downward pressure was at its greatest, and provided them in lengths up to twenty feet.

The wrought iron rails had exactly the characteristics that were needed; they flexed under the weight of the passing train instead of snapping. It is to Stephenson's enormous credit that he recognised the importance of this invention and decided to use Birkinshaw rails for at least some sections of the Stockton & Darlington. Losh was a good deal less impressed by the engineer's public spirited response that had lost his company a great deal of valuable business and relations between the two men were irreparably damaged. But it was a decision of huge importance for locomotive development, removing the issue that had bedevilled engineers for so long; the breaking rails.

Stephenson's line was mainly to be laid with Birkinshaw rails, but were still set, as in the old tramways, on stone sleeper blocks. There was a reason for this; although it was intended to work the line with locomotives for freight, passengers would be carried in a special stage-coach, fitted with flanged wheels and pulled by horses. It is doubtful if Stephenson gave much thought to the gauge; he simply set the rails 4ft 8in apart for no better reason than that was the Killingworth gauge and it was to fit that gauge that he had built his first locomotives.

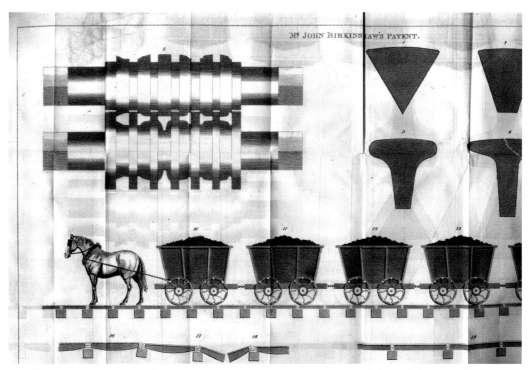

The illustration shows Birkenshaw rails and a typical horse-drawn tramway of the period. It also illustrates the grooved rollers used to provide different shapes, with cross sections of rails and both plain and fish-bellied rails. The use of such wrought iron rails was vital to the future development of the steam railway system.

They provided him with ready-made patterns to follow. At some time, the Stephenson gauge gained an extra half-inch and 4ft 8½in was eventually to become the standard for most of the country as it still is.

The line as finally constructed was an extraordinary mixture of transport systems old and new. The company's name is deceptive as Darlington, in fact, lies roughly half way along the line. The section from Stockton to Darlington presented comparatively few problems. It was to the north of the latter that the difficulties appeared, as the line headed off to Witton Park colliery to the west of Bishop Auckland. There were two ranges of low hills across the line and each was overcome by building inclines to go up one side and down the other. The heavy loads were always the ones heading south with coal from the colliery. So at the first inclines, Esserley West and East, trucks were helped on their way by a stationary 50hp engine. This was used to haul the loaded trucks up one side and lower them down the other. There was then a short gap, worked by horses, to the two Brusselton inclines, where a more powerful 60hp engine was installed.

Working the inclines produced all sorts of problems at the start of operations. Difficulties arose from the method of working with a single drum for the inclines on both sides of the hill. It was all too easy for the two sets of ropes to become entangled, and when that happened one was likely to snap. The result was that any trucks on the line went hurtling back down the

A sketch of the remains of the steam engine house and cable haulage system at the top of the Brusselton Incline at the northern end of the Stockton & Darlington. Originally there had been a single winding drum, and the second was added later to speed traffic movement. By the time this sketch was made it had long since fallen into disuse.

slope, smashing themselves and anything else that happened to be in the way. The obvious solution was to have two drums and with both set on the same shaft, the weight of descending trucks could help to raise trucks on the opposite incline. This was put in hand in 1826 and the system then worked far more efficiently. Loaded trucks were always heading south and empties coming the other way, so the weight of the full trucks lifted the empties. But it was a complex system that relied on trains of trucks being available in both directions at the same time. It worked, but it could hardly be said to represent the modern steam-powered railway that the Stockton & Darlington is often said to represent. It makes sense when one remembers Stephenson's advice to William James. It was not the only railway of the time to use this sort of system. The Cromford & High Peak railway, for example, authorised in 1825 was built with a similar alternation of level sections and steep inclines. Most of the route still exists, now used as a cycle path, and one of the engines has survived at Middleton Top, providing a very clear impression of how these systems worked.

Stephenson was faced with a dilemma from the outset. His initial idea had been to have locomotives built at Losh's works, but after the disagreement over rails this was now out of the question. His next thought was to turn to the company responsible for the very first

A surviving example of a fish-bellied rail mounted on stone blocks, from the Cromford & High Peak Railway, now on display at the museum based on the former maintenance yard near Cromford.

locomotive he had ever seen, Fenton, Murray and Wood in Leeds, but they had lost interest. Their reply was terse:

'It does not suit with the present arrangement of our Business to take orders for High Pressure or Locomotive Engines. We have not made any this 8 years.'

The only solution appeared to be to set up a locomotive works himself, but he needed partners to share the cost. Edward Pease agreed to join the enterprise and so did Michael Longbridge, the owner of the Bedlington Ironworks, where John Birkinshaw was the engineer, and who obviously saw a successful line run by locomotives as a valuable advertisement for his wrought iron rails. The other two shareholders were George and Robert Stephenson and the works at Forth Street, Newcastle, became Robert Stephenson & Company. The initial capital was £4000 divided into ten shares; four for Pease and two each for the rest. Pease actually loaned Robert Stephenson £500 to enable him to pay for his portion and was later to declare that it was one of the best investments he had ever made, even if at the time he thought he had little chance of ever seeing his money again.

George Stephenson made over all his patents to the partners and Robert, still only nineteen years old, was appointed to manage the works at a salary of £200 a year. Once established, the new company at once began work on the first two engines, *Locomotion* and *Hope* as well as the stationary engines for the inclines. This was the first engineering works in the world specifically set up to build locomotives and over the years was to prove to be one of the most successful. In a sense, the company was fortunate in that they could take advantage of improvements being made in machine tools that would produce parts with a degree of accuracy that would not have been possible even a few decades earlier. Wilkinson had showed that it was possible to bore cylinders with considerable accuracy for stationary steam engines. As mentioned earlier, Murray had been able to produce an effective slide valve because he had already invented a suitable planing machine to produce flat surfaces. It was not, however, an idea he was keen to share. A tool maker called March, who worked for Murray in 1814, described the situation:

> 'The machine was not patented, and like many inventions in those days it was kept as much a secret as possible, being locked up in a small room by itself, to which the ordinary workmen could not obtain access.'

But Murray was not the only one working on planing machines. Many of the early machines were designed for use in manufacturing machinery for the textile industry. James Fox built a machine in which, according to an account published in the *Transactions of the Society of Arts* in 1832, the bed ran on rollers that were so true that 'if you put a piece of paper under one of the rollers it would stop all the rest'. This sort of accuracy had seldom been achieved before. Another of the early designers was Richard Roberts, whose planer of 1817 is now in the Science Museum in London. He too began by making machines for the textile industry and he was to apply his knowledge to the locomotive industry through his company Sharp, Roberts & Co. In time, they were to rival Stephenson as engine builders, but in the 1820s Stephenson had the world of engine building to himself. The Newcastle Company was able to take on all parts of the construction process, from casting and boring cylinders to machining valve gear.

If the Forth Street development was, quite literally, at the cutting edge of technology, the same could not be said of its locomotive design, which showed little if any improvement over the Killingworth engines. The main difference was that the chains were dispensed with and the driving wheels conventionally coupled, in a 0-4-0 arrangement. The two cylinders were set vertically into the boiler and the drive transmitted through a form of 'grasshopper' arrangement. As originally built the engines had 8-spoked cast wheels, which proved unsatisfactory in

The replica of Stephenson's *Locomotion*, the engine that inaugurated services on the Stockton & Darlington Railway, under way at the Beamish Open Air Museum. The driver has a somewhat precarious position on a platform at the side, and the photo clearly shows the different position of the crossheads as the crankpins are set at ninety degrees to each other.

practice, due to the uneven track and lack of springs. A replica of the engine was built for the celebration of the 150th anniversary of the opening of the Stockton & Darlington and is now at the Beamish Open Air Museum. Seeing it in action shows just how complicated life was for the driver. Instead of occupying a conventional footplate position at the end of the boiler, he stands on a platform along one side. From this position he is able to carry out the complex operation of adjusting the valves and the gabs on the eccentrics to get the engine to change direction as on the Killingworth engines. Seeing it in action, it seems as complex to carry out as it is to describe and one can only admire the skills of the early drivers.

Once the railway was nearing completion it became obvious that the company would need some form of maintenance works and a qualified man to keep everything in working order. Timothy Hackworth was familiar with locomotives from his early days at Wylam colliery. He might well have remained there but was forced to leave on a matter of principle. He was a lay preacher and firm believer in the sanctity of the Sabbath. When he refused to work one Sunday he lost his job, but he was at once taken on as foreman smith at Walbottle colliery in 1816. He had been asked by Stephenson to join the Newcastle enterprise, an offer that he refused, but when he was again approached and offered the job as superintendent of the proposed new maintenance works he accepted. The official records of 13 May 1825 gave the details:

'John Dixon reports that he has arranged with Timothy Hackworth to come and settle on the line, particularly to have the superintendence of the permanent and locomotive engines. The preliminary arrangement as regards salary is £150 per annum, the Company to find a house, and pay for his house, rent and fire.'

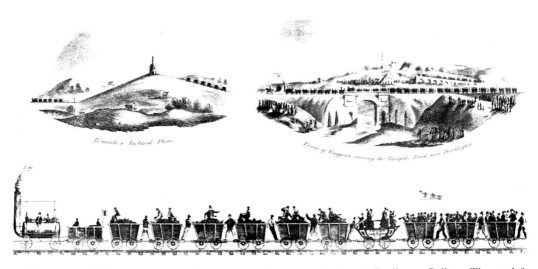

A lithograph of 1825 published to celebrate the opening of the Stockton & Darlington Railway. The top left illustration shows a somewhat exaggerated view of the Brusselton incline, with one set of trucks being hauled by the stationary engine, while another is pulled away by locomotive; the second illustration shows the inaugural train crossing the turnpike road at Darlington and the main picture gives a more detailed view of the first train, hauled by *Locomotion*, with some passengers precariously perched on top of the loads of coal.

The new works were built by the tracks at Shildon at the northern end of the line, near Bishop Auckland. The house is now home to the Timothy Hackworth Museum. He was to play an important role in the development of the Stockton & Darlington and in later locomotive development. He arrived just in time for the grand opening of the railway.

Locomotion was the only engine that had been completed and it was given a suitably imposing load to draw for the inaugural trip. The opening day was to be 27 September 1825 and spectators were invited to gather near the engine house on the Brusselton incline, a spot well known locally for a local folly tower. On the day a vast crowd assembled and the event received full coverage in the local papers, the *Durham County Advertiser* and the *Newcastle Courier*. Proceedings began with thirteen loaded waggons being drawn up the Brusselton incline; it took seven and a half minutes to pull them slightly over a mile up to the top and five minutes to lower them the half mile down the other side. The train was now made up for the journey to Stockton. Behind the engine and tender were six loaded waggons and behind them a specially built coach to take the members of the committee. There were then twenty-one waggons specially fitted with seats for the less important guests and then another six coal waggons bringing up the rear. This was a long train for the small engine and this was well before the introduction of through braking, so an unlikely safety measure was adopted. The typical waggons of the period each had a long handle attached to a brake on the wheels, so men were appointed to stand on the buffers between each waggon, ready to apply the brakes if needed. Quite how this was to be co-ordinated it is impossible to imagine. The engine set off and the *Courant* described the scene:

'The signal being given, the engines started off with this immense train of carriages; and here the scene became most interesting, the horsemen galloping across the fields to accompany the engine, and the people on foot running on each side of the road, endeavouring in vain to keep up with the cavalcade. The railway descending with a gentle inclination towards Darlington, though not uniform, the rate of speed was consequently variable. On this part of the railway it was intended to ascertain at what rate of speed the engine could travel with safety. In some parts the speed was frequently 12 miles per hour, and in one place, for a short distance, near Darlington, 15 miles per hour; and at that time the number of passengers was counted to 450, which, together with the coals, merchandise, and carriages, would amount to near 90 tons.'

The train was on the move for sixty-five minutes, but there were stops along the way, possibly to raise extra steam, and the entire nine-mile journey took two hours. The event greatly impressed everyone who was there that day, but it didn't exactly make a compelling case for the locomotive. Travelling downhill, the locomotive had averaged little more than four miles an hour, while the admittedly lesser load was hauled by cable up the incline at twice that speed. The argument in favour of the locomotive was yet to be won, and events after the opening did little to help the case. The engineers were moving into quite new territory, with the locomotives travelling far further than had been necessary on the earlier routes. Keeping up steam was the most obvious problem. One solution introduced by Hackworth was to follow in Trevithick's footsteps and use the exhaust steam blast up the chimney to increase the draught to the fire. This was certainly effective in improving the steaming ability of the engines and proved, if anything, rather too effective, throwing out the fire in all directions. As a result, trackside fires became a commonplace and the company had to employ full-time beaters to deal with them.

There was an intrinsic problem facing the footplate crew; judging how much water was actually in the boiler. The water-gauge that was to become a standard fitting on later locomotives had yet to be invented, so the only means of judging the levels was by the use of a number of test cocks. It was not simply a case of seeing what came out – water or steam. With the pressure inside the boiler, as soon as water hit the atmosphere it flashed into steam. The only difference between that and the actual boiler steam was in the noise each made. Whether or not this did cause real problems is uncertain, but in 1828 both *Locomotion* and the second engine *Hope* suffered disastrous boiler explosions, killing both drivers. The official verdict, however, was that the drivers had been trying to get extra power by tampering with the safety valves. These were simply held shut by a weighted lever; adding extra weight would allow anyone to increase boiler pressure without blowing the safety. Whether the explosions were due to low water levels or tampering could never be accurately determined but it was obviously in the company's interest to blame the driver. In any case, Hackworth designed a new, improved safety valve using springs that was far more difficult for the driver to adjust.

The other outstanding problem was the rough ride. Stephenson had abandoned the use of his 'steam springs' and had no available alternative. The problem was exacerbated by the fact that the wheels were all solid castings without any form of iron tyre. The Shildon works had no lathe capable of turning a large wheel, so casting was the only answer. Timothy Hackworth improved on the system by casting his wheels in two parts. The inner section could be turned on a lathe to produce a far more accurate circular outline than was possible by casting alone. The outer section was then added, secured by wooden plugs and iron wedges, hence its usual name – the plug wheel. An iron tyre was then added. The spoked wheels had regularly broken as they bounced along the uneven track, but at least with the new wheels it was comparatively easy to replace or repair the outer section. The problem was not specifically one of technological difficulty, but simply a failure to provide the appropriate machine tools for the job. Another line opened at the same time as the Stockton & Darlington, the Plymouth & Dartmoor, was a horse-worked line connecting stone quarries to the port. In that respect it was old fashioned, but the workshops had a lathe capable of turning the waggon wheels. The springing problem was solved by Nicholas Wood who developed laminated steel springs, but they were not initially used on the Stockton & Darlington.

Running the railway was far from straightforward. In a history of locomotives by Theodore West in 1885, there is a somewhat colourful account of what it was like to operate the line in wet weather:

'In awkward, slippery weather or on some long, greasy incline, the speed would flag rapidly; the engineman, first lavishing oil on the rods and bearings, and the prising the wheels round with a crowbar, would cry out to the fireman, "Give it to her, Bill, mon, give it to her!" As Bill, with his shovel, strode alongside, frantically scraping up small ballast and dashing it before the wheels in place of sand to make them bite (sand boxes were not then invented) – but in vain – puff! p–u–f–f–! engine and waggons at length stood still. Thereupon ensued a passionate rousing up of the fire, a brief and rather heavy swearing match at engines generally and this one in particular, then, hot and tired, the two men would sit down on the near railings or bank for a quiet pipe, whilst steam slowly rose to going pitch, then once more they mounted and went.'

In an attempt to improve the locomotive stock to the line, the company went to a new design by Robert Wilson of Forth Street. It was a four-cylinder engine in which each pair of wheels was worked by two pistons acting on cranks set at right angles to each other. It was not a success and the exhaust made a curious noise that gave it a local name – the *Chittaprat*. Rather than scrapping the entire engine, Hackworth was given the job of utilising the boiler to build a new locomotive. The engine he designed had a return flue boiler, providing far better steaming than the single flue used in the earlier locomotives on the line. There were two cylinders, set each side of the boiler at the end opposite the chimney, and the engine was mounted on six coupled wheels in a 0-6-0 arrangement. This meant that the fireman stood

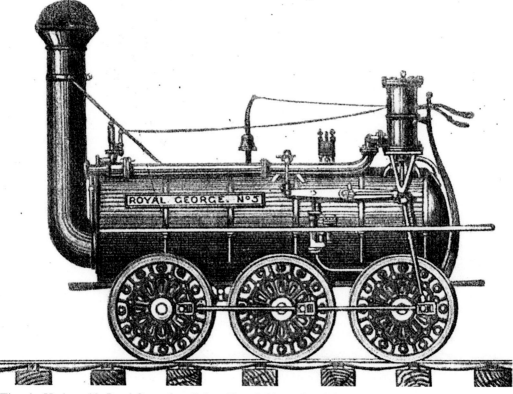

Timothy Hackworth's *Royal George* from Robert Young's biography of the engineer, simply described as being 'from an old drawing'. It shows the engine resting on typical fish-bellied rails. Apart from having three pairs of coupled wheels, it differs from *Locomotion* in having the two cylinders at either side of the boiler instead of on the mid-line.

next to the chimney and the driver at the opposite end, and there were two tenders, one for water at the driver's end and the other for fuel. It was unsprung but had plug wheels that had a certain amount of give in them. It also had a water feed pump that used water heated by the exhaust steam. It was renamed *Royal George* and proved to be a sturdy, workmanlike engine. It was built for heavy loads not speed and, being on six driven wheels, had the extra traction that meant it could be kept going in all weathers at a speed of around 9mph. The company reports for 1828 showed it hauling over 20,000 tons in the year at the rate of ¼d per ton. It was estimated that the cost worked out at £532 less than if horses had been used, so as the locomotive had only cost £425 it had already paid for itself. Yet, in spite of this success, the Newcastle & Carlisle Railway, incorporated in 1829, turned its back on the steam locomotive and decided to run the line using horses in the old way.

There was one other locomotive built to a new design that came from the Forth Street works. Although it still carried the name of Robert Stephenson, he was no longer in charge. No one has ever been able to say exactly why he had left; perhaps as a young man trying to make his own way in the world, having a strong-minded father constantly looking over his shoulder had proved just a little too much for him. Whatever the reason, he had signed up for a post as engineer to a South American mining company and set sail from Liverpool in 1824. In his absence, his father began to have new ideas about locomotive design. The new engine was aptly named *Experiment* and was the first Stephenson locomotive to be built with horizontal cylinders but, as with Trevithick's engine, they were embedded in the front of the boiler. The drive to the wheels was through a complex system of connecting rods that earned the engine the nickname

Hackworth continued to design locomotives for the Stockton & Darlington into the 1840s. *Derwent* was built in 1845 in Darlington and although the engine was retired in 1869, it was sold on and continued in use as a colliery engine and on a dam construction site. It took part in both the Stephenson celebrations of 1881 and the Stockton & Darlington centenary procession of 1925.

'Old Elbows'. Originally mounted on four wheels, it proved too much for the track and was remounted on six wheels. The idea of horizontal cylinders was not immediately followed up, but would re-emerge later on the next major Stephenson project.

Coal was the main reason the line was built, but it had been decided from the first that there should also be passenger coaches, but these would be worked by horses not locomotives. The first coach, called the 'Experiment' was leased to Thomas Close, who paid the company two guineas a week. When operations started, they were quite limited. The first journey began at Stockton at seven in the morning and left Darlington for the return journey at three in the afternoon. On Tuesday, it was a one-way trip from Stockton and for the next three days, return journeys from Darlington were run. On Saturday, it was a one-way trip back to Stockton, ready to restart services on the Monday morning. Passengers paid a shilling each for a single ticket and the trip took roughly two hours. The coach was like the other stage coaches of the day, with both inside and outside passengers and it seems there was no restrictions on numbers; health and safety rules and regulations had not yet surfaced. An eyewitness account, quoted in Robert Young's 1923 biography of Hackworth makes the journey sound quite hair-raising:

'We left Darlington with 13 outside passengers, and two or three inside, and picked up several others on the way. In regard to passengers, the coach appears to be in no way limited in its numbers. The coachman informed us that one day lately, during the time of the Stockton Races, he took up from Stockton nine inside and 37 outside, in all 46. Of these some were seated all round the top of the coach on the outside, others stood crowded together in a mass on the top, and the remainder clung to any part where they could get a footing. On that occasion he had two horses.'

It must have been an interesting journey, especially for those standing on top when the coach met one of the low bridges crossing the line. In time, more coaches were added, but run by different parties, resulting in frequent arguments over who had right of way on single-track sections and who would have to back up.

If the Stockton & Darlington was, it is often said to be, a model for later developments, then it was certainly not one without many problems. It remained a hybrid with all the attendant difficulties. Having two companies running the passenger service, neither under the direct control of the parent company, was not a recipe for smooth working. The locomotives, restricted to moving heavy goods, were built more with the idea of hauling the heaviest loads than with any idea of speeding on their way, but at least the inclines, once initial difficulties had been sorted out, worked well. One other railway was approved in the same year as the Stockton & Darlington opened, the Canterbury & Whitstable, described in the Act as 'a Railway or Tramroad', so the promoters were still keeping their options open. As built it had a number of steep sections, worked by stationary engines, and only used locomotives on short sections. Overseas there were railways being constructed in both Austria, opened 1827, and France, 1828, but both still relied on horses to do the work. The case for the steam railway had not yet been conclusively argued.

Chapter Five

The Great Locomotive Trial

Even before the opening of the Stockton & Darlington, Stephenson was already involved in another, even grander scheme. This was for a line to join Manchester, the rapidly developing heart of the Lancashire cotton industry, to the port of Liverpool, into which the raw material was imported from America. As with the earlier line, it was an idea that had been around for quite some time. The two centres were already linked by water, mainly based on the canal system built by the Duke of Bridgewater in the 1760s – now controlled by an influential body that was not at all enthusiastic about the idea of a railway arriving to challenge their monopoly. An early proposal had been for a Middleton type rack railway, but it was that great enthusiast for steam locomotives, William James, who finally got things moving. He approached Joseph Sandars, a successful Liverpool merchant who had been one of the most vociferous critics of the canals. Merchants were claiming that the system was so inefficient that it took less time to import cotton bales from America into Liverpool than it did to move them onward to Manchester. Sandars agreed to put up the money for a survey and James set to work in 1822, enlisting the young Robert Stephenson to help.

Surveying the route was not an easy task. The big landowners, many of whom had canal shares, opposed them all the way, refusing them access to their land and in the villages along the route they were showered with abuse and sometimes rather more solid objects. The only area where they could roam free was the marshy ground of Chat Moss. In spite of the problems, James completed his survey in October of that year and shared his ideas with George Stephenson, who James hoped would provide the locomotives. But then his financial world began to fall apart. His other business interests had been neglected, he had run up debts and he was being sued by his brother-in-law. He was bankrupt and the committee formed to promote the railway promptly dropped him, offering the job of chief engineer to George Stephenson. Sandars wrote to James to give him the news, explaining why he had been dropped and offering rather unconvincing consolation:

'I very much regret that by delay and promises you have forfeited the confidence of the subscribers. I cannot help it. I fear that you will only have the fame of being connected with the commencement of this undertaking. If you will send me down your plans and estimates I will do everything for you I can, and I believe I possess as much influence as any person. I am quite sure that the appointment of Stephenson will, under all circumstances, be agreeable to you.'

It is doubtful if the arrangement was at all agreeable to James, but he did receive a long and sympathetic letter from Robert Stephenson. It has been suggested by L.T.C. Rolt in his biography of the two Stephensons that the shabby treatment received by James might have been one of the factors in a disagreement between father and son that helped Robert in his decision to leave for South America. But, for now, George Stephenson was the man in charge. It soon transpired he was also a man with major problems, not least in completing a new survey in the face of the landowning opposition. In October 1824 he wrote:

> 'We have sad work with Lord Derby, Lord Sefton, and Bradshaw, the great Canal Proprietor whose ground we go through with the projected railway. Their Ground is blockaded on every side to prevent us getting on with the Survey – Bradshaw fires guns through his ground in the course of the night to prevent the surveyors coming on in the dark – We are to have a grand field-day next week, the Liverpool railway Company are determined to force a survey through if possible – Lord Sefton says he will have a hundred men against us – the Company thinks those Great men have no right to stop a survey.'

All very exciting stuff, but not circumstances that helped in producing well thought out plans. Stephenson, with so much to occupy his attention at this time, left much of the work to his juniors. As a result, when the plans were presented to Parliament, the lawyers employed by the canal interest tore into Stephenson and were all too easily able to show that the plans were hopelessly inadequate. In cross examination, for example, they were able to establish that a proposed bridge over the Irwell would be so low that it would be unable to take any flood water, leaving his proposed line under water. In short, he was made to appear an incompetent fool. The Bill was thrown out and it seemed for a time that Stephenson's involvement with the railway was at an end. In the event he was reinstated but with so many activities to look after, other concerns were beginning to suffer. In particular the Forth Street works were being sadly neglected. Longridge wrote to Robert Stephenson in South America to say how very much his presence was needed:

> 'I feel anxious for your return and I think you will find your father and your friend considerably older than when you left us.'

Robert had signed up with the mining company for three years and that period was coming to an end. It had not been a very good experience for him and he was very happy to head back to England. He was not, of course, the only pioneer who had gone to South American mines hoping to make a fortune. When we last met Richard Trevithick he had sailed to Peru to sort out problems with his high-pressure pumping engine for the Cerro de Pasco silver mines, high in the Andes. He was successful and thanks to the agreement he had made with the owners he had acquired a considerable fortune in silver bullion. Unfortunately, he had not been aware of the political situation in the region. Simon Bolivar's liberation army was marching across the continent and when it arrived in Peru it took over the silver mines – and appropriated all the stocks of the metal, including Trevithick's share. He had hoped to be heading home a rich man, instead of which he was co-opted into Bolivar's army as an engineer who might be able to help with their weapons. There followed years in which he tried to recoup his losses by various means, ending with the establishment of his own gold mines in Costa Rica. He was aware that to make money from the metal he needed to get it to the coast for shipment, but there were no roads and the only solution was to find a route for himself. After many adventures that included almost being killed by an alligator, he arrived at Cartagena, having lost virtually all his possessions en route and finding himself destitute with no chance of paying for a ticket back to Britain.

At this low point in his life, an amazing coincidence occurred that if one were to include it in a work of fiction would be considered too fantastical for serious consideration. Robert Stephenson arrived while Trevithick was recovering from his experiences. The two men met and Robert loaned the older engineer the money to get him home. No accurate records survive of their conversation, but they must surely have talked locomotives. Did Trevithick stress the importance of exhaust steam blast? It was to be a vital component of Robert's engines in the future. We simply do not know, and Trevithick slips out of the story again; his appetite for locomotive construction and design was never revived. Robert came back to Newcastle and was the driving force behind a vital period of locomotive innovation.

Back at Forth Street, Robert was able to take stock of what had happened in his absence, and he was particularly interested in the *Experiment* built in his absence. He was also looking at events outside the comparatively limited world of colliery-type engines. In January 1818 he wrote to Michael Longridge:

> 'I have been talking a great deal about endeavouring to reduce the size and ugliness of our travelling engines, by applying the engine either on the side of the boiler or beneath it entirely, somewhat similar to Gurney's steam coach'.

The Gurney referred to was Goldsworthy Gurney, one of the pioneers attempting to develop steam coaches for use on the road. His first efforts involved the use of legs rather in the manner of Brunton's walking locomotive. He soon abandoned this in favour of more conventional wheels. He had his own patent boiler that was tested to what was then the very high pressure of 200psi and regularly worked at up to 120psi. As Stephenson's letter suggests, the two-cylinder engine was tucked away under the chassis, driving a cranked axle. Like other engines of the day it had no brakes, but Gurney assured the authorities that it could safely be stopped from running away downhill by putting the engine into reverse. This was not strictly true, as the engine could only be reversed when completely stationary. It went into service at Bath in 1828 but was not very successful. Gurney was to abandon that design and built a steam drag, in effect a tractor, to pull a coach, which proved far more efficient and was used to provide a regular service between Cheltenham and Gloucester. A Gurney drag was restored by the Bristol Industrial Museum and provides a remarkably smooth ride. The success of the Gurney experiments certainly encouraged Robert Stephenson to begin on an improved locomotive design.

A new line had been authorised in 1825, the Bolton & Leigh Railway which, in spite of its quite imposing title, was simply a 7¾ mile long route linking collieries to the Leeds

& Liverpool Canal. It was to be worked by a mixture of locomotives on the level and two inclines were included to be worked by stationary engines, so there was nothing new about the route. An order was placed with Forth Street for a locomotive, which was built in 1828 and named the *Lancashire Witch*. The cylinders were steeply inclined at about 40 degrees driving directly to one pair of wheels, which were then coupled to the other pair of wheels in a 0-4-0 arrangement. There had been a certain amount of difficulty in constructing return flue boilers, specifically in making the curved section of the U. Stephenson solved this, while still providing a greater heating surface, by having two parallel flues, each fed from its own fire and each leading to the single chimney. It proved effective, but must have represented something of a nightmare for the fireman. Other engines of this pattern were built, including a 0-6-0 version for the Stockton & Darlington and a construction engine for the Liverpool & Manchester. Another locomotive of this type was sent to America to the Delaware & Hudson Canal. It was not the first appearance of steam on American canals.

A canal was designed to join Philadelphia and Pittsburgh, but the Alleghenies, rising to a height of 2,291 feet stood across the line of the track. The engineers James Geddes and Nathan Roberts came up with an ingenious solution. Steam powered inclines would cope with the hills. A boat would be hauled to the foot of the first incline, but the passengers had no need to change to a different vehicle. The boat was designed to be broken in half and each portion was floated onto a wheeled carriage. At the top of the slope, the two boats on wheels would be hauled along rails to the next incline to take them down the other side of the hills and the halves reunited to continue the rest of the journey by water. The company were considering using a locomotive for the summit section. Among those who travelled this remarkable system was Charles Dickens.

Dickens was not impressed by what he described as 'a barge with a little house in it' and even less impressed with the accommodation inside. He found:

The unique system of the main line of the Philadelphia Canal, in which the canal packet boats were divided in half and hauled up and down the inclined plane by steam engine.

'suspended on either side of the cabin three long tiers of hanging book-shelves, designed apparently for volumes of the small octavo size. Looking with great attention at these contrivances (wondering to find such literary preparations in such a place), I descried on each shelf a sort of microscopic sheet and blanket; then I began dimly to comprehend that the passengers were the library, and that they were to be arranged edge-wise, on these shelves, till morning.'

A Philadelphia Canal poster, advertising the three modes of transport in use: steam railway, horse-drawn canal boat and river steamer. It is not a notably rapid service; 3½ days for what is a 305-mile journey on modern roads.

The Delaware and Hudson Canal also had sections that had to be linked by inclines and these were suitable for working by locomotives. The man entrusted with the job of travelling to England to purchase locomotives was Horatio Allen. It was originally assumed that the engines would all be supplied by Stephenson, but having been to see Stephenson engines at work, Allen also visited the 3¾ mile Shutt End Railway. This was a typical short colliery line with two inclines and a level section linking with the Staffordshire & Worcestershire Canal. Here John Urpeth Rastrick had designed a locomotive *The Aegenoria*. It had two vertical cylinders, set at the firebox end of the engine, with the drive being transmitted by the method used for the so-called grasshopper stationary engines. Each cylinder operated through a beam which, instead of pivoting in the centre, was permanently attached at one end. The connecting rod was fastened half way down the beam to the drive wheels. In this respect it was a fairly conventional 0-4-0 engine of the period.

Like Stephenson, Rastrick had tried to find a different solution to the steam-raising problem. Instead of a single flue, the boiler divided at the end of the fire grate into two separate riveted tubes. They ended in an immensely tall chimney the tip of which was 22 feet above the rails.

Allen was clearly much more impressed by the Stourbridge engine than with Stephenson's and instead of ordering four *Lancashire Witch* type locomotives, he ordered just one, which it appears was never used, and the other three engines came from the Stourbridge company, Foster, Rastrick, one of which was named after the town in which it was built, the *Stourbridge Lion*. It was on this engine that Allen made the first trial run back in America. He described the experience:

'I took my position on the platform of the locomotive alone, and with my hand on the throttle-valve said 'If there is any danger in this ride, it is not necessary that more than one should be subjected to it.' The locomotive having no train behind it answered at once to the movement of the valve; soon the straight line was run over, the curve (and trestle) was reached and passed before there was time to think … and soon I was out of sight in the three miles' ride alone in the woods of Pennsylvania.'

What he did not record was that the trestle bridge he had passed over had swayed alarmingly and that many of the rails had been knocked out of line. This is perhaps not too surprising as the rails in use were of the older tramway strap-rail type, wooden with an iron strip on top. The first railway experiments in America were short lived; the Stephenson engine was not even tried. The Philadelphia Canal was also to get locomotives in time, but successful locomotive trials in America were still to come. In Britain, however, there was about to be a fundamental change.

The original Bill for the Liverpool & Manchester had been thrown out and George Stephenson had been publicly humiliated. His engineering expertise had been thrown into doubt and fun had even been made of his Geordie accent. 'One member asked me if I was a foreigner, and another hinted that I was mad.' He had lost his role as chief engineer and the company had to start all over again, appointing two new engineers, George and John Rennie, sons of John Rennie, the famous canal and bridge builder. They took on a comparatively young assistant, Charles Vignoles. He came from a distinguished Huguenot family and had practical experience of civil engineering when he had worked on modernising the northern section of the Oxford Canal. It is a mark of just what a small community the world of engineering was at that time, that the man who gave Vignoles the job was Marc Brunel, father of Isambard.

Between them the Rennies and Vignoles produced a new and accurate survey and the Bill successfully passed through Parliament in 1826. The post of chief engineer was offered to George Rennie and he was to have the help of an 'operative engineer' and two names were put forward – George Stephenson and Rastrick. Rennie refused to accept either of them. The company found this attitude unreasonable so Rennie had to go and they began looking around for an alternative, coming up with another son of a famous engineer, Josias Jessop, whose father William had been responsible for some of

John Urpeth Rastrick designed *Aegenoria* for the short colliery line, the Shutt End Railway – a route that obviously included no low overbridges. It inspired Horatio Allen to order similar locomotives from Rastrick for use in America, of which the *Stourbridge Lion* was the first to be tried.

Britain's most important canals. Stephenson was accepted as the operative engineer under his direction. Stephenson was not a man to take kindly to a subsidiary role and when inevitably he and Jessop disagreed it was Jessop who failed to get the committee's backing. He went and Stephenson was in charge, appointing his own man, Joseph Locke, as his assistant. That left just Vignoles from the Rennie era and it was not long before he was off as well. Vignoles' own version of events has the smack of truth about it:

'I also plead guilty to having neglected to court Mr. Ss favour by crying down all other engineers, especially those in London, for though I highly respect his great natural talents, I could not shut my eyes to certain deficiencies.'

Vignoles, however, will shortly reappear again in the Liverpool & Manchester story. Stephenson was now back where he wanted to be – in sole charge with people he knew and trusted around him. The task was to prove far more difficult than anyone expected, especially the task of pushing a railway across the great bog that was Chat Moss. But there also remained one vital question that still had to be answered; how was the railway to be worked?

The original Act had left the whole question of how the line would be run quite vague, with mention of both stationary and locomotive engines. It was equally uncertain about whether the company would run all the traffic themselves or lease it out to carriers as had been done on the canals. Tonnage rates were laid out as well as special rates for 'Persons, Cattle and Other Animals', the first time a railway had publicly admitted that they might treat their passengers like cattle. Eventually they took the sensible decision that they would control all the traffic themselves, but were divided over how things were to be moved. One idea was to follow the lead of the Stockton & Darlington and use a mixture of horses and locomotives, but that had already been shown to be a recipe for chaos and the idea was quickly dropped. That left two options. One group favoured a cable haulage system for the entire line, in which carriages and trucks would be moved from engine house to engine house. There was an obvious disadvantage to this idea; a fault in any one section would bring everything to a halt. If a locomotive broke down, it could be moved out of the way. If a stationary engine was stopped, nothing could be done until it was repaired. On the other hand, this was a tried system, used mainly on inclines but adaptable for use on the flat as well – and it was safe. And as the Stockton & Darlington had shown, things moved along just as fast with cable haulage as they did when worked with locomotives – indeed rather faster if anything. The other faction, led naturally enough by Stephenson, wanted everything to be run by locomotives. The question to be answered was this – could a thirty-mile journey followed by a return to the start be managed at a reasonable speed by a locomotive and its train?

The committee was divided so a deputation was sent over to the Stockton & Darlington to see what how that was faring. Everyone was aware of the importance of the visit and Edward Pease at once wrote to Hackworth asking him to get 'the engines and men as neat and clean as he can' and to have statistics available to show how much money was being saved by using locomotives. The deputation arrived, saw the spruced up men and machines and also inspected the two inclines. The result was not what Stephenson expected; they recommended stationary engines. It was not at all clear that they had any idea of how the system would work in practice. The method used on the Cromford & High Peak, for example, had a cable running in a continuous loop to which trucks were attached. It is difficult to see how that would work with a main line railway anticipating a considerable passenger traffic. The alternative of preparing a whole train to be hitched up and moved in a series of stops and starts was hardly more appealing. The committee remained unconvinced and decided that they probably needed a rather more experienced party to carry out the assessment. They chose James Walker and John Urpeth Rastrick. They set out on their tour of inspection in January 1829.

Their first call was the Middleton Colliery and they were well pleased with what they found there:

'Here we examined Mr. Blenkinsop's Engine upon the Middleton Rail-Road. We saw it make a journey with 38 waggons, and containing 45 cwt. of coals, which, considering the small size of the Engine, exceeded our expectations.'

One up to the locomotive it seemed. They then went round Durham and Northumberland and at the end decided that either locomotives or stationary engines would be suitable. It seemed the final decision would come down to cost. To run the Liverpool & Manchester with stationary engines would require fifty-four engines spread down the line at a capital cost of £81,000. The capital cost for locomotives would only be £28,000. Again, locomotives seemed to be winning, but then the engineers declared that running costs for the stationary engines would be twenty-five per cent below those of the locomotives, so in the long term the stationary engines would be a better investment. That was the course they recommended.

The locomotive camp at once challenged the figures and set to work producing counter-arguments. Robert Stephenson wrote to Hackworth that:

'they have increased the performance of fixed engines beyond what practice will bear, and, I regret to say, that they have deprecated the locomotive engines below what experience has taught us.'

Hackworth, in turn, wrote to George Stephenson:

'Do not discompose yourself my dear Sir; if you express your manly, firm, decided opinion, you have done your part as their adviser. And if it happens to be read some day in the newspapers – "Whereas the Liverpool and Manchester Railway has been strangled by ropes", we shall not accuse you of guilt in being accessory either before or after the fact.'

Hackworth offered his own figures to boost the locomotive case, showing that *Royal George* regularly moved seventy tons at five mph and the new Stephenson engine shifted more. The report had also said that to achieve a speed of ten mph the load would have to be limited to ten tons – Hackworth argued that thirty tons could be hauled at that speed. He also added his own rather telling argument against rope haulage:

'Admit it to be possible, who would dare to be near when a mass of matter standing at rest, say, 20 or 30 tons is first put into motion by a rope, moving at the rate of ten or 15 miles per hour? It need not be added what will follow – a scene of endless confusion.'

There was another very persuasive argument. The rope haulage system required every engine house to be built and paid for before anything could run on the line. On the other hand, a trial could be made with a single engine; if it was not a success, the loss would have been comparatively small. Rastrick and Walker had already pointed out that there was a comparatively straight, level section of track near the centre of the route at Rainhill, which would be ideal for trying out rope haulage. The locomotive faction, headed by the treasurer Henry Booth, proposed that the section could do equally well for mounting a trial to see if locomotives could do the job, and it need not cost the company a penny. Engineers would enter their own locomotives at their own expense. If any of them proved wholly satisfactory, it would receive a prize; if none of them proved up to the mark then no payment would be made. The idea was accepted and a locomotive trial was arranged; everything was to be decided at Rainhill in October 1829.

Advertisements were placed in the leading northern newspapers offering a premium of £500 over and above the cost of the engine to the successful competitor. This was a considerable sum – roughly £25,000 at today's prices, but much more importantly the winner could expect to get more lucrative contracts. The conditions were exact. The engine had to 'effectively consume its own smoke', which in practice meant that it would have to burn coke, not coal. The engine could weigh up to six tons if carried on six wheels and up to four and a half tons on four wheels. The six-ton engine 'must be capable of drawing after it, day by day, on a well-constructed Railway, on a level plane, a Train of Carriages of the gross weight of Twenty Tons, including the Tender and Water Tank, at the rate of Ten Miles per Hour, with a pressure of steam in the boiler not exceeding Fifty Pounds on the square inch .' The weight to be hauled was to be reduced proportionately with the weight of the locomotive. Other conditions included springing to support the boiler and two safety valves, one of which had to be out of the driver's reach; the latter clause was a precaution against tampering and boiler explosions.

Work began at once at Forth Street on what was then known as 'the premium engine'. It was decided to build the lighter, four-wheeled version and to base the design on the successful *Lancashire Witch*. Henry Booth, who had always been a keen supporter of both George Stephenson and locomotives now showed that he had taken more than merely the economic view of locomotives; he had also been aware of the technology involved. On 15 October 1829 he wrote to Robert about a new idea for improving the steam raising capacity of an engine. He proposed that instead of the single or return flues that had been in use up to then, the engine should be built with a separate firebox, from which the hot gases would pass through a number of copper tubes immersed in the water in the boiler. He included

GRAND COMPETITION

OF

LOCOMOTIVES

ON THE

LIVERPOOL & MANCHESTER RAILWAY.

STIPULATIONS & CONDITIONS

ON WHICH THE DIRECTORS OF THE LIVERPOOL AND MANCHESTER RAILWAY OFFER A PREMIUM OF £500 FOR THE MOST IMPROVED LOCOMOTIVE ENGINE.

I.

The said Engine must " effectually consume its own smoke," according to the provisions of the Railway Act, 7th Geo. IV.

II.

The Engine, if it weighs Six Tons, must be capable of drawing after it, day by day, on a well-constructed Railway, on a level plane, a Train of Carriages of the gross weight of Twenty Tons, including the Tender and Water Tank, at the rate of Ten Miles per Hour, with a pressure of steam in the boiler not exceeding Fifty Pounds on the square inch.

III.

There must be Two Safety Valves, one of which must be completely out of the reach or control of the Engine-man, and neither of which must be fastened down while the Engine is working.

IV.

The Engine and Boiler must be supported on Springs, and rest on Six Wheels; and the height from the ground to the top of the Chimney must not exceed Fifteen Feet.

V.

The weight of the Machine, WITH ITS COMPLEMENT OF WATER in the Boiler, must, at most, not exceed Six Tons, and a Machine of less weight will be preferred if it draw AFTER it a PROPORTIONATE weight; and if the weight of the Engine, &c., do not exceed FIVE TONS, then the gross weight to be drawn need not exceed Fifteen Tons; and in that proportion for Machines of still smaller weight—provided that the Engine, &c., shall still be on six wheels, unless the weight (as above) be reduced to Four Tons and a Half, or under, in which case the Boiler, &c., may be placed on four wheels. And the Company shall be at liberty to put the Boiler, Fire Tube, Cylinders, &c., to the test of a pressure of water not exceeding 150 Pounds per square inch, without being answerable for any damage the Machine may receive in consequence.

VI.

There must be a Mercurial Gauge affixed to the Machine, with Index Rod, showing the Steam Pressure above 45 Pounds per square inch; and constructed to blow out a Pressure of 60 Pounds per inch.

VII.

The Engine to be delivered complete for trial, at the Liverpool end of the Railway, not later than the 1st of October next.

VIII.

The price of the Engine which may be accepted, not to exceed £550, delivered on the Railway; and any Engine not approved to be taken back by the Owner.

N.B.—The Railway Company will provide the ENGINE TENDER with a supply of Water and Fuel, for the experiment. The distance within the Rails is four feet eight inches and a half.

THE "ROCKET" OF MR ROBT STEPHENSON OF NEWCASTLE.

WHICH DRAWING A LOAD EQUIVALENT TO THREE TIMES ITS WEIGHT TRAVELLED AT THE RATE OF 12¼ MILES AN HOUR, AND WITH A CARRIAGE & PASSENGERS AT THE RATE OF 24 MILES. COST PER MILE FOR FUEL ABOUT THREE HALF PENCE.

THE "NOVELTY" OF MESSRS BRAITHWAITE & ERRICSSON OF LONDON,

WHICH DRAWING A LOAD EQUIVALENT TO THREE TIMES ITS WEIGHT TRAVELLED AT THE RATE OF 20¾ MILES AN HOUR, AND WITH A CARRIAGE & PASSENGERS AT THE RATE OF 32 MILES. COST PER MILE FOR FUEL ABOUT ONE HALFPENNY.

THE "SANSPAREIL" OF MR HACKWORTH OF DARLINGTON.

The official document, listing the competition rules for the Rainhill Trials, illustrated by drawings of the three main contestants.

Rastrick was one of the judges at the Rainhill Trials, and this page from his notebook shows his sketch of the multi-tubular boiler and firebox of *Rocket*.

two sketches to illustrate his idea. Robert realised that this was a hugely important advance and at once began to plan to build the premium engine on the basis of Booth's design. The engine would now be entered in the Forth Street books under the names of both Booth and Stephenson. To ensure that there was sufficient heat from the fire, the engine would also use blast–pipe exhaust.

The 6-foot long boiler was to have 25 3-inch diameter copper tubes; this gave a total heating area of 138sqft. For comparison, if we look at one of the rival engines, *Sans Pareil* built with a conventional return flue boiler, which had only 90sqft of heating surface, and to accommodate that the boiler had to be far larger at 4ft 2in diameter against the premium's 3ft 4in. The firebox in the premium engine was separate and surrounded with a water jacket connected to the boiler by copper pipes. Steam from the boiler was passed to two inclined cylinders connected to a pair of 4ft 8½in drive wheels, giving the locomotive a 0-2-2 wheel arrangement. Reversing was through slip eccentrics on the left side of the driving axle and direction could be reversed through 'drivers' operated by a foot pedal on the footplate.

Robert had difficulty deciding how to fasten the copper tubes onto the body of the boiler; he experimented with screw threads and nuts but eventually decided on 'clunking', riveting the ends of the tubes to the boiler. Robert invited Booth along to see the tests on the boiler. Although working pressure was limited to 50psi, the rules demanded that for safety reasons the boiler had to be tested to 150psi. The test did not go well, as Robert reported: 'The boiler ends at 70 lb per square inch came out full 3/16 of an inch – This you may easily conceive put

Rocket is now preserved in the Science Museum in London, but has been considerably altered since first built. The most obvious difference is the lowering of the angle of the cylinders to nearly horizontal.

a severe strain on the clunking of the tube ends.' The problem was solved by adding stays to help the boiler retain its rigidity. He was aware that the engine should look good to impress the judges. The wheels, which were wooden spoked and rimmed with an iron tyre, were painted yellow: 'The same character of painting I intend keeping up, throughout the engine it will look light which is one object we ought to aim at.' On 5 September, Robert was able to write to Booth to tell him they had taken the engine over to Killingworth and that the trials had gone well, though there were still 'some nick nacks' to be added. It was to be sent off to Carlisle on the start of its journey to Rainhill at the end of that week.

There were three other contestants, two of which made no impression on the event. One was built by Timothy Burstall, who had begun by building steam carriages in Scotland. We know very little about it, as the cart carrying the engine down from Scotland overturned causing so much damage to the locomotive that, although it eventually reached Rainhill,

The replica of *Sans Pareil* was built for the 150th anniversary of the Rainhill Trials. This sturdy, workmanlike engine is seen here in the old engine shed at Shildon, where the original was built.

it was so badly damaged it was unable to compete. We do know, however, that 'Mr Burstall Junior' was not short of chutzpah. He turned up unannounced at Forth Street and was found wandering around the works taking notes before his identity was discovered and he was sent packing. The other non-starter was entered by a Mr. Brandreth of Liverpool and could hardly be said to qualify for the contest. Instead of being steam powered, it was worked by a horse walking in a treadmill. That left just two serious competitors to the premium engine which had by now been named – *Rocket*.

Sans Pareil was entered by Timothy Hackworth. Essentially it was a scaled down version of *Royal George* but built to a 0-4-0 configuration. Unlike Stephenson he was unable to build everything himself; Longworth built the return flue boiler and the cylinders were cast at Forth Street – the latter were to be the source of controversy that has echoed down the years ever since.

The third competitor was aptly named *Novelty* for it was quite unlike any other locomotive being built in Britain. The men responsible were John Braithwaite and John Ericsson. Braithwaite's father was one of that rare breed of inventors who managed to make money from his own inventions. He had run a small engineering business in St. Albans but later moved to London, where he designed a diving bell that he used himself to bring up some £130,000 of bullion from a sunken East Indiaman the *Earl of Abergavenny*. He died in 1818 leaving the business to his two sons, Francis and John and when Francis died in 1823 John took over the company. He soon began developing high-pressure steam engines and the world's first steam powered fire engine. It performed well when wheeled out to deal with a fire in the House of Commons, but the regular firemen were unimpressed by the rival. They turned their hoses on the firebox and the experiment came to an end.

In 1827 he actually met George Stephenson and the same year he met the young Swedish army officer Captain John Ericsson. The latter had already established a reputation as a brilliant engineer and was given extended leave to pursue some of his ideas. Unfortunately he got too involved with the work and overstayed his leave; luckily the army took a lenient view and instead of court martialling him, allowed him to resign his commission. He was to have a distinguished career in later life, designing one of the first screw propellers for ships and building the first iron-clad battleship, the *Monitor*, that saw service in the American Civil War. During that conflict he made the case to Lincoln that to win a war you needed superior weapons – 'By a proper application of mechanical devices alone will you be able to destroy the enemies of the Union'. They were a formidable pair, and they were joined by Charles Vignoles, who was no doubt looking forward to bettering his old adversary.

The Rainhill Trials were not advertised widely and the pair heard about the competition in a letter from a friend in Liverpool, leaving them only seven weeks in which to design and build their engine. All previous railway locomotives had developed out of a need to haul heavy loads, with speed of very little interest. The Braithwaite-Ericsson locomotive had very different origins. It was inspired by the fire engines, where speed in getting to the blaze was the first consideration. The differences were very apparent in *Novelty*. For a start it was very light, weighing in at less than three tons and that included the tank for the boiler water that was slung beneath a sprung platform holding the engine. It had two vertical cylinders that drove down to a bell crank, and via a connecting rod to a cranked axle, very much in the road vehicle tradition. The firebox was rather like a closed stove, from which an exhaust pipe snaked away, doubling back on itself twice before finally bending up to the vertical to form the chimney. The boiler was partly vertical, built round the stove, and partly horizontal enclosing the exhaust pipe. The whole boiler assembly was sheathed in copper, giving it what

This lithograph, based on an original drawing by Vignoles, shows *Novelty* as it never appeared in actuality, drawing a very mixed passenger train.

one of Stephenson's assistants called a 'very Parlour-like appearance' like 'a new tea urn'. The fire was assisted by mechanically operated bellows, which in order to work effectively required the whole stove to be closed off, with a sealed ash can and shutters at the top. The shutters could be opened to allow the fireman to add more fuel – presumably first turning off the bellows or he might have ended the trip with no eyebrows and burnt hair. With its narrow, spoked metal wheels it looked very sporty and when it arrived at Rainhill it was much admired and considered a clear favourite to win the competition. George Stephenson had a different view; 'no guts' was his comment.

The trials at Rainhill began on 6 October 1829. There was a crowd, estimated at between ten and fifteen thousand, a huge number for those days when few people had leisure time to spend watching anything. Among the crowd were scientists, engineers, potential railway builders and, far outnumbering them, the merely curious. The vast majority of those who turned up would never have seen a locomotive and were fascinated by the idea of these panting, fiery beasts hurtling down the track. Not only had most not seen a locomotive, but they also had no notion of the safety measures involved and to the consternation of the organisers, kept wandering across the track in the way they might cross a main road in front of a horse-drawn carriage. Rainhill itself was little more than a village, and the landlady of the newly opened Railroad Tavern set aside rooms for 'better class visitors' and, as the local paper wryly noted, she would have 'substantial reasons for remembering the trial of Locomotive Carriages'. All in all it was a great event, with a special grandstand erected for spectators, bands playing the inevitable 'patriotic airs' and a keen sense of anticipation in the air as everyone waited for a sight of the first locomotive.

There was a surprise right at the start. It was generally thought that the slope on the approach to the level section on which the trial would be run would require a stationary engine for hauling. *Rocket* stormed straight up it in a rather cheeky demonstration run before the actual trial got under way. Before proceedings could begin, the engines had to be weighed. To Hackworth's consternation, *Sans Pareil* was declared over the limit. The engineer at once demanded it should be reweighed. The judges refused but allowed it to compete anyway; quite what would have happened if the engine had won the trial we shall never know, but it would certainly have given the judges a few headaches. They were a distinguished trio. John Rastrick and Nicholas Wood have already put in appearances in this narrative, and they were among the few men with any practical experience of steam railways, though the Hackworth supporters were later to claim that Wood's early connections to Stephenson made him unduly prejudiced in his favour. The third member was John Kennedy, probably the biggest cotton manufacturer in Lancashire, who had an obvious interest in seeing a successful railway run by the best locomotive.

The first day was rather like the practice day at a modern Grand Prix, with each engine showing off its abilities. *Rocket* and *Sans Pareil* both made runs at a modest twelve miles an hour, while pulling loads and *Rocket*, running light, gave a demonstration dash that was variously estimated at between fifteen and twenty-five miles an hour. But it was little *Novelty* that stole the show, dashing along at great speed and at one point reaching just over thirty miles an hour. A contemporary account gives an idea of the overwhelming effect it had on the crowd:

'It seemed to fly, presenting one of the most sublime spectacles of mechanical ingenuity and human daring the world ever beheld. It actually made me giddy to look at it, and filled the breasts of thousands with lively fears for the safety of the individuals who were on it, and who seemed not to run along the earth, but to fly as it were, on the wings of wind.'

If the event had been decided there and then on popular acclaim, there would have been a clear winner. But this was a test of endurance as much as speed and tough conditions had been laid down. Each engine with its stipulated load had to make ten double runs up and down the track, the equivalent of the distance between Liverpool and Manchester. There would then be a pause to take on fuel and water, after which it would repeat the runs. At the end of the equivalent of a return run between the two cities, the engine had to average ten miles an hour – and as a measure of efficiency, the amount of fuel used would be recorded. On the first run of 8 October, *Rocket* was put to the test with George Stephenson driving. It started steadily, but with each pass, confidence grew. On the very last run, Stephenson opened the regulator wide and the little engine and its load raced along at thirty miles an hour. It had done everything asked of it by the judges. Now all that remained was to see if any other engine could beat or even match it.

Hackworth had been having all kinds of problems with mechanical faults of one kind or another, particularly with a leaking boiler, that had been made for him at the Bedlington Iron Works. His team worked through the night, but it was not until the 13th that it was ready to go. The engine made seven successful runs, but on the eighth, the boiler feed pump failed, no water reached the boiler and as a result one of the fusible plugs did what it was supposed to do as a safety measure, melted and allowed the water to dowse the fire. Hasty repairs were made, but on the next run the same thing happened and *Sans Pareil* was out of the contest. John Dixon wrote in rather understandably triumphant if ungenerous terms about the events of the day:

'Timothy has been very sadly out of temper ever since he came for he has been grobbing on night and day and nothing our men did for him was right, we could not please him with the Tender or anything; he openly accused all GS's people of conspiring to hinder him of which I do believe them innocent, however, he got many trials but never got half of his 70 miles down without stopping. He burned nearly double the quantity of coke that the Rocket does and mumbles and roars and rolls about like an Empty Beer Butt on a rough Pavement and moreover weighs above 4½ tons consequently should have had six wheels and as for being on Springs I must confess I cannot find them out.'

The tales of chicanery did not end there. Although nothing appears to have been mentioned at the time, there were rumours that many of the problems were actually caused by a crack in the cylinder – a cylinder that had, of course, been cast at the Robert Stephenson works. But all official accounts are clear; the engine was stopped due to a faulty water pump.

Novelty had an equally disastrous trial. On one early trip the bellows broke and had to be repaired. Back in working order it set out for another run, but the driver inadvertently closed

This photograph of a locomotive stripped down for restoration on the preserved Bluebell Railway shows very clearly how the modern steam locomotive developed out of *Rocket* and its immediate successors: the separate firebox and multi-tubular boiler are self-evident.

the stopcock between the boiler and feed pump, bursting the water feed pipe. When that was repaired, the boiler gave way and that was the end of that. It was always the crowd pleaser, and, fully repaired, it was to give a demonstration running light in which it was said to have reached a speed of 60mph, faster than man had ever travelled before. It could be said the engineers were unlucky. They had so little time to prepare that everything had been rushed, but even if it had behaved immaculately it is doubtful whether it had the endurance to run the course with a full load.

The fact that only one locomotive completed the course led to a lot of speculation at the time and for years to come. *Novelty* and *Sans Pareil* never had the chance to show their capabilities due to mechanical failures, but what would have happened if they had finished the trial? This is necessarily speculation, but there was an opportunity to see the three engines perform when replicas were made for the 150th anniversary of Rainhill. *Sans Pareil* was built at Shildon and turned out exactly as one might have expected; a solid, reliable locomotive based on tried and tested principles. I was fortunate enough to be asked to present a TV programme during which we followed the whole construction process and I was present when the engine was fired up for the first time. Among those who were there for the big day was Jane Hackworth Young, a direct descendant of the engineer, and she was given a footplate ride. It was all she needed to convince her that this was a great locomotive and given the opportunity would have been a potential winner – even if she wasn't quite prepared to accuse the Stephensons of deliberate sabotage. *Novelty*, however, was a very different story. Built together with the replica *Rocket* at Locomotion Enterprises, an organisation that had been set up originally to construct the replica of *Locomotion* for the Stockton & Darlington celebrations, the little engine had scarcely left the shed before things started to go badly wrong. In the event it proved impossible to make it work satisfactorily and on the grand celebration at the original site at Rainhill it had to be ignominiously displayed being carried on a flat truck. There was some consolation for the Hackworth camp. *Rocket* was derailed on the way to join the procession, and *Sans Pareil* was the only engine to steam down the course on a memorable Saturday afternoon – apart from on the pages of one Sunday newspaper that contained a thrilling account of *Rocket*'s appearance in front of the cheering crowds.

This event has been described in some detail because it represented one of the great turning points in the history of locomotive development. It was as well that the Stephenson engine won as it was the one that contained all the elements that were to be crucial for later development: the multi-tube boiler and separate firebox; exhaust steam blast; and cylinders lowered from their former vertical position. Had *Sans Pareil* succeeded it could well have been selected if only because it was based on well-established practices and could have been thought more reliable than the rivals. But it was built by an engineer looking back over previous successes, not forward to new developments. *Novelty* would never have had the power for working a busy line. It was *Rocket* that proved that a railway really could be worked more efficiently by steam locomotives than by any other means then available. It was the future.

Chapter Six

Coming of Age

Once the Rainhill Trials had established that locomotives could work a main line railway, work continued on finishing the line between Liverpool and Manchester. Thanks to the success of *Rocket*, plans to include three inclines on the route were drastically revised and the only rope-worked incline was used on the steep section on the approach to Liverpool. *Rocket* itself was comparatively light simply because it had to meet the rigorous conditions laid down for the competition, but now Stephenson began making changes to the basic design. A series of new engines came out of Forth Street: *Meteor, Comet, Dart and Arrow* being the first. In these the angle of the cylinders was gradually dropped down to be nearly horizontal. The next two *Phoenix* and *North Star* introduced a new element, the smoke box at the foot of the chimney. This both improved the effect of the exhaust blast and made maintenance, such as cleaning the boiler tubes, far simpler. The number of tubes had been steadily increasing and by the time the last of the group, *Northumbrian* and *Majestic*, had

Invicta built for the Canterbury & Whitstable Railway in 1829 by Robert Stephenson & Co, on display in Canterbury in the 1970s.

been built the number of tubes had been increased to 130. Heating was improved by having the firebox integrated into the boiler end. The locomotives were also becoming bigger and more powerful. Cylinder size was gradually increased, from the 8in bore of *Rocket* up to the 11in of *Phoenix*. By the time the last of the group had been built, the locomotive weight had risen from *Rocket*'s 4½ tons to 8 tons. These were important changes, but the similarities are more striking than the differences. One other *Rocket* type locomotive was built at the same time, ordered by the Canterbury & Whitstable Railway. For some reason, *Invicta* was built with cylinders steeply inclined as in the original, but with the cylinders at the opposite end of the boiler, next to the chimney.

The Canterbury & Whitstable was a decidedly modest line. There was a rope-worked incline to take trains up from the river valley at Canterbury, leaving only a short run to be worked by the locomotive. Nevertheless, the engine earned its place in railway history when in May 1830 it inaugurated the first passenger service in the world to be worked on a regular basis by a steam locomotive. The engine was not a great success and was much altered over the years – alterations that included removing the multi-tubular boiler and replacing it with a straight flue in a lengthened boiler. Its working life was short. Offered for sale in 1839, there were no takers but fortunately it was decided that it was an object of historic importance so it was kept by the company until 1906 when it was donated to the city of Canterbury. It now stands in a place of honour in the city.

Although *Rocket* had done more than enough to demonstrate its superiority over the Rainhill rivals, the directors were still impressed by light, speedy *Novelty*. One of the directors of the new company, James Cropper, had been among those who had argued for fixed engines and whether out of pique at being defeated in the argument by the Stephensons or from a genuine admiration for the little engine, he now began campaigning to use similar locomotives on the line. This time he won his case and two locomotives were ordered – *William IV* and *Queen Adelaide*. The engineers were still having problems with the boiler and Ericsson redesigned it, this time with a fan mounted on the top to draw air through the fire. In Ericsson's own, very frank words, it was 'very classical but miserably inefficient'. The engines, each of which cost more than Stephenson's, were never brought into service. *Novelty* itself was sold on to the St. Helens & Runcorn Gap Railway where it enjoyed a brief run before being sold on again to the North Union Railway where, instead of enjoying a glamorous existence as an express locomotive hauling excited passengers at high speeds, it was reduced to the humble role of use by the contractors building the Ribble viaduct. When it came to the opening of the Liverpool & Manchester every engine that took part in the ceremony came from the Robert Stephenson works.

There was inevitably speculation about how the public would react to this new form of transport. A passenger service was planned and an entirely new type of building had appeared in the landscape, the railway station. But would anyone want – or dare – to use the service? Even before the official opening there were opportunities to try this novel form of transport and reactions were very mixed. Thomas Creevey was a gentleman who moved in aristocratic circles and was invited by Lady Wilton to join her party for a trip on 'the Loco Motive machine'. The trip took place on 14 November 1829 and was, according to Creevey to be 'a

Northumbrian, from an 1831 lithograph by I. Shaw; the locomotive is at once recognised as a close relation to *Rocket*, but the main changes can also be easily seen. The cylinders have been lowered to the horizontal and the firebox has now been integrated into the boiler assembly.

lark of a very high order'. He treated the trip seriously enough, however, to take the trouble to time the journey with his pocket watch, watch, which , as he seemed proud to note, was equipped with a second hand. He reported that the five mile trip took just a quarter of an hour, but in places where the 'machine was made to put itself or *go it*' they reached 23 miles an hour, yet Creevey was not a happy man.

> 'But the quickest motion is to me *frightful*: it is really flying, and it is impossible to divest yourself of the notion of instant death to all upon the least accident happening. It gave me a headache which has not left me yet … The smoke is very inconsiderable indeed, but sparks of fire are abroad in some quantity: one burnt Miss de Ros's cheek, another a hole in Lady Maria's silk pelisse, and a third a hole in someone else's gown. Altogether I am extremely glad indeed to have seen this miracle, and to have travelled in it. Had I thought worse of it than I do, I should have had the curiosity to try it; but, having done so, I am quite satisfied with my *first* achievement being my *last*.'

The best-known account of travel at this period was given by Fanny Kemble, a member of a famous theatrical family who had made her first appearance as Juliet in 1829. Portraits show a beautiful slender young woman and she clearly won the heart of George Stephenson who invited her to share a footplate ride with him. Like Creevey, she described it as being like flying, but unlike that nervous gentleman she found it exhilarating:

> 'You cannot conceive what the sensation of cutting the air was; the motion is as smooth as possible too. I could have either read or written; and, as it was, I stood up and with my bonnet off "drank the air before me".'

If she was enthusiastic about the engine, she was equally struck by her eminent driver:

> 'Now for a word or two about the master of these marvels, with whom I am horribly in love. He was a man of from fifty to fifty-five years of age; his face is fine though careworn, and bears an expression of deep thoughtfulness; his mode of explaining his ideas is peculiar and very original, striking, and forcible; and although his accent indicates strongly his north-country birth, his language has not the slightest touch of vulgarity and coarseness, He has certainly turned my head.'

How flattering for the engineer to have such open admiration from one of the great beauties of the day; though he would have been less pleased by her guess at his age – he was still only forty-nine. Fanny Kemble herself was to have a remarkable later life. On a theatrical tour of America she met and married the owner of a Southern cotton plantation, and discovered for the first time the horrors of the slave system. It was to turn her into a passionate and eloquent abolitionist.

There must have been a certain amount of nervousness among the investors as opening day approached. Would the public react with horror like Creevey or with delight like Fanny Kemble? The engines were ready and they represented the pinnacle of engineering achievement at that time. The track had been completed and represented a mixture of the old and new. Unlike the Stockton & Darlington, which had used a mixture of cast iron and wrought iron rails, Stephenson had this time settled for wrought iron fish bellied rails throughout, but mostly they were still mounted on stone blocks, even though there was no longer any intention to use horses for any part of the traffic. However, on some sections, especially over Chat Moss, he had set his rails on transverse wooden sleepers. It was soon discovered that with the heavier, faster traffic of the new line, stone blocks were easily shifted out of place, while the wooden sleepers remained firm. Within seven years of the opening, the stone blocks had all been replaced by the new wooden sleepers that would become the norm for railway construction for many years to come. The changes to the track were important. With an improved permanent way, engineers could feel confident in building bigger, more powerful locomotives. The Liverpool & Manchester would show whether there was a real demand for this kind of transport.

The opening of the Stockton & Darlington had attracted large crowds of local people, but had made less impact on the world at large. This opening was very different. The chief guest was the Duke of Wellington, who may have been the hero of Waterloo but for the industrial communities of the north, and especially those of Manchester, he was better known as the villain of Peterloo, the infamous massacre of 1819 in which a peaceful political protest had been broken up by the military, causing death and injury. Many also disliked his reactionary political views, which can easily be imagined by his criticism of railways; he disapproved of them because 'they encourage the lower classes to travel about'. He was also at odds with the local MP and enthusiastic supporter of railways in general and this one in particular, William Huskisson. In many ways he was an unfortunate choice for the position of guest of honour, but he undoubtedly helped to place the whole event as one of national importance.

The report of the event in the local press described people coming from all over Britain for the occasion and such was the demand for horses that when the Duke arrived at Warrington and needed fresh horses for his carriage all he could get were 'two sorry jades'. However, he was more than compensated by a journey in style with the Marquis of Salisbury on the railway. A special carriage had been built in a most extravagant style and it is worth quoting the contemporary account to give an idea of its opulence:

> 'The ducal carriage was a costly and splendid car. The floor was thirty two feet long by eight feet wide, supported on eight wheels, which were partly concealed by a basement, ornamented with bold gold mouldings and laurel wreaths on a ground of crimson cloth. An ornamental gilt balustrade extended round each end of the carriage and united with one of the pillars which supported the roof. Handsome scrolls filled up the next compartments on each side of the doorway, which was in the centre of the carriage, protected with balustrading similar to that at each end. A lofty canopy of crimson cloth 24 feet in length, rested upon eight carved and gilt pillars, the cornice enriched with gold ornaments and pendant tassels, the cloth fluted to two centres, surmounted with two ducal coronets. The canopy was, by the aid of a windlass in the basement, made to rise or fall, and so constructed that, when down, the coronets were concealed in the roof ….The whole had a magnificent and imposing effect, in the Grecian style of architecture.'

Everything got off to a splendid start; the ducal carriage appeared to the accompaniment of a band playing the most obvious choice imaginable – 'Hail, the conquering hero comes'. The organisers must have been delighted, but the day was famously to end with tragedy. There had been a temporary halt at Parkside, where the Duke of Wellington spotted Huskisson on the far side of the tracks. He held out his hand in greeting and Huskisson decided to accept the gesture of friendship and hurried forward to stand on the track beside the carriage. At that point spectators spotted *Rocket* speeding down the line, and in spite of shouts of 'get in', Huskisson seemed confused. He hesitated and the engine was upon him, crushing his thigh. He was placed on a flat car and rushed off to hospital, but in spite of everything he died.

It was agreed that the event must proceed and what had been a triumphant procession was now funereal. The crowds along the way, unaware of the tragedy, cheered but at Manchester the cheers turned to boos and cries of 'Remember Peterloo'. It was not the opening the organisers had hoped for and planned so carefully yet it did mark a major turning point.

Robert Stephenson

A portrait of Robert Stephenson in later years, from Smiles'. *Lives of the Engineers.*

It was soon evident that there was a real hunger for rail travel. Up until then, railways had been all about freight, with passenger traffic an afterthought. Now it was becoming obvious that the two types of rail transport were achieving something like parity, and engineers would have to plan accordingly. No one cared very much how long it took a coal truck to get from the colliery to a waiting barge but passengers would be taking a keen interest in their journey time, and the faster the railways could deliver them to their destination the less likely they were to use the old stage-coaches.

Robert Stephenson was already planning for the future before the Liverpool & Manchester was officially opened. He was busy designing a whole new class of locomotives, named after the first in the series, *Planet*. These engines were to incorporate a number of important changes. Nearly all early locomotives had used the boiler as the main foundation for the whole engine, but this engine had a separate frame consisting of a sandwich, made up of a stout wooden beam with iron plates to either side. The beams were outside the wheels, allowing Stephenson to achieve his ambition of following road carriage design by having the cylinders inside the frame, bolted onto the smoke box. The introduction of the latter increased the efficiency of the exhaust blast and that, together with a larger grate improved the steam raising capacity. They were set horizontally and drove a cranked axle. The original had a 2-2-0 wheel arrangement with 5ft diameter drive wheels. Cranked axles caused trouble on these early examples; they were difficult to forge in the first place and were prone to breaking in use. Nevertheless, the new arrangement, with a rigid frame and springs and bearings outside the wheels, made for a very compact engine and a relatively smooth ride.

The valve gear was based on slip eccentrics as in *Rocket* but required two long eccentric rods, passing between the cylinders, to gabs, notches at the end closest to the valve, which could engage or disengage with the rocking shaft to operate the valves. Reversing was achieved by manually operating levers attached to the rocking shaft. Once the engine was under way, these rocked backwards and forwards with the movement of the valve, making the footplate seem as dangerously interesting to the driver as it had been on the earlier Trevithick engines. Other innovations included the dome, where steam collected above the boiler before being fed to the cylinders, ensuring the steam remained dry and no liquid water was carried over to the cylinders. Boiler pressure was increased, allowing Stephenson to use smaller cylinders than previously at 11in diameter, while still maintaining power.

Shaw produced this companion piece to *Northumbrian*. This time the locomotive is *Planet*. The overall boiler assembly is more or less unchanged, but now it has changed from the 0-2-2 arrangement of the former to 2-2-0 and the cylinders have been moved inside the frame, beneath the boiler.

As with many early locomotives, a replica has been built for the Museum of Science and Industry in Manchester. It was completed and first steamed in 1992. It is currently run on a length of track outside the original Liverpool Road Station in Manchester. The building itself is of considerable interest, looking from the road side rather like an elegant town house of the period, or perhaps a rather grand office. This no doubt was intended to reassure nervous passengers that really there was nothing sensational about rail travel. Behind the façade are the usual booking hall, waiting rooms and platform. Across the tracks are the goods sheds, all of which helps to create a splendid historic setting for seeing the locomotive and its replica carriages at work.

Michael R. Bailey, who supervised the construction, has written an account of some of the difficulties that the team faced, first in constructing the replica and then in making it work. His paper, *Learning through replication*, was published in the *Transactions of the Newcomen Society*, Vol. 68, 1996-97. A certain number of changes had to be made; some, such as the addition of air brakes, were required by modern safety standards. The team consulted Mike Satow, who had set up Locomotion Enterprises and by then had considerable experience in building replicas, including *Locomotion* and *Rocket*. He suggested a few more changes to make the engine more manageable in everyday use, including the replacement of the original

This working replica of *Planet* is regularly steamed at the Museum of Science and Industry in Manchester. One can see the details of construction that are missing from the Shaw illustration, such as the actual frame assembly and rivet heads on the metal plates that form the firebox and smokebox.

feed pump by an injector. This required a higher boiler pressure, raised from the 50psi of the original to 100psi which in turn meant reducing the size of the cylinders from 11in to 8in to compensate. But as far as possible, the original design was closely followed.

The first problems arose from trying to fit all the mechanism within a very confined space. Stephenson had been restricted by various factors. In the first place, in manufacturing the boiler he could only use plates up to the maximum size that could be rolled using the technology of the day, and that was 2ft 6in width. With a short boiler, there had to be a short wheelbase of just 5ft 2in and the space between the front of the firebox and the back of the smoke box was a modest 7ft. This left very little space, which was further reduced by the timber cladding that provided insulation for the outside of the boiler. As a result the cranks in their rearward horizontal position cleared the edge of the firebox by just 17/32 of an inch, and there was a danger of them actually scraping the wooden cladding of the boiler. There were also problems in setting the valves to compensate for the fact that connecting rods could not work horizontally for lack of space.

One of the most interesting features of the construction was learning how to drive an engine so very different from more modern steam locomotives. I cannot do better than quote

Michael Bailey's own words. There was no problem when the engine was to be restarted in the same direction as before as the slip eccentrics would normally be correctly set. If, however, it had to start in the opposite direction or if it had stopped in the stall position, then things became much more difficult:

'To achieve a manual valve change, the gabs at the leading ends of the eccentric-rods are first lifted off the valve-drive cranks. The lifting mechanisms are two pull-rods, the handles for which are located on the footplate hand-rails. The valves are then free to be re-positioned by the hand-levers, to suit the new steam as determined by the crank position. The left-hand crank can be observed by the driver looking down over the firebox. At the same time, the foot pedal is depressed by the driver in readiness for the eccentric sheave to engage with the dog, as the crankshaft rotates through approximately half a turn.

'When the regulator is opened, and movement commences, the valve-levers are pulled and pushed for the requisite valve movements, the operation requiring both understanding and dexterity by the driver. When the dog is engaged, the eccentric rods are lowered ready for their gabs to re-engage the valve-drive cranks. With the eccentric rods engaged and driving the valves, the valve operating levers continue to reciprocate and drivers quickly learn their threatening presence … the dexterity required in re-starting the train 'on the handles' soon encouraged the practice of reversing the valves while slowing to a halt. We can be certain that the footplate crews of the 1830s were also soon encouraged to adopt this practice. The technique requires that, on the last few revolutions of the driving wheel, and with the regulator closed, the eccentric cluster be released from the driving dog by the foot-pedal and, correspondingly, delayed and re-engaged by the alternative directional dog. The foot-pedal spring keeps the eccentric sheave rubbing on the new dog until it coincides with its slot.'

If this seems a complex procedure and difficult to understand immediately that is not too surprising, because it is almost equally complex in practice. Having watched the replica being put through its paces from the footplate, one comes away filled with admiration for the men who first drove such locomotives and had to master such difficult skills for themselves, with no precedents to follow. Stephenson went on to design a modified version, beginning with *Samson*, which was adapted as a 0-4-0 instead of a 2-2-0. Altogether the factory was to turn out about twenty Planet Class engines with the 0-4-0 arrangement and the same number with 2-2-0. They were not just built for the home market but were also sent overseas. These will be looked at in more detail in the next chapter.

Stephenson was not the only engineer working on similar ideas at this time. The Stockton & Darlington directors, encouraged by the success of passenger traffic in the north-west, decided to abandon their horse-drawn coach and asked Hackworth to design them an appropriate, speedy locomotive to take over the task. The locomotive he produced, which he christened *Globe*, was a strange affair with a unique boiler. It was over nine foot long and consisted of a single flue, with the firebox at one end and the chimney at the other. A series of small tubes passed transversely through the main flue and it was these that carried the water. It had a copper dome, four coupled five-foot diameter drive wheels and a cranked axle. There was a platform with an ornamental rail all round the boiler, and the general appearance was far more like a road locomotive than a railway engine. Parts had to be made at the Stephenson factory in Newcastle and Hackworth made the journey to explain exactly what was needed. This was in 1830 while Robert was working on the *Planet*, so it was inevitable that in later years the Hackworth family, who remained convinced they had been cheated out of winning Rainhill, now decided that the Stephensons had simply borrowed an idea that originated with Hackworth. In 1852, Timothy's son, John Hackworth, received a query from another engineer, John Gray, about the origins of the crank axle. Hackworth replied that, he could not say when *Globe* was first tried on the line:

> '…but that is of slight importance when you are made aware of the fact that no sooner had Messrs. Stephenson & Co. secured the order for the "Globe" than they commenced and finished an engine with a "crank shaft" (called by the name of some Planet or Star, no doubt of the first magnitude), I believe for the L. & M. Railway Co. previous to sending the "Globe" there.'

The sarcasm is all too evident, but Stephenson had no need to hear about Hackworth's engine in order to consider a cranked axle; he had already seen it a year earlier on *Novelty*.

The other new engine designer to appear on the scene was Edward Bury. Born at Salford in 1794, he took a conventional route into his profession. He went to school in Chester, where he discovered a talent for model building that led him to take an engineering apprenticeship and eventually to set up in business for himself in Liverpool. 1830 was an important year in his life. He married the distinguished botanical artist, Priscilla Susan Falkner, who by a happy coincidence was actually born at Rainhill, and designed his first locomotive, *Liverpool* for the Liverpool & Manchester. It too had a cranked axle and a general arrangement similar to that of *Planet*, but with a few important differences. Bury used large 6ft diameter drive wheels in a 0-4-0 arrangement, and attached them to an iron frame, consisting of metal bars set on each side of the boiler, attached by brackets to boiler, firebox and smokebox. The wheels were outside the frame. The main difference was in his design for the firebox. This was contained in a vertical cylinder attached to the end of the main boiler and closed off by a dome. The grate was D-shaped, instead of the square found in Stephenson's engines. Bury was to continue with a distinguished career as a locomotive builder, and also as a theorist, one of the few engineers of the day given to serious analysis of design and performance.

One other innovation of the period was a great boon to footplate crew. On the first engines, the only method of checking water levels in the boiler was by opening cocks set in the boiler end. In 1829, Foster & Rastrick introduced the water gauge. Connected to the boiler by tubes, the level of water in the glass gauge is the same as that in the boiler. It is

This 0-4-0 locomotive was designed by Edward Bury in 1835 for the Liverpool & Manchester. It is a very compact and workmanlike engine.

then always clear whether water levels are high enough to clear the firebox crown, but not so high that a large amount of water is carried over with the steam. It is a constant visual indicator, and safety no longer depended on the crew remembering to test levels at regular intervals.

Although it was the passenger locomotives that attracted the most attention, there were more mundane duties for engines to perform. In 1837, they acquired two locomotives from a brand new company, specifically designed for hauling luggage trains. The company, based at Hunslet in Leeds was Todd, Kitson and Laird. James Kitson was the chief promoter of the enterprise. He was born in Leeds in 1807, educated at local schools and the Leeds Mechanics' Institution, where he studied engineering and mathematics. He also read Nicholas Wood's *Treatise* that convinced him his future lay with the railways. Charles Todd had connections going back to the beginning of the railway age, having served his apprenticeship at Matthew Murray's foundry, while Laird was a wealthy farmer who provided the finance. It was said that the very first locomotive was built in one corner of a textile mill, but by 1837 they were already advertising a specialist railway engineering works in purpose-built premises. Their first engine, *Lion*, was conventional enough, a 0-4-2 inside cylinder locomotive, but it was to enjoy fame denied to far grander machines. In 1859 it was sold to the Port of Liverpool and might have been scrapped but it was rescued by local engineers who recognised its historic significance. In 1930 it went home to Hunslet where it was restored to full steaming capability. In its renewed form it became a film star, most notably as the eponymous hero of *The Titfield Thunderbolt*. At the celebrations to mark the 150th anniversary of the Rainhill Trials, it was *Lion* that led the grand procession of locomotives, the world's oldest working steam locomotive. It has now been retired and has a place of honour in the Liverpool Museum.

Passenger traffic on the Liverpool & Manchester proved very popular with all classes, although they received very different treatments. A well-known pair of illustrations of the time show a train of first class passengers headed by a Planet class locomotive. The coaches are rather like three old stage-coach bodies stuck together to create three separate compartments, in which passengers face each other, the whole assembly carried on four wheels. Baggage is piled on top and some passengers clearly preferred to remain aloof. They are carried in their own coach, mounted on a flat truck. There are guards perched on high seats at the front and rear of the train. The second illustration has second and third class carriages headed by a Rocket class locomotive. The second class have an open-sided carriage, with a canopy for cover; third class are crammed into vehicles little different from freight trucks, with a few benches but with many passengers standing. The lack of comfort for third class passengers was to be a feature for many early railways. The Glasgow, Paisley, Kilmarnock & Ayr Railway originally provided wooden bench seats but when they discovered how many more people they could squeeze in if they all stood up, they had the seats removed. These 'carriages' are often referred to as being like cattle trucks, and in the case of the Sheffield, Ashton & Manchester Railway this was literally true. When the company ordered cattle trucks they had them fitted with sprung buffers so that if no cows were available they could be used

Lion was the first locomotive to be designed by James Kitson, founder of the famous locomotive works at Hunslet, Leeds. Fans of Ealing Studios comedies will recognise it as the eponymous hero of The Titfield Thunderbolt

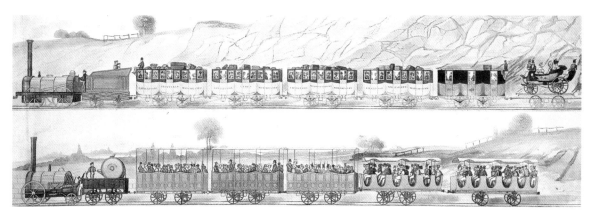

This 1833 lithograph based on the original by artist I. Shaw show passenger trains on the Liverpool & Manchester Railway. The upper picture shows a train of first class carriages, clearly based on contemporary stage coach design. Some wealthy families preferred to travel in their own coaches on a flat truck. The train is shown as being hauled by a Rocket class locomotive, *Jupiter*, but the artist portrays it as having equally-sized wheels. The lower illustration shows a train hauled by *North Star* – not to be confused with the Great Western locomotive of the same name – and here the second and third class passengers have to make to do with glorified cattle trucks.

for people. In spite of the discomfort, railways were proving immensely popular, and they began to spread rapidly, not just in Britain, but internationally as well. British engineers had dominated the first decades, but now others appeared with their own ideas and designs in different countries.

Chapter Seven

Across the Atlantic

T he failure of the *Stourbridge Lion* in the trials was not the first attempt to interest Americans in steam locomotives. One would have expected America to be in the forefront of developing steam for use in transport. It was, after all, an American, Robert Fulton, who had inaugurated the world's first commercial steam boat service in 1807. It was to be another American engineer who also worked at developing steamers on the water, who was to become the first eloquent advocate of railways and who backed up his words with a practical demonstration.

John Stevens was born at Perth Amboy in New Jersey in 1749, the son of an eminent political figure. He studied law, but his career was interrupted by the American War of Independence. At the age of twenty -seven he was appointed a captain in Washington's army

The replica of John Stevens' original experimental locomotive shows the simple drive mechanism. The crank turns a central cog that engages with one below, which in turn provides the motive power through the connection with the toothed rack rail, running between the lines. Although the basic form of the original is known the details are not and this represents the likeliest arrangement of the engine.

and then rose to the rank of colonel. He was later to be made the treasurer of New Jersey. At this time, he purchased a large farm estate at what was then Hoebuck, the site of modern Hoboken. Stevens was convinced that transport was going to be a key factor in helping the young nation to develop. His early work involved the construction of steamboats and in the process he developed a form of multi-tubular boiler, which was unlike the later developments in that the tubes contained the water and were clustered round the firebox. He used this in his vessels, which went into commercial service shortly after Fulton's pioneering efforts had proved successful.

Early in the nineteenth century, America was beginning to develop an extensive canal network, with such major waterways as the Erie Canal, but Stevens felt that the answer lay with railroads. He published his ideas in a pamphlet of 1812, the title of which is lengthy but self-explanatory, *Documents tending to prove the Superior Advantages of Railways and Steam Carriages over Canal Navigation.* In it he argued that the government should help to promote railways as a cohesive system, and if that was accomplished then it could be 'truly said that these States would constitute one family, intimately connected'. The arguments may have been sound, but there was little enthusiasm for the idea either in the government or among private investors. Over the years he made valiant attempts to promote railway construction. He suggested a steam railway between Philadelphia and New York but no one was interested. In 1815 the New Jersey legislature approved a Bill for a line to connect the rivers Delaware and Raritan; it too was never built. In 1823, the Pennsylvania Railroad Company was formed with powers to construct a line from Philadelphia to Columbia 'under the superintendence and direction of John Stevens'. It hardly seems necessary to add that it too was never started.

In 1825 Stevens was in correspondence with DeWitt Clinton, a New York politician and as passionate an advocate for canals as Stevens was of railways. In the hopes of convincing the latter, Stevens wrote to him putting the case for 'steam carriages' running on rails. Clinton accepted that the idea was important, but remained dubious:

'Until your plan can be tested by actual experiment, on a small scale at least, I think it will be almost impracticable to procure an adequate investment of capital on the magnificent scale you have contemplated.'

What is remarkable about this letter is that it seems to suggest that Clinton had no knowledge of the many successful experiments that had already been carried out on the other side of the Atlantic. In the event, Stevens took up the challenge. He built a circular track in the grounds of his Hoboken estate and designed a locomotive to run on it. Although very little is known about the details of the engine, a replica was built and is now in the Railroad Museum of Pennsylvania. The track was very short, just 660ft long and the curvature on such a short radius would have greatly hampered any attempts at speed. The engine was very light. In appearance it is quite similar to *Novelty*, with the boiler and engine mounted on a four-wheeled, flat top carriage. The vertical boiler is assumed to be similar to those he designed for ships, consisting of twenty vertical water tubes set in a ring round the firebox. It is reported as producing steam at what was for that time the very high pressure of 100psi. The steam is passed to a horizontal cylinder that provides drive through a crank. He is said to have tried various ideas, but the replica shows the half crankshaft linked to a cogged wheel, engaging with a toothed rack placed centrally between the rails. At least one historian has suggested that he was thinking ahead to a possible use on mountain railways, or at least on steep inclines. A more likely explanation is that he was facing exactly the same problem as that which had confronted Blenkinsop – how to provide sufficient traction on an engine that had to be light enough to avoid breaking fragile rails. As the engine was only designed to go round in circles, there was no need for any reversing mechanism. He seems to have had a problem with finding a suitable method of keeping his machine on the rails. The engine suffered from the severe friction between track and wheels – hardly surprising when the engine was being run round such a tight circle. He solved that problem with an ingenious system:

> 'I sent the carriage to Van Belsen's shop and directed him to insert rollers into each end of two bars: one to be placed in front of the fore-wheels and the other behind the hind wheels, extending beyond their track on each side, so as to roll against the upright pieces placed on the outer side of the way. This improvement, as far as I know, is original.'

Visitors were invited to come and ride on his little railway and one is inevitably reminded of Trevithick's attempts to interest investors in his locomotive run in a similar fashion in London. Stevens was to prove no more successful. He could at least claim the distinction of being the very first American to build a steam locomotive, even if it was destined never to go into service. He remained a visionary in spite of his failure to convince others that his dreams could become reality, and he was certainly ambitious, declaring that he saw no reason why a locomotive should not reach speeds of 100 miles an hour, though he thought that 'in practice, it may not be advisable to exceed 20 or 30 miles an hour'. He was a man ahead of his time, but it was not to be long after these initial experiments that an American locomotive would be put to work.

Baltimore businessmen began to talk about constructing a railroad in competition to the proposed Chesapeake & Ohio Canal. Among the leading promoters were two brothers, Evan and Philip E. Thomas. Evan had visited Britain and had been to look at the Stockton & Darlington. He successfully argued the case that the new line should operate on the same principles, as a common carrier for both freight and passengers. There the similarity with the English line ended. Because it was going through difficult country, the line had so many twists and turns that it was generally considered unsuitable for locomotives, so was designed for horse-drawn traffic. It had strap rails, similar to those already described for the Delaware & Hudson. A contemporary illustration of the first passenger coach, if it can be dignified by such a name, shows what looks like a wooden shack on four wheels being drawn along by a single horse. One man at least thought that it was time to change this antiquated system for one using locomotives.

Peter Cooper was an intriguing mixture of inventor, engineer and businessman. Born in New York in 1791 he started work as an apprentice in a company manufacturing cloth-shearing machinery. He was soon starting up on his own, making enough money to diversify into groceries and then into manufacturing glue. It was while working with extracting different basic materials in the glue works that he developed an edible form of gelatine. It was eventually to be marketed as a product that was to delight generations of American children – Jell-O. He was then to buy an estate that he discovered had substantial reserves of iron ore, and that took him into a new direction and he acquired an iron rolling mill. It was now that he made one of those imaginative leaps that bring about great changes. He realised that if railroads were going to flourish, they would eventually need to be worked by locomotives – and if they were worked by locomotives, the old strap rails would be inadequate. They would need iron rails and he could supply them. First he had to convince the railroad company to use a steam locomotive, and as no one else seemed interested, he decided to build one himself.

Like Stevens' steam carriage, the locomotive was based on a four-wheeled platform. He bought in parts from various sources, including the vertical boiler, and the 3¼-inch diameter cylinder that was mounted vertically. The cylinder was supported in an A-frame and had crosshead and slide bars. Cooper experimented with a chain drive, but soon opted for using gears. A connecting road and crankshaft turned a gearwheel that engaged with a pinion on the axle. It is normally referred to as a 0-2-2 engine, though it is difficult to decide which is the front and which the back. He used anthracite coal as a fuel and increased the draught to the fire by means of a rotary fan at the top of the stack – a device first tried unsuccessfully on *Novelty*'s successors.

In August 1830, he invited the directors of the Baltimore & Ohio to join him for a trial run. The platform had a railing all round the edge, so six were invited to travel on the engine, while another 36 passengers were carried in a special carriage. At that time, the railway only extended 13 miles from Baltimore, and the outward journey took 76 minutes. There is a popular legend, though there appears to be no contemporary account to back the story, that on the return journey the locomotive raced against a horse-drawn vehicle and was well in front until the belt driving the fan slipped, pressure dropped and the horse galloped ahead. The locomotive may have lost that race, but Cooper won the argument.

The obvious answer to the question of the type of locomotive that might be used was to go to the world's leading manufacturer, Robert Stephenson and Co. and a six-wheeled engine was duly ordered. However, the ship foundered on its trip across the Atlantic, and the locomotive was lost. The next alternative was to get an American manufacturer to build one instead. The Baltimore & Ohio decided that the best way of finding a suitable engine was to hold a competition along the lines of Rainhill, with a first prize of $4,000 and one of $3,500 for the runner-up. The main concern was keeping down the weight, which was limited to 3½ tons, with four wheels and springing – a weight limitation that the Stephenson engine would never have met. It had to be able to haul 15 tons on a level track at a speed of 15mph and to be capable of working for thirty days. Boiler pressure limitation was set very high for the time at 100psi and the engine had to have two safety valves and a pressure gauge, which at that time would have to be a mercurial gauge.

There were five locomotives entered for the competition, but only one came even close to satisfying the conditions – the engine designed by Phineas Davis. He was born in New

PETER COOPER'S LOCOMOTIVE, "TOM THUMB," RACING WITH A HORSE CAR

Tom Thumb is an obvious development of Stevens' original, but without the rack and pinion. It was originally built with a chain drive, but this soon altered to the geared drive shown here. An illustration from a 1902 history of American technology, giving an impression of how the race between *Tom Thumb* and a horse drawn carriage might have looked. Other artists produced different versions, but it is not even certain that the event took place at all.

Hampshire in 1792, but moved to York, Pa. in 1809 where he set up in business as a watch and clockmaker. He was extremely successful and invested in an iron works in York and it was here that the first iron steamship to be built in America was constructed. The *Codurus* was launched in 1825. This appears to have kindled an enthusiasm for engineering and steam in Davis and he formed a company with Israel Gartner, Davis & Gartner, to manufacture engines. His locomotive, named *York* after the town in which it was manufactured was an immediate success in the trials. There is no accurate record of exactly what the engine was like, but again a replica was built based on the best available information and extrapolating backwards from later locomotives designed by Davis. As with *Tom Thumb* the locomotive had a vertical boiler sat in the centre of a flat platform, carried on 4 wheels, coupled in a 0-4-0 wheel arrangement. It had two cylinders, set vertically on each side of the boiler, with cross heads and connecting rods that led down to the centre of the couplings, constructed as diamond-shaped trusses.

An account of the trials was given in the *History of Baltimore City and County* by John Thomas Scharf, published in 1881. The date of the trial had originally been set at 1 June 1831 but it was postponed and the first runs only took place on 12th July:

'Only two competitors put in an appearance at the first trial, the 'York', manufactured by Davis & Gartner, at York, Pa., and an engine from New York City, the name of which is not recorded in the local chronicles. Another engine, built at Gettysburg, Pa., by George Welsh, had been entered for the prize, but it was not ready to take the track on the day finally set for the contest. At this exhibition the 'York' won all the honors. On the first trip it made a mile in three minutes, drawing a car containing forty persons, and rounded the curves without checking speed. Several trips were made, and the engine ran a mile in two minutes and a half on some portions of the road, After the Davis engine had astonished the assembled multitude with its splendid performance, the New York engine made a short trip, but it fell so far behind the competitor in the essential quality of speed that not much notice was taken of its merits, whatever they may have been.'

With the company now committed to steam, Peter Cooper reappeared, offering to build six locomotives. This was agreed but when he failed to supply the engines, the contract was withdrawn and he sold on his patent to the Baltimore & Ohio. Davis now took over the task of constructing an improved version of his original *York* engine. He was helped by Ross Winans, an engineer who had worked with Cooper in developing *Tom Thumb*. The new engine, named *Atlantic*, was completed in 1832. Once again, the engine had a vertical boiler and two cylinders, but a very different drive arrangement. The crossheads above the cylinders connected to oscillating beams, from which the two long connecting rods led down to a cranked axle. A gear on the axle, engaged with a second, smaller gear that provided the drive to the two pairs of connected wheels. The motion of the beams and their connecting rods seemed like those of an insect's legs, so that the locomotives of this type were known as 'Grasshoppers'. *Atlantic* was a success, maintaining an average speed of 13mph over an 82-mile run that included comparatively steep gradients, up to 1:93. Altogether some twenty Grasshoppers were built, though the design was improved over the years.

In 1832, Davis went for a trip on a Grasshopper on the recently opened Washington branch of the line. He had got into the tender so that he could have a good view of the working of the locomotive and then the engine derailed. The following coaches crashed into the tender, and Davis was killed. Winans was to carry on his work with the Baltimore & Ohio, continuing to develop vertical boiler engines.

Other American railroads were opening up at this time and choosing a variety of different locomotives to run them. The Camden & Amboy Rail Road & Transportation Co. was an interesting enterprise, intended to work as part of a complete transport system in association with the Delaware & Raritan Canal Co. to form a link for freight and passengers between Philadelphia and New York. The President of the new concern, founded in 1830 was Robert L. Stevens, son of Colonel John Stevens. It was an ideal venture for him, combining his successful steamboat enterprise with his developing interest in steam railways. He had already visited England and the Stephenson works, which had given him the opportunity to see the first of the Planet class in action. He was sufficiently impressed to place an order and this time there was no shipwreck, and the engine parts were safely delivered, ready for assembly. The only striking difference in the American engine was that it had the round firebox developed by Edward Bury. Although it was later to be named *John Bull*, when trials on the line began it was simply Number 1.

The locomotive was satisfactory up to a point and although it had been designed to fit the slightly wider gauge of 4ft 10in, it was still basically planned with British track in mind. American routes were notable for their extravagant curves and the 0-4-0 wheel arrangement was proving difficult to manage, so the company decided to adapt it. It reappeared in 1833,

John Bull at the Columbian Exposition of 1893. The locomotive was provided by the Robert Stephenson works but was adapted for American conditions. It is quite clear that the front truck is simply a bolted-on addition to the original engine.

with the wheels uncoupled to give a 2-2-0 arrangement and a two-wheeled truck was added at the front to convert it into the first 2+2-2-0 locomotive. It was probably at this time that the 'cow catcher' was added at the front, giving it the appearance that was to characterise American locomotives for some time. There were to be more modifications over the years and the locomotive was kept at work right through to the 1860s. It was then decided to preserve it as an important part of American railroad history and as a result it is the only engine of the Planet class that has survived anywhere in the world.

Early railroad development had been largely limited to the north-eastern states of America, but there were important developments further south. The cotton plantations were booming and there was a great trade in raw material that was brought to Augusta, Georgia and then shipped downriver to Savannah before being sent across the Atlantic to feed the mills of Lancashire. This was not good news for the port of Charleston so it was decided to build a railroad to link to the town of Hamburg, on the opposite side of the river from Augusta to try and capture some of the lucrative trade. The chief engineer was Horatio Allen who, in spite of his experiences driving the *Stourbridge Lion*, remained as enthusiastic as ever for the locomotive. He wrote to the Board:

> 'in the future there was no reason to expect any material improvement in the breed of horses, while in my judgement, the man was not living who knew what the breed of locomotives was to place at command.'

He was also aware that, as the new line would also be built using strap rails, there was little point in trying once more to use imported engines from Britain. The company, he felt, would have to design its own locomotives with the track limitations in mind.

The Board, with one notable exception, were unconvinced by the arguments. The one man who agreed with Allen was Ezra L. Miller. He was born in 1784 in Simsbury, Connecticut and was a studious boy, with early ambitions for becoming a minister, but had to give up his studies through bad eyesight. He travelled south, and took up a teaching post in South Carolina. He later moved to Charleston, where he prospered. By the 1820s he owned a tannery, a shoe factory and a steam saw mill and was, according to a census of 1820, the owner of several slaves. Like other Charleston businessmen he was concerned with the port's decline and joined the new Railroad Board in 1828. He was convinced by Allen that the future lay with steam locomotives and the two men were sufficiently enthusiastic to make the long voyage to England to see the Rainhill Trials. No record of what they thought of the event has survived, but based on earlier experiences with British engines they were probably more interested in light, speedy *Novelty* than in the winner *Rocket*.

Neither was able to convince the Board to invest in building a locomotive but the sceptics made a suggestion. If Miller cared to put up the finance to build a locomotive that proved to be up to the task of pulling three times its own weight at a speed of 10mph., then they would purchase it. He accepted the challenge and he, Allen and a German immigrant, Christian Detmold, set about the work of designing the engine. It was built at the West Point Foundry in New York and delivered in parts to Charleston in October 1830. At the rear end of the platform was a tall, vertical 'porcupine' boiler, in which the hot gases passed up small tubes before entering the outer jacket and exhausting up the chimney. The whole assembly looked exactly like an enormous bottle. The steam pipe from the boiler went down one side of the frame to a manifold, which distributed the steam to the two cylinders set inside the frame at the front end. They drove a cranked axle and the exhaust steam passed through a water tank slung beneath the platform, providing a pre-heating arrangement. The two pairs of wheels were coupled.

There were problems with the original wheels, which had iron hubs, wooden spokes and rims with iron tyres. A local machinist provided the answer, replacing them with wrought iron wheels. By the middle of December, the engine was put through its trials, and given a name – *Best Friend*. It proved successful, reaching speeds of 30mph when running light and 12mph when pulling around 14 tons, the required load of three times its own weight of 4½ tons. It had satisfied the conditions laid down by the Board and made its first run with paying passengers on Christmas Day and went into regular use the following January, the first American built locomotive to go into service.

The *Best Friend* replica outside its engine house in Charleston, South Carolina. The distinctive bottle-shaped boiler is larger than the original, a deliberate choice made to enable the museum to use the locomotive for giving rides to visitors.

Best Friend had a successful but short career. The engine was equipped with a single safety valve. On 17 June1831 the locomotive was on a turntable and the driver was away from the engine inspecting the trucks that were due to be attached. Apparently, the fireman became irritated by the noise of the steam whistling out of the safety valve, so he sat on it. The result was an explosion and nothing would ever bother that fireman again. Some parts of the locomotive were recovered and used to assemble a new engine, appropriately named *Phoenix*. By 1831 the line had a new locomotive, named *West Point* after the foundry, with identical running gear to *Best Friend* but with a more conventional horizontal boiler.

Travel on the line was a somewhat leisurely and, it seems, uncertain, affair. A timetable from 1841 shows details of the 136-mile journey from Charleston to Hamburg, with trains starting 'not before' 7am and arriving 'not before' 4pm. In case passengers were worried about excessive speed, they were assured they would not move at more than 25mph. There were five intermediate stations. At one station passengers were to get off the train for a twenty-minute breakfast stop and there would be another twenty-minute break for dinner. At the remaining stations, there would be five-minute stops to take on water and fuel. There were also numerous halts, where would-be passengers could stop the train by waving a white flag. The greatest danger facing the travellers was from the track itself. The iron straps were nailed to the wooden stringers. If the nails came loose, the heads – known as 'snake heads'

TRIAL TRIP OF THE "WEST POINT" ON THE SOUTH CAROLINA RAILROAD

By 1831 the West Point foundry had delivered a third locomotive to join *Best Friend,* named *West Point* after the foundry. Now, however, the boiler is horizontal instead of vertical. This imaginative reconstruction of the trial run is distinctly short on accurate detail: there is no indication, for example, that this is actually a 0-4-0 locomotive, since no coupling rods are shown. It does, however, give a sense of the excitement caused when a new engine was delivered.

– would protrude and could cause an accident. So each day track walkers had to cover the whole length of the system knocking down the snake heads.

In 1830, America had one British locomotive, with a horizontal boiler, but other lines were working with home built engines each with vertical boilers. This pattern was soon to change and developments in America were to move on rapidly as we shall be seeing in a later chapter.

Further north, railway construction was getting under way in Canada at the start of the 1830s. Navigable rivers and lakes had always been the key to transportation in Canada, with long portages where the goods had to be carried round sections with rapids and other obstructions by pack animals. There was another disadvantage to rivers; they seldom ran in straight lines. Traffic from New York to Montreal went up the Hudson to Lake Champlain, then into the Richelieu River that heads north for seventy-seven miles with a final leg of forty miles turning back south on the St. Lawrence to Montreal. Yet from the tip of the lake to St. Johns on the opposite bank from Montreal was only fourteen and a half miles overland. It was a very obvious candidate for a railway. The Canadian authorities took the framing of the Bill for the new railway very seriously. It was a masterpiece of bureaucratic language, containing one memorable sentence of 1,453 words. It was approved in 1832 but work only got under way two years later.

The line was constructed on American principles. James Hodges who left England to work in Canada explained the difference; in America economy ruled:

'With this object in view, timber is universally substituted for the more costly materials made use of in this country. Tressel [sic] bridges take the place of stone viaducts, and, in places in which in this country you would see a solid embankment, in America a light structure is often substituted.'

He could have added that the well-ballasted, solid foundations accepted as essential in Britain were not thought necessary. Yet the railway company turned inevitably to Britain for its locomotives. The first engine was a 0-4-0 sent over from the Robert Stephenson works. An admirable engine, it was not, however, suited to the bumpy ride offered over Canadian rails. For a time it was even withdrawn from service, and horses were used to work the line. The Canadians had not yet learned the lessons of America; that they would eventually need to design their own, more appropriate engines. The other line brought into use in these early years had an even less likely locomotive to start its operations.

The first railway in Nova Scotia was initially surveyed by a local schoolteacher, Peter Crerar, in 1817. As there were no qualified engineers locally, the plans were sent to England for assessment and returned with this encouraging comment: 'What need is there of our sending you an engineer when you have Mr. Crerar in the County? Let him supervise the construction.' So he did and made an excellent job of it, providing a route through difficult country but with no gradient

Timothy Hackworth's *Samson* built for the Albion Coal Mining Co. in Nova Scotia in 1839 remained in service until 1882. The photograph shows it on show at the Chicago Exhibition of 1882.

greater than 1:360 and no extravagant curves. It was originally worked by horses, but by 1834 it was decided to try to use locomotives. For once the order did not go to Robert Stephenson but to Timothy Hackworth, who by now had set up as a manufacturer in his own right, based on a new Soho workshop near his house in Shildon.

Hackworth had not changed his fundamental ideas of how to build locomotives in the years following Rainhill. He was to build three locomotives for the line, one of which, *Samson*, survived in use until 1882 and was put on show at the Chicago Exhibition of 1893. This was a 0-6-0 locomotive with vertical cylinders, connected using a form of Watt's parallel motion and a return flue boiler. It hardly represented the latest thinking in engine design and an account of it in use makes it appear even more old-fashioned:

'The cylinders and driving gear are at the back end of the locomotive, and this was the engineer's place so that he could keep a good look out ahead. The fireman was at the other end. The "sandbox" consisted of two buckets of sand, one at each end of the locomotive, the sand being thrown by hand on the rails. This duty was attended to by the engineer or "driver", as he was termed in those days, when the locomotive was moving ahead, and by the fireman when it was going backwards.'

Given the severity of Canadian winters this must have kept them busy. The driver also had another awkward task to perform. He 'was compelled to leave his place at the front of the locomotive whenever desirous of ascertaining the height of water or pressure of steam and go around to the side of the boiler where the water and steam gauges were located.'

Canada was slowly and hesitantly joining the railway age, largely relying still on British expertise. In the meantime, the first steam-powered railways were also coming into use in mainland Europe.

Chapter Eight

On the Continent

While it now seems inevitable that Britain, the country in which the Industrial Revolution had blossomed in the eighteenth century, should have led the way in the development of railways, so it was equally inevitable that it would not be long before the rest of Europe joined in. In fact the first primitive railways had actually been developed in what is now Germany as early as the beginning of the seventeenth century. However, the first move towards steam railways took place in France. In the last chapter, Fulton's early experiments with steam on the water were mentioned, but the very first steamship was the work of an aristocrat, Marquis Jouffroy d'Abbans, whose vessel *Pyroscaphe* puffed its way down the Saône in 1783. But the late eighteenth century in France was not a good time for either industrial experiments or aristocrats and the river steamer was not immediately developed. It was not until the beginning of the nineteenth century that France's industrial life was renewed and railway construction began.

The Saint-Étienne à Lyon railway was opened in 1827 and was originally worked entirely by horses. From Saint-Étienne it descended on gradually diminishing gradients, over which the horses rode in carts, only taking over when the track levelled out for the final section up the Rhone valley to Lyons. The heavy goods traffic was down to Lyons, so the horses were able to haul the empties back up the slopes. It also carried passengers and a contemporary illustration shows a train, pulled by two horses. The first class passengers were carried in coaches very similar to those used on the Liverpool & Manchester, but the rest were in double-decker carriages. The lower deck seemed quite comfortably seated, with curtained windows, while the rest rode on the open top deck.

The chief engineer was Marc Seguin, a man from a family who had already shown inventive genius. His uncles were the Montgolfier brothers, famous as the pioneers of balloon flights. Most of the British engineers who had developed the steam locomotive had done so from the basis of practical experience, working in industries such as mining. Seguin was very different. He was well educated having studied science in Paris under the tutelage of his great uncle Joseph de Montgolfier and at the Institut des Arts et Métiérs. This was an institution for which there was nothing comparable in Britain, offering professional training in mechanics and engineering. French engineers had always taken a different line from their British counterparts. The first professional institute for training engineers was the École des Pont et Chaussés established as early as 1746 and it would eventually merge with other similar schools to form the École Polytechnique, in which the emphasis was as much on theory as on practice. Seguin was to travel to England, where he met the leading scientists of the day, including Michael Faraday and Humphry Davy. He also took time to visit the north east to see what was happening in the new world of steam railways. On his return he established a reputation as a civil engineer, and was responsible for developing Europe's first wire-cable suspension bridge.

As chief engineer for the new railway, he was obviously thinking about steam locomotives and his visit to the Stockton & Darlington, when he set the gauge at 4ft 8½in. He took the obvious step of ordering two locomotives from the Stephenson works in Newcastle, one of which went to the workshops for testing and the other was set to work at once on the line. They proved inadequate, mainly because of their poor ability to raise and maintain a sufficient head of steam. Seguin had already experienced problems with poorly performing boilers in another of his enterprises, when he had designed a steamship for use on the Rhône. It had been ordered from a London company and Seguin used scientific methods and ideas in correctly diagnosing the problem; the heating area of the flue was simply too small in relation to the size of the firebox. He set about designing a multi-tubular boiler, which acted just as the boiler on *Rocket* had done, passing the hot gases through the tubes. He had taken out a patent in 1828 and though it made no mention of locomotives and appeared to be intended for use primarily for stationary engines, he now decided to use a similar arrangement in a locomotive that he would design himself.

A replica of Marc Seguin's locomotive, which shared the claim with *Rocket* to be the first to include a multi-tube boiler. It is obvious from the photograph, however, that in its drive mechanism, via a pivoting beam, it has similarities to earlier locomotive designs.

This photograph of the Seguin replica in steam shows a clearer view of the fan mechanism mounted on the tender. It is clear that such a huge device would have used a lot of the power generated by the improved boiler.

In some ways the engine can be seen to have its origins in those he had seen in England, with two vertical cylinders to either side of the boiler, driving the two pairs of coupled wheels. The big differences were in the boiler and the firebox. The firebox was constructed out of thick cast iron and the gases passed through forty-three 40mm diameter tubes and then through a flue that served to heat the feed water for the boiler. His biggest problem was in raising enough heat from the fire. If he had heard of blast-pipe exhaust he did not use at it this stage. Instead he used two big four-bladed fans placed on the tender to blow air into the firebox through a flexible tube. The fans were driven by belts from pulleys on the tender wheels. It was a cumbersome arrangement, and a waste of power. In later models he reverted to exhaust blast. The locomotive was first tested in October and November 1829 and successfully hauled 15 tons of iron up the steepest part of the line with a 14:1000 incline. It was even stopped and restarted on the slope. Orders were immediately placed for more locomotives of the same design.

Historians have inevitably argued over the years as to who should have the credit for bringing the multi-tubular boiler to the world of railways. Seguin's locomotive was certainly the first to go into service, but had Stephenson or Booth heard of it? There is no evidence that they had. When the French engineer Jean Albert Perdonnet had a medal struck to commemorate the invention, he only confused the matter further by having two heads represented – Seguin and George, not Robert, Stephenson. What we can say is that Seguin was certainly first to use a multi-tubular boiler but Stephenson was the first to combine it with an efficient firebox. Seguin was to continue with locomotive construction for a while, but after an argument with the other directors, he left the Saint-Étienne à Lyons in 1834. After the split the main emphasis on his working life remained bridge construction, especially suspension bridges. In spite of his hectic professional life he obviously had a busy home life as well, being father to nineteen children. Apart from the commemorative medal, he was also one of the elite group of French scientists whose names are engraved on the Eiffel Tower.

Seguin's success did not lead to any great rush to employ French engineers in either railway or locomotive construction. Indeed there was no great rush to build railways at all. In 1833 Charles Vignoles was surveying lines that would link London to Paris; London to Southampton on one side of the Channel and Dieppe to Paris on the other, with a branch to Rouen. It was hoped that the French government would lend its support and the Minister of Public Instruction, Monsieur Thiers came across to England to see the new railways and declared himself so horrified by the sight of those monstrosities that he would never support them being introduced into France. It was to be 1839 before a scheme would get under way and even then it relied almost entirely on British expertise. The first section, Paris to Rouen, was begun under the direction of an English engineer, Joseph Locke, and the greatest part of the actual construction work went to two British contractors, Thomas Brassey and William Mackenzie. They even brought over their own workforce of hardened British navvies, whose capacity for hard work astonished the French. 'Mon Dieu!' declared one onlooker, 'les Anglais, comme ils travaillent!' Various British locomotives were ordered in these early years and it was to be some time before France again became a leading country for locomotive development.

Among the list of countries that might be expected to embrace the new age, Russia would probably not rate very highly as a likely candidate. But if one remembers Grand Duke Nicholas's enthusiasm for the Middleton Colliery Railway, then it is not perhaps quite so surprising. The story begins with the Demidov family who owned a number of factories manufacturing many kinds of machinery. The chief mechanic at the works at Nizhny Tagil was Yefim Cherepanov, who, although he held an important position, was still a serf. From the start of the 1820s, the company began manufacturing stationary engines, mainly for pumping water from mines. In 1832, Yefim's son Miron was sent to Britain to see what he could find out about what they referred to as 'road steam engines'. No written records survive but it is clear that what most impressed him were Stephenson's Planets on the Liverpool & Manchester. He made sketches and on arrival back in Russia the Cherepanovs began constructing Russia's first locomotives of the Planet type. They had to be made to fit the gauge of the local railways which was 2 *arshim* 5 *vershak*, roughly 5ft 5in. A half-scale replica was made by the students at the St. Petersburg Institute of Engineers' Communication Network in the nineteenth century. The similarities to the British engines are striking apart from a complete lack of springing. Perhaps it was not thought important since the track was little more than two miles long. It is said that the performance fell far short of the original, which is not perhaps too surprising, as Cherepanov seems to have had only limited chances to see the British engines at work.

Whatever success the first locomotives may or may not have had, Russia was to do as so many others had done and turn to Britain for motive power for its first railway designed to carry both passengers and freight. It was an Austrian, Franz Anton von Gestner, who first put forward plans for a line designed to appeal to the Tsar. It would link the capital St. Petersburg to the Imperial Summer Palace at Tsarskoye Selo. It is a mark of either the poor state of Russian technology or the wretched state of transport in the country at that time, that it was decided to order rails from Merthyr Tydfil rather than try and fetch them from ironworks beyond the Urals. Soon orders were going out for everything from locomotives to rolling stock. Realising that British manufacturers might have problems working in *arshims* and *vershaks* it was decided to use measures they could understand; the new gauge was set at 5ft 5in.

As with the orders for Canada, locomotives were built by both Stephenson and Hackworth. The Hackworth engine was very different from that supplied to Nova Scotia. It was a 2-2-2 locomotive with inside cylinders of rather unusual dimensions, 17in diameter but only 9in stroke. This particular development was rapidly abandoned. The drive wheels were 5ft diameter and the rest 3ft 6in. He had finally given up his return flue boiler and the new version had 138 1½in. pipes. One of the attractions of early records is the very precise costings that are often included, and none has ever been more precise than this; the total cost of engine and tender was £1,884 2s 9¾d.

The task of delivering the engine was entrusted to seventeen-year-old John Hackworth, who had followed his father into the engineering profession, and a Shildon foreman George Thomson. It was an interesting and exciting experience. Winter was setting in by the time they arrived in Russia and they had to make their way from the Baltic port to the site by sleigh. It was so cold that spirits froze in their bottles and for part of the journey they were pursued by a pack of wolves. They were received by the Tsar, who declared himself amazed to see how far design had progressed since his visit to Leeds just over twenty years previously. Before going into service the engine had to be blessed. John Hackworth gave an account of the proceedings:

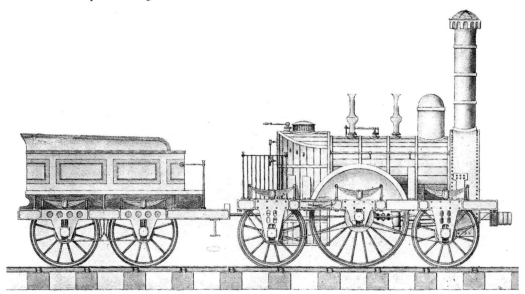

Timothy Hackworth's locomotive built for Russia is typical of the work being done at the Soho works in Shildon at the time.

'The engine, before being brought into public requisition, had to be put through a baptismal ceremony of Consecration according to the rites of the Greek Church. This was done in the presence of the assembled crowd. Water was obtained from a neighbouring bog or "stele" in a golden censer, and sanctified by immersions of a golden cross amid the chanting of choristers and intonations of priests while a hundred lighted tapers were held round it. This was followed by the invocation of special blessings on the Tsar and Imperial Family, and fervent supplications that on all occasions of travel by the new mode, just being inaugurated, they might be well and safely conveyed. Then came the due Administration of the Ordinance by one priest bearing the holy censer; while a second, operating with a huge brush and dipping in the censer, dashed each wheel with the sign of the cross, with final copious showers all over the engine, of which John Hackworth was an involuntary partaker.'

The elaborate ceremony didn't prevent all accidents. After just a few days at work, one of the cylinders cracked. Thomson set off on a 600-mile journey to the ordnance factory in Moscow. There he made a pattern, had a new cylinder cast and machined, returned to fix it to the engine and service was resumed.

The 1830s saw railways spread to more European countries: Belgium and Germany 1835; Austria, 1838; the Netherlands and Italy, 1839. Belgium, which had only recently separated from the Netherlands as an independent country was unusual in that the system was built by the state, not by private companies. However, they still turned to Britain and the Stephenson family for support. George and Robert both made visits to the country during the planning

A rare photograph of Hackworth's locomotive *Middlesboro*, built in 1841 for mineral traffic on the North of England Railway. Although it has many typical Hackworth features, it differs from his earlier engines in having sloping cylinders and a multi-tubular boiler.

stage and the King rewarded George with the Order of Leopold. They returned for the opening of the line from Brussels to Ghent, dined with the King and Queen and travelled on the inaugural train, hauled by a locomotive built by the Robert Stephenson works. Two locomotives had been delivered, one named *Flèche* and the other named in honour of the engineering family, *Stephenson*. Germany also opted for a Stephenson locomotive to inaugurate their first line. In spite of its very grand name, Bayerische Ludwigbahn, named after King Ludwig of Bavaria, this was a modest waggon–way, running for just four miles between Nuremberg and Fürth. Like most such lines, originally worked by horses, it was laid with light rails. In order to cope with the track, the Planet-type locomotive *Adler* was rather lighter than most of the others in this class. It had a smaller boiler and a pair of trailing wheels was added to give a 2-2-2 arrangement. A replica is now on display in a museum in Nuremberg. Austria also opted for Stephenson Planet-type engines for their inaugural service. The line from Vienna to Kraków was financed by the Rothschild family and operated by the Emperor Frederick North Railway. Robert Stephenson sent over his assistant, John Haswell, to Vienna to oversee the arrangements and he was to stay on and help to develop locomotives in that country. The Netherlands and Italy were also to start operations with British locomotives, but by the time they were constructed, locomotive design had moved forwards and the type of locomotive they used will be discussed in the next chapter.

Ireland had actually become part of the United Kingdom at the beginning of the nineteenth century, but that did not mean that its railway system had to conform to anything that had happened in the rest of Britain. It all began conventionally enough, when a short line, the Dublin & Kingstown Railway was constructed. It had been authorised in 1826 but was not actually built until 1834. It was a modest affair just six miles long and has aptly been referred

A replica of *Adler*, a locomotive of the Planet type built by Robert Stephenson & Co. Although in the photograph it looks as grand as the original *Planet* it is obvious from the engine in relation to the people on the footplate that it is actually considerably smaller, the original engine weighing just six tons.

to as the world's first commuter line, relying largely on bringing passengers from the suburbs into the city. As it was to use British locomotives, it seemed only sensible to adopt what was rapidly becoming the standard gauge of 4ft 8½in. Then life got complicated. Two other companies were formed in 1836. The Dublin & Drogheda decided that a few more inches were required so settled on 5ft 2in for their line, while the Ulster Railway was even more ambitious and went for 6ft 2in. So Ireland started into the railway age with three lines and three gauges. This meant that two of the three could not order 'off the peg' locomotives, but had to have them specially constructed to meet their individual needs. It also, of course, meant chaos once a joined–up system was developed. Eventually a gauge commission was to agree on 5ft 3in as the Irish standard.

During this period, it was inevitable that British manufacturers, and especially Robert Stephenson & Co. would provide the lion's share of manufacturing. Their successful Planet Class locomotives or designs based on them were now at work on two continents, but back home the search was on for more power and other engineers were staking their claims as innovative designers.

LOCOMOTIVE ENGINE–DUBLIN AND KINSTOWN RAILWAY.

Hibernia, the locomotive built for the Dublin and Kingstown Railway. The drawing shows the interesting arrangement of the running gear, including the prominent bell crank (labelled M), linking the piston rod and connecting rod. It also has a spark arrester stuck on top of the chimney.

Chapter Nine

Broad Gauge

The 1830s saw a great burst of enthusiasm for railway construction, following the success of the Liverpool & Manchester. Previously, steam railways had been largely limited to the north of England. Now the system was spreading throughout the country. London got its first rather modest line to Greenwich in 1838, but soon developed more important connections to Birmingham and Southampton. Other trunk routes soon followed in the Midlands and in Scotland. They all had one thing in common; they were built to the gauge set by George Stephenson, now accepted as in such widespread use that it could be thought of as the British standard gauge. There was one maverick engineer who had different ideas – Isambard Kingdom Brunel. He has become something of an idol to the British public, regularly appearing at or near the top of any list of famous Britons. It is not difficult to see why. He had a charismatic personality and was a man always ready to go his own way regardless of what alleged experts might say to the contrary. His contribution to the development of railways in general and locomotives in particular is, however, somewhat less than a story of continuous triumphant success.

Brunel was born at Portsmouth in 1806. His father was the eminent engineer Marc Brunel, who, during his stay in Portsmouth, had developed what could be thought of as a very early example of mass production. The wooden blocks that were essential parts of the rigging of all sailing ships had previously been made by hand. He broke the manufacturing process down to a series of individual processes, each of which could be carried out by a different specialist machine. He was later to go on to create one of the engineering masterpieces of the age, the tunnel under the Thames – a project that had defeated Richard Trevithick. The family moved to London, where Isambard received a conventional education in his early years. Marc Brunel was from a French Huguenot family and was well aware of the superiority of technical education in that country. At the age of 14, his son was sent to France but he failed to gain admission to the École Polytechnique. He did, however, spend two years with Louis Bréguet, a leading French clockmaker and had a chance to study both practical and theoretical engineering. At 16, he was back in London, working with his father on the Thames tunnel, a project in which he nearly lost his life when the workings were flooded. He needed a long convalescence to recover from the experience.

His great opportunities came in Bristol. His lesser-known achievement there was the improvement of the docks, but the work for which he is remembered is the Clifton suspension bridge. Although this has nothing to do with railways, it shows a great deal of the young man's character. The idea of bridging the Avon gorge had been around a long time when a committee was formed in 1829 and invited engineers to submit designs. The first batch, including Brunel's proposal, was submitted to the foremost civil engineer of the day, Thomas

Brunel is at once recognisable in this photograph as the little man with the big cigar. Unlike the familiar posed photograph, this is Brunel at the troublesome launch of his famous ship the *Great Eastern*, with an anxious looking John Scott Russell, the ship builder, on the far left. It is a reminder that not all the great engineer's works went according to plan.

Telford, for assessment. He rejected the lot. The committee then invited Telford to enter a design of his own. The result has generally been agreed to be a monstrosity. It, too, was a suspension bridge, but instead of crossing the whole space, was slung between two vast Gothic towers rising up from the river bank. The committee were appalled and eventually returned to the Brunel design and gave him the commission.

The story has generally been presented as an old fogey who was past his best competing with the young forward-looking pretender. It is not quite that simple. Telford already had one outstanding suspension bridge to his credit, carrying the Holyhead Road across the Menai Straits, from the mainland to Anglesey. He had found great difficulty in stabilising the bridge and had decided, on that basis, that it would be unwise and potentially highly dangerous, to try and build with a greater span. The Brunel design exceeded that limit by a considerable amount, and Telford saw no alternative to his own idea of intermediate towers rising the full height of the gorge. Events were to prove him wrong but his arguments were sound and based on personal experience. Brunel was heading blithely into the unknown and was quite ready to back his own judgement. This was to be the pattern of his life. He would, in the words of a well-known TV series 'boldly go' where others would hesitate. In the event, the Clifton bridge was never completed in his lifetime, simply because funds ran out. However, his two Bristol schemes made him a great favourite in the city. When the idea was first mooted of a line to link Bristol to London, he was the man they turned to for the post of chief engineer. It was 1833 and he was not yet thirty years old.

When George Stephenson selected the gauge for the Stockton & Darlington he had simply continued on from Killingworth. The line was after all primarily a mineral railway, on which passenger traffic was of almost negligible importance. He saw no reason to change as he moved on to other lines where different considerations came into play. Brunel took a very different approach. He recognised that there was a rapidly developing public appetite for rail travel, and the successful line would be one that offered both speed and comfort. That would depend on having the right locomotives running on the best possible track to meet those needs. He did not see a gauge selected for a colliery as being appropriate. He had travelled on the Liverpool & Manchester and been unimpressed, considering the carriages to be cramped and the ride uneven. His ideal railway would have sound, firm tracks, running as far as possible on the flat – and the rails would be set wider apart, enabling the company to build wider, more comfortable coaches. It would be a broad gauge, nominally of 7ft but actually of 7ft ¼in and he would build it on a completely new system.

The line that would eventually be known as the Great Western Railway was to be unlike any other ever built. One of the limitations for locomotive engineers in the early days had been attempting to cope with a track that could scarcely bear the weight of the engines. Brunel ignored everything that had gone before and simply sat down to work out how to achieve the best possible results. For a start, he opted for a completely different rail design. The rail has been described as like an inverted 'u' with widespread serifs or a broad-brimmed hat seen in profile. The top of the rail was flat, roughly 2½in. across and rising 4½in above the sleeper. From the crown, it sweeps down in a curve to a base measuring 12in across. The rails were heavy, initially weighing 55lb per yard, though later versions were even heavier. They were supported on a rigid grid. Instead of the conventional transverse sleepers, which were beginning to come into use elsewhere to replace the old stone blocks, these rails were laid on continuous baulks of pine with a hardwood top. They were braced by transverse ties, which in turn were secured by piles sunk deep into the ground. For double tracks, the transverse ties ran across both sets of lines. The final touch was added by ballasting. It was, in theory, the most rigid permanent way ever built. In practice, it was not quite so successful. If the ballast shifted after rain, the piles tended to push up the track rather than hold it down, and there were frequent complaints of an uneven ride and even derailments. Brunel had discovered that a successful track could not be too rigid; it needed a certain amount of give in it.

Where the engineer was successful was in producing a remarkably level route, which included some imposing engineering features, such as the brick viaduct over the Thames at Maidenhead and Box tunnel. One very good reason for Brunel paying little attention to 'experts' was that they were so very often entirely wrong. Among those who were to challenge him time and time again was a well-known writer on scientific topics, Dr Dionysius Lardner. Box tunnel was actually built with the lines on a gradient, and the self-proclaimed expert 'proved' by scientific calculations that if a train entering the tunnel suffered a brake failure, it would emerge at a speed of 120mph and no passengers would survive moving with such rapidity. Brunel pointed out that the learned doctor had taken account of neither air resistance nor friction. The predictions were, however, taken seriously by some passengers, and for a time the company had to lay on a conventional coach to take nervous passengers over the top of the tunnel. What was beyond doubt was the fact that the Great Western was a magnificent line, offering every opportunity for fast, comfortable travel – provided the locomotives were up to the job as well. That, however, proved to be a different affair altogether.

Whatever Brunel's virtues as a civil engineer, his ideas about what was needed to operate the new line were simply bizarre. He decreed that the locomotives should be built to provide a speed of 30mph and at that speed, the piston speed should not exceed 280ft per minute; on other lines piston speeds had already risen to 500ft per minute with no ill effects. Having correctly decided that a locomotive could only be as good as the track on which it ran, and having gone to considerable trouble to provide a uniquely solid track, he now stipulated that the weight of a locomotive carried on four wheels, with water and fuel, but discounting the weight of the tender, should be limited to 8 tons, but could rise to 10½ tons on six wheels.

It is all very well ignoring contemporary opinions and practices, but it only works if you have something better to offer. On this occasion, Brunel was taking several steps backwards, not moving forward. He went to manufacturers with his requirements and they struggled to meet his conditions. Certainly the most bizarre solution was found by the manufacturers Hawthorns of Newcastle, who built two locomotives, *Thunderer* and *Hurricane*. In order to keep within the weight limits, the boiler was mounted on a separate carriage and connected to the power unit by flexible pipes. *Thunderer* had four 6ft coupled wheels, geared to the crankshaft, while *Hurricane* had single 10ft diameter drive wheels. On trial over a short length of track, *Thunderer* was recorded to have reached a speed of 60mph running light. However, the engines proved unsatisfactory in many ways. The flexible tubing created problems from the first and the engines were so cumbersome that there was difficulty moving themselves let alone hauling heavy trains. Two others, both geared locomotives, built at the Haigh works in Wigan turned out to be even worse. The locomotive situation was desperate but fortunately help was on hand and an alternative was soon made available.

It was clear that Brunel needed someone to take charge of his motley array of locomotives and attempt to coax them into doing useful work. The man he chose for the post of Superintendent of Locomotives was Daniel Gooch, who, when he was appointed in 1837 was just one week short of his 21st birthday. Gooch was born at Bedlington in Northumberland in 1816, where his father worked for the local ironworks. He was educated at a private school until the age of fourteen, but his main interest was always in engineering, not surprising given that the family connections included the Stephenson family. When his father moved down to South Wales to take a post as manager at the Tredegar iron works, the boy began his apprenticeship there. He was later to look back on those years as 'the most important in my life', during which he acquired his basic engineering skills. He was to move around to other engineering works and spent some time at Robert Stephenson & Co. in Newcastle. It was there that he was asked to help with the design of a locomotive. There is some confusion about who ordered the locomotive; George Stephenson said it was intended for the New Orleans Railway, Gooch later in life claimed it was meant for Russia. All are agreed, however, that it was built to fit something in the region of a 5ft 6in gauge. Gooch was impressed, writing, 'I was much delighted in having so much room to arrange the engine.' He was so pleased, in fact, that he tried to arrange a meeting with Brunel to see if he could get a job working on the broad gauge line. The meeting didn't happen, so he took a job with his brother, Tom Gooch, on the Manchester & Leeds Railway. But he still felt drawn to the broad gauge, and wrote to Brunel. This time he managed to set up a meeting, the two got on and Gooch was given the job. He now had the rather thankless task of looking after the locomotives built to satisfy Brunel's requirements. He must rapidly have discovered their inadequacies and then remembered the locomotives he had worked on in Newcastle and recalled that the order had been cancelled with only one of the two actually having been delivered. Here was a chance to adapt this engine that belonged to a class of proven worth.

The locomotive was one of a series known as the Patentees, introduced by Robert Stephenson in the early 1830s. Already there was a demand for more power and speed. Stephenson responded by developing the basic Planet design, increasing the size of the firebox, giving a larger grate area and also increasing the size of the boiler. To carry the extra weight he added a pair of trailing wheels to give a 2-2-2 arrangement. The drive wheels had no flanges, which improved the performance on tight curves, an idea that he patented, hence the name of the first locomotive *Patentee*. Like the Planet engines it had an outside frame and leaf springs. There was also an improved valve arrangement. Instead of the old arrangement for reversing, the gab was redesigned in a V-shape, which allowed the drive pins to slide into place and be repositioned by means of a lever on the footplate. The 5ft 6in gauge locomotive that still remained at the Stephenson works had been built as a Patentee and this was now adapted to the Brunel broad gauge and given a new name, *North Star*.

Gooch and Brunel had very contrasting temperaments; the former somewhat dour, the latter mercurial. Early in the relationship, Brunel invited him to a party at his mother's London home. Gooch later wrote that he 'did succeed in getting as far as the staircase' before leaving in disgust at what he considered unseemly behaviour. That they were unlikely ever to share a social life was less important than their ability to get on professionally. That ran into trouble almost as soon as Gooch took up his post. He found that while *Thunderer* may have shown a remarkable turn of speed it was dismally lacking in tractive power. He struggled to get useful work from any of the engines and when the Board asked him for a report he had to admit that Brunel's ideas on how the locomotives should be limited were at the heart of

North Star was originally built for an overseas client by the Robert Stephenson works in Newcastle, but when the order was cancelled it was bought instead by the Great Western and adapted to the 7ft gauge. It was the first successful locomotive to work the line. For many years it was on display at the Swindon works.

the problem. It says a great deal for the honesty and the courage of the young man that he was able to criticise the man who had just appointed him, but it did nothing to improve the relationship between the two. Fortunately, it was not in Brunel's nature to hold grudges for long, and the arrival of *North Star* restored the partnership. Brunel wrote at the time:

> 'We have a splendid engine of Stephenson's, it would be a beautiful ornament in the most elegant drawing-room'.

More importantly, it proved to be up to the job of running the railway.

In some ways it might seem surprising to hear Brunel praising Stephenson. After all, the battle of the gauges between the two railway systems that had now appeared would seem to have set the Stephenson camp against the Brunel faction. Certainly each was ready to argue its case vehemently, but that was never reflected in the personal relationship between Isambard Brunel and Robert Stephenson. They were rivals but personal friends, always ready to offer each other support in times of crisis. When Stephenson was erecting his revolutionary box girder bridges on the Holyhead Railway, Brunel was there to offer his support; and when Brunel faced one of his greatest crises, the attempts to launch his huge ship the *Great Eastern*, Stephenson was at his side.

Brunel's faith in Gooch was to be rewarded for he was to go on to design locomotives that would help to secure the reputation of the Great Western and the reinterpretation of the

One of the famous series of lithographs of the Great Western Railway made in the 1840s by J. C. Bourne. This one shows *Fire Fly* emerging from Box tunnel. The man in the tall hat is not a spectator, but a signalman giving the 'all clear' sign to the driver.

initial GWR as God's Wonderful Railway. It had been usual for railway companies to give a list of requirements to manufacturers and then leave it up to them to decide how to meet them. The result was likely to be a line run with a mish-mash of engines, each presenting its own unique maintenance problems. Gooch appreciated that a far better solution would be to provide detailed design specifications and drawings which the manufacture had to agree to adhere to in every detail. The result would be a standardised class of identical locomotives. The success of *North Star* encouraged him to develop the design into a Star class of locomotives. The first of the class, the 2-2-2 *Fire Fly* went into service in 1840, a handsome locomotive with a domed firebox, in a style that came to be known as 'Gothic' and with the outside frame arching over the 7ft drive wheels. On initial trials, *Fire Fly* was recorded as travelling at 58mph while pulling three vehicles. Over the years, sixty-two locomotives of this class were built, doing sterling work and the last was retired as late as 1879. It is a remarkable achievement for one class to remain in use for almost forty years. A replica has been built and it still impresses one as a remarkably good-looking engine. However, like many early locomotives, it was not without its share of early problems. Stephenson himself wrote in his notebook number one on 18 March 1833:

'This engine wanted some stays near the bottom tubes which had been put in at Liverpool or Manchester, and it was likewise found with seams [cracks] in the plates of the inside firebox. When she had run 3000 miles she began to burst tubes and by 15 May when she had run 49-miles she had burst 8 or 10 copper tubes, the brass ones all stand. She broke her crank axle after running 28,500 miles.'

Not exactly a glorious record but, as Brian Reed wrote in his book *150 Years of Steam Locomotives* from which this quote was taken, it was not uncommon. By 1840, there were some thirty works turning out locomotives and few arrived in a condition that allowed them to go straight into service without tinkering or more major adjustments, and servicing and repairs left much to be desired.

Gooch was to develop the basic *Fire Fly* design to create a larger experimental version, *Great Western* with 8ft diameter drive wheels, and when that proved successful moved on

Hirondelle was built in 1848, as one of the Iron Duke class, which was developed from the earlier Great Western engines, with an extra pair of leading wheels, 4-2-2 instead of 2-2-2.

to establish a new class. The first of the new locomotives *Iron Duke* was built in 1847, with a much larger firebox, and without the Gothic dome. It proved too heavy for the 2-2-2 arrangement, so an extra front axle was added. It shows how rapidly locomotive engineering had developed, as in just a few short years since the first Patentee had appeared, tractive effort had been increased five-fold. With a load of over 100 tons *Iron Duke* achieved an average speed of over 50mph and on a downhill gradient of 1:100 was recorded at almost 80mph. Gooch's engines were to prove the mainstay of the GWR throughout its first half century. It is somewhat ironical that such a splendid locomotive should have been named after the Duke of Wellington, a man who may have been a national hero, but had publicly expressed his dislike of railways.

The Great Western empire soon began to spread westward, with the first extension reaching as far as Exeter. By now the success of Gooch's locomotives was well assured, but the next stage of the extension proved far more difficult to plan because of the nature of the ground it had to cover. The route that was eventually chosen began easily, following the west bank of the Exe, then turning to follow the coast through Dawlish to Teignmouth, then following the Teign to Newton Abbot. It was after that that things became problematical, with a route running across the edge of Dartmoor, which involved three sections with heavy gradients at Dainton, Rattery and Hemerdon. Brunel had doubts about the ability of locomotives to cope with such steep slopes. The most forbidding of the three was Dainton, two miles long and varying from 1:38 to 1:57. He was right to worry. I remember being on a steam excursion to mark the 150th anniversary of the GWR. Double, headed by a Hall and a Castle out of Exeter; things were going well until we met Dainton Bank. It was already clear that one of the engines, the Hall, was not steaming well and unfortunately the train was stopped by a signal at the foot of the slope. It got going again but as we huffed and puffed up the bank, the Castle was forced to give up the struggle. We were all ignominiously rescued by diesel, and these were engines far more powerful than anything available to Brunel. The answer that most engineers would have come up with would have been the well-tried methods of cable haulage by a stationary steam engine, or providing banking engines. But being Brunel he was never ready to accept the obvious solution if something newer and more exciting was on offer.

The idea of either using compressed air as a source of power to push a train along, or evacuating a tube and using ordinary air pressure to do the work had been around in various forms since 1810. There was a brief, but failed attempt in 1835, but another experiment in 1840 proved a great deal more successful. The Birmingham, Bristol & Thames Junction Railway – one of several at that time with ambitions which were greater than its finances could bear – had a short length of track available for experiment for Mr. Clegg's Pneumatic Railway. Clegg's ideas were improved on by two brothers, Jacob and Joseph Samuda. In between the rails of the 1¼-mile long track, they laid a 9-inch diameter pipe that could be evacuated by a steam engine set at one end. Inside the pipe was a piston, with a flange projecting through a slit running the length of the pipe. As air pressure pushed the piston along, the slot was kept airtight by means of leather flaps, reinforced with iron. It proved capable of hauling a considerable load up a gradient of 1:120. Several engineers came to see the experiment, including George Stephenson, who declared the whole thing to be 'a

Another Bourne lithograph, this time showing Bath station. It is a very good illustration of the spaciousness of the broad gauge track. It is interesting to note, however, that the rolling stock does not extend beyond the limits of the wheel base, unlike most trucks and carriages on the standard gauge.

great humbug', but Brunel was a great deal more impressed. So too were the directors of the Dublin and Kingstown Railway who installed the system on the branch line between Kingstown and Dalkley. It proved to be quite successful and one passenger had the dubious pleasure of discovering just how powerful it could be. Normally, a full train was hauled up, but Frank Ebrington was sat on the little truck attached to the piston that provided the motive power. Before it had been linked to the train, the system was started and he hurtled up the track at the unprecedented speed of over 80mph.

It was one thing to apply the system to a short length of just less than a mile and a half and running an entire main line with it. That, however, is exactly what Brunel decided to do. Exeter and Plymouth were to be joined by an atmospheric railway. Robert Stephenson made the point that his father had made when opposing the proposed haulage system for the Liverpool & Manchester; a problem in just one pumping station would bring the whole system to a halt. However, Brunel was confident that it would prove to offer a safer and faster system than a conventional railway. It was a hugely ambitious scheme that caused trouble from the start, when it proved extremely difficult to cast the pipes with accuracy, and when the first piston carriage arrived and was put to the test in February 1847 it was not the success everyone had anticipated. P. G. Margary, an engineer on the line, described that first experimental run:

The atmospheric railway at Dawlish. The tubes are set between the rails, with the slot closed by flaps. The steam-powered pumping station used to create the vacuum is seen to the right of the line.

'Started at 6.0 p.m. for Turf, towing a locomotive behind. Went on very slowly to Turf, there being a large quantity of water and dirt in the pipe.'

By February 1848, the system was in operation between Exeter and Newton Abbot – not yet having to deal with the banks that had caused it to be built in the first place. Now freight and passengers were being moved using the system, and the local press was enthusiastic:

'The novelty of the thing begins to disappear: passengers go in and out with the same indifference and confidence they would manifest towards a stage coach. Master Piston is getting a general favourite. Indeed many prefer his noiseless track to the long drawn out sighs of "Puffing Billy".'

Brunel was initially delighted, but then problems began to appear. Winter had a devastating effect on the leather valve. It froze solid, so that it could no longer act effectively. It was also found that the leather was deteriorating rapidly, and it was becoming clear that if the system was to be run, it would all have to be replaced at frequent intervals at great expense and with inevitable hold ups. Brunel bit the bullet and admitted failure. The atmospheric railway was abandoned. In time, banking engines would be used to help trains up the various inclines.

Very little remains as a reminder of this bold but ultimately misguided experiment, apart from a few pumping houses; the one at Starcross was for a time a museum devoted to the atmospheric railway in which visitors could be whizzed for a few yards down a length of track, powered by a vacuum cleaner. A small length has been recreated at the Didcot Rail Centre.

For Brunel it was a bitter experience; he had, it seems, really thought that the system would replace locomotives as the most efficient way of running a railway. It was not to be. Brunel has been feted as Britain's greatest engineer, but if he were to be judged purely on his contribution to railway technology it would be difficult to uphold the verdict. His genius can certainly be seen in the civil engineering, culminating in his bridge over the Tamar that brought rails from the rest of Britain to Cornwall. Its opening was to be one of the last events of his life; he was already sick and was carried across on a bed mounted on a flat car. However logical his decision to build to a broad gauge might have been, it ignored the needs of a national system that was already well under way. It was to be his fellow broad gauge enthusiast, Daniel Gooch, who was to have the unwelcome task of overseeing its dismantling. Brunel's instructions for constructing locomotives for the start of the Great Western were perverse and the atmospheric railway was a costly failure. Looked at solely as a locomotive pioneer, he would be no more than a footnote in most reference books. He was, however, to move on to new worlds, when he famously declared that he saw no reason why the Great Western should stop at Bristol – why not go on to New York? His steamships represented a quite extraordinary achievement and opened up the world to steam navigation. In this he proved himself to be a true genius and worthy of his place in the engineering pantheon.

The line at Dawlish was rapidly converted into a conventional railway, worked by locomotives. This view shows some of the difficulties encountered in its construction along the rugged coast. The locomotive has just left Dawlish for Teignmouth.

Chapter Ten

Valve Gear

Valve gear had developed a great deal since the earliest days when a simple four-way cock either let steam in or let it out. The slide valve was a comparatively sophisticated piece of machinery that did more than merely cover or open ports to the cylinder. When fully developed, it had a rather more complex arrangement, involving 'lap' and 'lead'. 'Lap' is the amount by which the valve overlaps the steam port at dead centre – 'steam lap' on the live steam side, 'exhaust lap' on the exhaust side. 'Lead' is the amount by which the steam port is open when the piston is static at dead centre. These can be adjusted according to the work the locomotive is required to do. Exhaust lap, for example, is particularly useful for locomotives designed for heavy work where speed is unimportant, as it allows the maximum effort to be obtained from the expanding steam by delaying the exhaust. The movement is controlled by the eccentrics, which have to be set according to the amount of lap and lead being used. In the simplest case, where neither is used, when the valve is in mid position, the eccentric would be set at 90° in advance of the crank, so that as the eccentric moved the valve would begin to open. The position would have to be slightly adjusted to take account of lap and lead. The problem that engineers struggled with was finding a convenient way of reversing the engine. The common method developed was for fixed eccentrics, activated by either V, Y or X-shaped gabs that would engage with different pins to change direction. Some used a single eccentric for each valve, driving a rod with a pin at the end connected to a rocking arm, pivoted at its centre. When a pin at the other end of the rocking arm was moved, it changed the direction of the eccentric.

A major advance was made by the Liverpool engineer James Forrester. In 1834 he introduced a new type of valve gear, using two eccentrics on

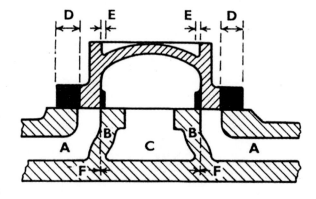

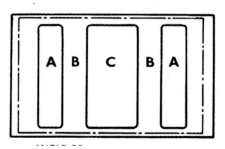

The diagram shows the main features of a traditional slide valve: A steam port; B bridge; C exhaust port; D steam lap; E exhaust lap; F exhaust clearance.

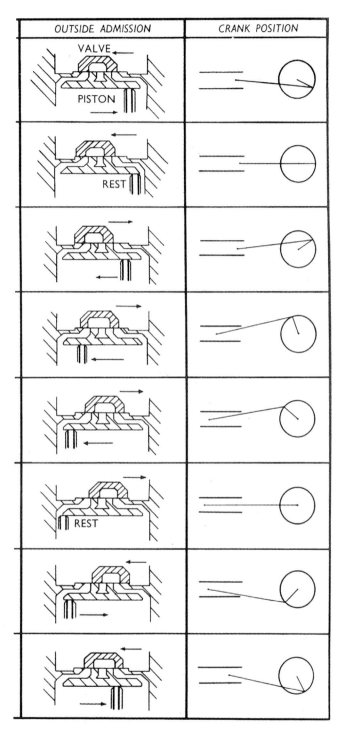

This diagram shows the full set of events for one revolution of a locomotive wheel. The relative positions of the slide valve and the piston can be seen on the left, the position of the crank on the right.

the driving axle, one for forward movement and the other for reverse. He used two gab hooks, in between which was a pin attached to the valve spindle. To move forward the upper gab was lowered onto the pin. To reverse the engine, the upper gab was raised out of the way and the lower gab lifted to engage. It was a simple arrangement that was soon widely used.

One thing that each of the early versions had in common was that they all had a fixed cut off point for admitting steam into the cylinder. A modern analogy would be a motorcar with just two gears, one forward, one reverse. One man who tried to solve the problem was John Gray, who patented what became known as the 'horse leg' gear in 1838. He first applied it to the Liverpool & Manchester locomotive *Cyclops* in 1839, and shortly after took on the job of Locomotive Superintendent of the Hull & Selby Railway, using the mechanism in a number of the locomotives built for that line. In his patent he made it quite clear that he fully understood all the advantages of his system, not just in simplifying the reversing process but also in allowing variable cut off. Perhaps it was because he worked for one of the smaller railway companies or simply that he did not have a great reputation, such as that of Stephenson, but whatever the reason, his work was largely ignored. If other engineers read his patent, they failed to heed the message that using his gear could bring in a new age for economical and efficient working of locomotives. There were, however, also technical problems. The system was complex and hard to work, so difficult in fact that it needed a double reversing handle to provide extra leverage – rather in the way that 'the waiter's friend' bottle opener, uses one lever to start moving the cork, then engages with a second to give greater purchase. Whatever the reasons for ignoring Gray's breakthrough, the gear had limited application and others would come up with a different answer.

The next practical solution to the problem was found almost by accident in 1841 by two men who worked on improving valve gear at the Robert Stephenson works in Newcastle. William Williams was a 'gentleman apprentice', a young man of comparatively wealthy parents, who had paid for him to be taught draughtsmanship, without having to go through the arduous job of working his way up the grades as other apprentices would have done. He was looking at ways for improving the complex X-type gab gear, in which different pins were engaged. It was difficult to work and if not firmly pushed home could cause damage. He devised a slotted link; the fore-gear eccentric is coupled to the top and the reverse-gear to the bottom of the link. The links are raised and lowered via the reversing rod that can be operated from the footplate. This enabled the change from forward to reverse to be made smoothly as a continuous operation, rather than as before in a single change from one to the other. Williams worked on the idea with a pattern maker, William Howe.

Edward Cooke, the Chief Clerk at the Newcastle works, sent Robert Stephenson a model of the new arrangement in August 1842. He replied:

'On the first blush it is very satisfactory and I sincerely hope on a more mature investigation will prove really so …If it answers it will be worth a Jew's eye and the contriver of it should be rewarded.'

But who was the contriver, Williams or Howe – both of whom were to claim the credit for the idea? The question was never really answered, but whichever it was, the gear would be named after neither man, but after the company for which they worked. What is not clear is just when someone made the discovery that if the reversing gear was moved slightly while the engine was running, it would effectively reduce the length of the stroke during which steam would be admitted to the cylinder. In other words, the dream of the early engineers had been unwittingly realised; the cut off point for the admission of steam could be varied. The new gear was fitted to a 2-4-0 in 1842 and immediately proved its worth. The working of the gear is explained more fully with reference to the diagram below.

The introduction gave the driver two means for adjusting the flow of steam to the piston. He could use the regulator, to open a valve in the dome by different amounts to allow more or less steam through and he could use the reverser to change the cut-off point at which steam stopped being admitted. By careful using of the reverser, the engine can be run as economically as possible. If the cut-off is late, the steam is used to maximum force, which is exactly what is needed when starting up or coping with steep gradients. The steam leaving the cylinder will still be under considerable pressure, and anyone who has travelled on a steam train will have been aware of the loud chuff-chuff of escaping steam at the start of a journey. However, once the engine is travelling at speed, the cut-off point can be much earlier, allowing the steam to expand – and again this will be obvious to the traveller in the quieter sound of the engine. One of the reasons enthusiasts like to stick their heads out of carriage windows – disregarding stern warning notices – is so that they can listen to the changing noises of the engine and mentally follow the way in which the driver is handling his locomotive. Thanks to the introduction of the Stephenson linkage, the driver had far greater

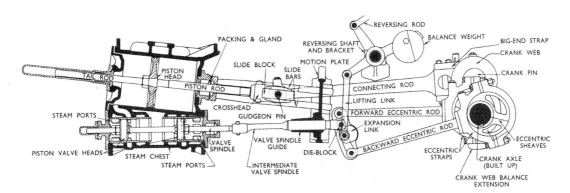

Stephenson valve gear: the diagram was published in the British Transport Commission's *Handbook for Steam Locomotive Enginemen* of 1957 and shows the gear being used in conjunction with a piston valve as opposed to the slide valve of earlier engines, but the general arrangement of the gear remains the same. The forward and backward eccentric rods are suspended from the common reversing shaft and can be raised and lowered by means of a lever on the footplate. The movement is transmitted from the eccentric via the slotted expansion link, allowing for a continuous movement and thus variable cut off, instead of the either/or arrangement of earlier types of gear, where the cut-off point was fixed.

control over the efficiency with which he could work the engine, saving fuel and thus saving costs – to the delight of the railway operators.

Other engineers quickly realised the advantage of the new system, which Stephenson at once patented, and they began looking for variations of their own – either to try and improve the arrangement or to avoid paying royalties on the patent by declaring theirs to be entirely new inventions. Among those who took this path was Daniel Gooch. Looking at the diagram of the Stephenson gear (p.121) it is clear that the valve spindle is fixed, and the reversing rod moves the expansion link and the forward and backward eccentric rods. In the Gooch system, the arrangement was effectively reversed; the expansion link was attached to a fixed bearing and this time the reversing rod moved the valve rod. It found very little, if any, use other than on the broad gauge lines.

Yet another variation was used on the Grand Junction Railway. This had opened in 1837, joining Birmingham to Warrington, where it linked with the Warrington & Newton Railway to provide a through route to the Liverpool & Manchester. It was decided early on that the company would need its own locomotive works for both repair and construction and in 1840 the new works were opened at Crewe. The engineer in charge, Alexander Allan, the works manager, devised his own variation in which the reversing lever moved the eccentric rods, the link and the valve rod. How far the engineers thought their systems were an improvement or were merely attempts to avoid paying royalties to Stephenson is open to question. What is certain is that the Stephenson system became the most commonly used on British locomotives throughout the second half of the nineteenth century. In one part of Europe, however, a completely new system was being developed.

The development of railways in Belgium followed a very different pattern from that of the rest of Europe. Instead of being promoted by private enterprise, it was built from the first by the state and run by Belgian State Railways. The very first line was opened in 1835 between Brussels and Mechelen, a town roughly halfway between Brussels and Antwerp. It must have been an exciting time for the locals and especially for 15-year-old Egide Walschaerts, a boy who was already showing a keen interest in all things mechanical and became a skilled model maker. At the age of eighteen he was displaying his work at a local exhibition – work that was so impressive that he was encouraged to study engineering at the University of Liège. By the time he was ready to start work, the railway had established their workshops in Mechelen and he got a job there, rapidly rising through the ranks – first as foreman then as works superintendent, a position he was to hold for the rest of his life. It was during this period that he began thinking about valve gear. The first locomotives to work the line had been, as they were on so many lines at that time, supplied by Robert Stephenson – *La Flèche* and *Stephenson*. But by the 1840s, European engineers were already developing ideas of their own.

The Walschaert valve gear – the final 's' was dropped from the engineer's name when naming the device – also allowed for both reversing and variable cut off, but by different means from those used by Stephenson. This time there is just a single eccentric, attached to the eccentric rod, which in turn was attached to the expansion link that allows for both reversing and varying the cut-off point. A second system, based on a radius rod attached to

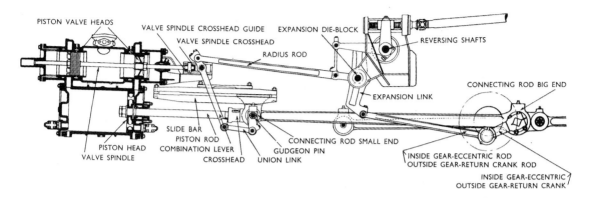

The Walschaert valve gear: the diagram from the same British Transport book as before. Once again, the expansion link is the key to variable cut off. The arrangement is simpler than in the Stephenson valve.

both the piston cross-head and the valve spindle, ensures that the lead on the valve remains constant in both directions, regardless of the cut-off point. In the Stephenson system, when the cut-off was less than a quarter of the way through the stroke, the excessive lead allowed steam to enter in front of the piston. As with the Stephenson linkage, the arrangement of the different parts can be understood more clearly by reference to the diagram above. The Walschaert came into use on many European lines, but never into regular use in Britain until the latter part of the nineteenth century.

I came across a little book in a second-hand bookshop, published by *Model Railway News* on the Walschaert gear. It has no date, but it is many decades since a 64-page book was available for just one shilling (5p). In the Preface it describes the importance of the mechanism as 'the most perfect gear in its accuracy of function in all positions of the drivers' reverse lever that we have'. The author also adds a caveat that everything depends on the correct attachment rod to the link. 'Once the link is wrongly made no amount of tinkering with cranks, links or rods, or with the position of the valve on its spindle, will ever put matters right.' And what is true of the model was no less true of the full-sized locomotive. In other words, locomotive construction was becoming more and more dependent on accurate machining. Things had come a long way from the simple four-way plug of Trevithick's day that could easily be cobbled together, and, in many respects the changes would not have been possible without improvements in the manufacture of machine tools. It is all too easy when discussing the pioneering work of locomotive engineers to forget how far they depended on others to design the tools for the job. One has only to look at the diagrams for the Stephenson and Walschaert gears to see how complex they are and how essential it was to design the individual parts with great accuracy so that they all worked together as a smooth whole, and after that to make each part with equal accuracy. One man at least operated in both worlds.

Richard Roberts had an extraordinary career. He was born in Wales in 1789, had little or no education and as soon as he was big and strong enough went to work as a labourer in a quarry. It was soon apparent that he had a knack for working with machinery, and was always being asked to take on all sorts of odd mechanical jobs. He realised that he would be better off as a mechanic than as a labourer and he went to work for local engineers, including for a time John Wilkinson. It was an interesting place to be, on the site where the first successful machine tool had been made for accurately boring steam cylinders. He travelled widely, picking up knowledge, eventually ending up in 1814 at the works of the most important machine manufacturer of the age, Henry Maudsley. By 1817 he felt he had learnt enough to set up in business for himself in Manchester, and soon new machines were appearing on a regular basis: one of the earliest planers; a new type of lathe; gear-cutting and slotting machines; and the first successful gas meter. By 1825, his reputation was so well established that he was approached by Manchester cotton manufacturers to see if he could improve on the spinning mule, by making it self-acting. He achieved his goal, and the result was a machine that was to remain in use in the British textile industry until the second half of the twentieth century. He was a man always looking for the latest thing, and quickly saw that the railways offered an ideal opportunity for him to use his skills. In 1828 he went into partnership with iron merchant Thomas Sharp to form Sharp, Roberts & Co. to manufacture locomotives at their new Atlas Works in Manchester.

Roberts' own interest in locomotive construction faded, though not his inventiveness and the company continued to thrive, building some 1,500 locomotives over the years. They were among the first companies to use templates and gauges to standardise production, using the types of systems introduced by companies such as Colt in America. Roberts himself, though a brilliant mechanical engineer, was a terrible businessman and he died in 1864 in poverty. He may not rank as one of the great locomotive engineers, but he was one of those who made it possible for those who were to realise their designs. Without men like him, the necessary accuracy of construction for complex valve gears could never have been realised. It is difficult for us to understand just how badly equipped in terms of machine tools even the best workshops were at the start of the railway age. George Bruce was an apprentice at Robert Stephenson & Co.'s Newcastle factory in 1837. Looking back at that time fifty years later when he had become President of the Institution of Civil Engineers, he wrote this description of the works that had 400 men at work, but surprisingly sparse resources:

'In 1837 there were no small planing or shaping machines: there was only one slotting machine, the use of which was very restricted. Wheels were driven onto their axles by sledge hammers, wielded by strong arms alone. Steam hammers were, of course, unknown, and only hand labour was available for the ordinary work of the smiths' shop and boiler yard, with the exception of the punching and shearing machinery. Riveting by machinery was unknown. It is scarcely credible, but it is a fact, that there was not a single crane in Robert Stephenson's shop in 1837. There were shear-legs in the yard by which a boiler could be lifted onto a truck, and there were portable shear-legs in the shop, by the skilful manipulation of which, at no little risk of life and limb, wonders were done in the way of transmitting heavy loads from one part of the shop to another.'

The availability of machine tools able to work within ever-finer tolerances was the key to the development of more complex mechanisms, such as the new valve gears, and the development of the Walschaert gear showed that increasingly manufacturers outside Britain were beginning to move down different paths. This was still true to a limited extent in Europe, but Americans were beginning to develop locomotives that were suitable for their conditions, so very different from those of Great Britain.

Chapter Eleven

New Directions

In the early years of development, American railroads had first depended on British imports and had then begun experimenting with their own locomotives, rather lightweight affairs with vertical boilers. One notable exception was the *Dewitt Clinton* built for the Delaware & Hudson Canal Company, home to the unsuccessful trial of the *Stourbridge Lion*. It was designed by the company's engineer, John B. Jervis, and built at the West Point Foundry. It was the first locomotive to be built in that country with a horizontal boiler. It was an ungainly machine, with a massive chimney and an equally huge dome mounted on a rather slender boiler, less than three-foot in diameter. It had four large, 4ft 6in diameter coupled driving wheels, each built up from wrought iron spokes attached to a cast iron hub. The valve mechanism was similar to that used on the *Stourbridge Lion*. On its initial trials on the 17-mile track it hauled a train with 125 passengers at 25mph. It was a useful beginning, but from the first there were problems with running the engine on the poor track and it would later be modified. A working replica is now housed at the Henry Ford Museum in Michigan.

From a tentative start, the network began to spread with remarkable speed, so that by 1850 the country had some 9,000 route miles of track. There were different approaches to construction. One line, the New York & Lake Erie, was built on the grand scale with a broad, 6ft-gauge and featuring equally grand structures, notably the Starrucca viaduct, a thousand feet long, rising a hundred feet above the creek and carried on seventeen stone arches.

The *DeWitt Clinton* would certainly win a prize for the oddest looking of all early American locomotives, with its oversized chimney and dome and rather spindly spoked wheels. It was built for the Mohawk & Hudson by the West Point Foundry – a company whose usual business was making armaments.

Most other lines took a very different approach. The engineers tried to avoid major civil engineering works by sweeping round hills on what were often very tight curves, accepting tougher gradients than would have been thought practical in Britain at that time and building many of their bridges and viaducts out of locally available timber. There was another major difference that developed between American and British practice that was to have a profound effect on locomotive construction.

In Britain, the old system of stone sleeper blocks had mostly been replaced by wooden sleepers, to which metal chairs were attached to hold the rails rigidly in position. The entire system was then stabilised with stone ballast. In the early 1830s the Americans produced a different system, originated by Robert Stevens. It too used wooden sleepers, or 'ties' as they were known on that side of the Atlantic, but dispensed with the chairs. The T-shaped rails had a flat base that was fastened directly to the ties by means of metal spikes. One advantage was that rails could be laid very quickly as was famously demonstrated during the construction of the Central Pacific when a team of eight men laid ten miles of track in a single day, 28 April 1869. Using the American system resulted in a track that was far less rigid then the British version, which could make for a rougher ride and this combined with sharp bends created

Norris's 1836 *George Washington* has the cylinders bolted to the smoke box, with an unusually long piston rod and connecting rod to the large driving wheels. Built in 1836 it is an early example of the developing pattern of having a four-wheel leading truck.

problems for locomotive engineers. With an extended system, they needed more power from their locomotives, while at the same time they had to make allowances for the vagaries of the track. In solving this dilemma they eventually arrived at what was to become the archetypal American steam locomotive.

Engineers were finding difficulty with their imported engines and began making their own adaptations. The first difference introduced allowed for easier negotiation of tight bends, by having a 4-2-0 arrangement, where the front four wheels were mounted on a swivelling truck. One of the innovators was John B. Jervis of the Mohawk & Hudson railway. Born in New York State in 1795, the son of a carpenter, he began his working life as an 'axeman' – literally using an axe to clear the way – for the construction of the Erie Canal. He soon rose through the ranks until by 1827 he had become the Resident Engineer. He moved on to the Delaware and Hudson and was to become acquainted with both *Stourbridge Lion* and *John Bull* in these early years. He later said that he had recognised the problems presented by these engines and had already by 1830 thought up the idea of the four-wheel truck. It was only later, however, when he was appointed engineer to the Mohawk & Hudson railway that he was able to put the design into practice. The result was his locomotive *Experiment*, completed in 1832 that established itself as a good, practical machine, achieving speeds of 50mph. Jervis did not stay long with the railway and by 1837 he was back at work again as a canal engineer, though he was to return to the railways much later in life.

The establishment of the 4-2-0 locomotive as the first American standard came largely through the success of the Norris locomotives. The story starts with two men, William Norris and Colonel Stephen H. Long, who had been experimenting with locomotive construction for some time and actually built a locomotive for the Boston & Providence Railroad before finally setting up the American Steam Carriage Company in 1832. It was a grand name for a very small operation, based on a workshop in a converted stable in Philadelphia. Long was as famous as an explorer as he was as an engineer, and it was not long before he was off on his travels again, surveying in Quebec. William was now joined by his brother Septimus and together they formed the Norris Locomotive Works, and Septimus was to prove an inspiring partner, introducing many new ideas into the company.

In September 1836, the company gave a spectacular demonstration of the power of their new 4-2-0 locomotive *George Washington* on the Philadelphia & Columbia Railroad. As with British railways at that time, some slopes were considered too much for locomotives to handle, so inclines worked by stationary engines were built. One of these on the edge of Philadelphia was the 2,805-foot incline that took the double track up from the Schuylkill River that contained a 187-foot section with a gradient of 1:15. The 6½-ton locomotive hauled a freight car, together with twenty-four passengers sitting on the tender, up the slope at a speed of 15mph. When the event was reported in the technical journals of the day it aroused great scepticism, so the whole thing was repeated in a formal trial in front of expert witnesses nine days later on 19 July 1836.

As a result of the experiment, the company received an order for a locomotive for the Baltimore & Ohio. The *Lafayette* was named after one of the heroes of the War of Independence, the Marquis de Lafayette. Like the *George Washington* the new locomotive had several features based on the Bury locomotives, in particular the D-plan firebox with its domed top and the bar frame. In other respects it was very different. It had outside cylinders attached to the smokebox and sloping at an angle of ten degrees. A replica of this engine was constructed in 1927 and is now housed in the Baltimore & Ohio museum in Baltimore. It is slightly different from the original, being built to fit the standard 4ft 8½in gauge rather than the 4ft 6in gauge of the original line. The success of the Norris locomotives in conquering

As late as 1838 some American railroads still ordered their locomotives from Britain. *Rocket* was built by Braithwaite, Milner & Co. of London, one of a set of eight delivered to the Reading Railroad. It continued in service right up to 1879, though in latter years it was converted to a tank engine. It was restored to its original condition for the 1893 Columbia Exposition.

quite steep inclines caught the attention of British railway companies. The Birmingham & Gloucester line included a famous 2½-mile long Lickey incline with a gradient of 1:37. The company ordered fourteen engines from Norris, specifically to cope with this section of the line. They served well as banking engines, joining their more conventional running mates to overcome the obstacle.

By 1839 the company had started to build more powerful 4-4-0 locomotives and in 1847 they produced the *Chesapeake* the country's first 4-6-0 engine. Only one of the Norris 4-4-0s has survived, the *Copiapó*, named after the silver and copper mines of Chile and it worked on the line that joined those mines to the port of Caldera. Built in 1850 it has a version of the Norris cut-off valve – in effect a valve serving the main valve. This was driven by a third eccentric and was placed above the conventional slide valve, a complex arrangement compared with the variable cut-off valves of Stephenson and Walschaert, and less successful in varying the cut-off point.

It is a mark of how rapidly construction had advanced that they had moved in just eleven years from a four-wheeled 6½-ton engine to a ten-wheeled locomotive weighing 22 tons. Norris went on to become one of the leading manufacturers of locomotives in the world and

Copiapó is the oldest surviving example of a Norris locomotive, virtually unchanged since its working days. It was built for the Copiapó Railroad in 1850 and has the Norris cut-off valve mechanism.

A Norris business card, showing a typical locomotive of the 1850s – the date was added by hand at some time.

Lafayette, built by Norris for the Baltimore & Ohio in 1837 was the first American-built locomotive to have a horizontal boiler. This replica is housed in the historic roundhouse of the Baltimore & Ohio Railroad Museum, Baltimore.

by the start of the 1850s they were employing about a thousand men and the works were said to be capable of turning out 150 locomotives a year. It is doubtful if it ever achieved that figure, though they did produce a hundred engines in 1853. By the 1850s, the process of construction had become so sophisticated that the time from drawing board to rolling out onto the track had been reduced to around thirty working days.

The best known of all the American manufacturers was Baldwin. Matthias W. Baldwin was born in New Jersey in 1795 and at the age of sixteen was apprenticed to a local jewellery-maker. In 1817 the family moved to Philadelphia where he went to work for one of the most important jewellers and silversmiths of the region. Two years later he was ready to set up business on his own and in 1825 he went into partnership with a skilled machinist, David Mason. That could have set him up in a career for life, but as their business expanded they found that in order to increase productivity, they needed a new power source for their machinery. They purchased a steam engine for use in the workshop. It proved unsatisfactory, so Baldwin decided to design an engine himself. Space was limited and the engine he produced was both efficient and very compact. It attracted a great deal of interest and soon he was getting orders for engines as well as jewellery and was gaining recognition as a steam expert.

As news began to spread about the wonders of steam travel, the Philadelphia Museum asked him if he could build a miniature locomotive to run round a circular track and give rides to a few passengers. Although he had no experience he agreed, and based his design on drawings of the engines that had taken part in the Rainhill Trials. In 1831 his little engine was set to work, hauling two trucks, each carrying four passengers. It was a small beginning but was sufficiently impressive to encourage the owners of the Philadelphia, Germantown & Norristown Railroad Co. to invite him to design and construct a locomotive for their line, which at the time was carrying passengers in horse-drawn coaches. He agreed but now he had a different model to work from.

The Camden & Amboy Railroad had just taken delivery of *John Bull* from the Stephenson works in Newcastle. Baldwin and a friend went to inspect it and found the locomotive still in pieces waiting for assembly. They took copious notes and measurements and used them as the basis for the new engines, popularly known as 'Old Ironsides'. Externally, it was very clearly based on the Stephenson Planet class, but there were significant differences. Baldwin had clearly not quite recognised the idea of exhaust steam blast. The two cylinders exhausted into a single horizontal tube, with a hole in the centre, from which a vertical pipe led steam up the chimney. This meant that the exhausts from the cylinders arrived in the tube from opposite directions and met at the centre. This inevitably soon proved unsatisfactory and a more conventional system was adopted, in which the exhaust gases passed united in a tube that was curved to point vertically up the chimney. The valve gear was quite simple with single loose eccentrics for each cylinder.

The local press was full of enthusiasm for the new engine. *The Chronicle* of 24 November 1832 wrote:

'The principal superiority of this engine over any of the English ones known, consists of the light weight – which is but between four and five tons – her small bulk, and the simplicity of her machinery. We rejoice at the result of this experiment, as it conclusively shows that Philadelphia, always famous for the skill of her mechanics, is enabled to produce steam-engines for railroads combining so many superior features as to warrant the belief that her mechanics will hereafter supply nearly all the public works of this description in the country.'

It was perhaps more than a little chauvinistic to praise the locomotive's superiority over British models, since Baldwin had happily borrowed most of his ideas from the Stephenson engine. It also turned out that praising its light weight was also a little premature as it was to prove unable to cope with one section where the gradient was too great. And once passenger services started, the advert made it clear that passengers would only be able to travel behind the engine 'when the weather is fair'. On wet days, the hoses would be back on duty. It was a disappointment to Baldwin, who gloomily forecast it would be his 'last engine'. His pessimism was short lived.

It was suggested to Baldwin that he ought to go over to the Mohawk & Hudson Railroad, where another Planet type locomotive, built by Robert Stephenson & Co. was running, but had already been adapted from its original 2-2-0 configuration by the replacement of the two leading wheels by a 4-wheel bogey. Once again, Baldwin decided that he could improve on the original. He designed a new type of half-crank axle. The cranks were set at the far end of

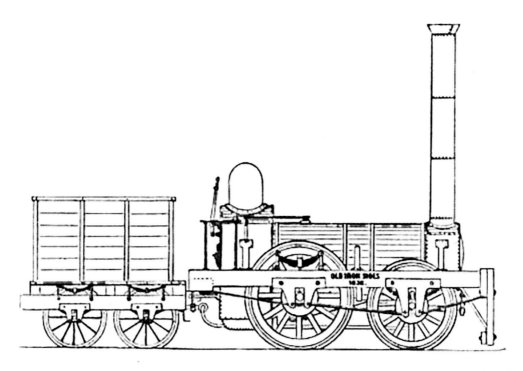

Old Ironsides was the first locomotive to be built by Baldwin. It is clearly modelled on *John Bull* as it was originally delivered, but without the additional truck for leading wheels.

the axle and attached to spokes on the wheel, so that in effect the wheel itself was part of the crank. This allowed more space inside the frame to extend the boiler. The engine again had outside cylinders, and the wheels were made of cast bell metal, a form of bronze. The earlier iron and wood composite wheels had not proved very successful and the new versions were no improvement, wearing out very quickly. On later models Baldwin designed a new type of composite wheel with cast iron spokes, a wooden rim and iron tyre.

In 1835, the company moved to bigger workshops and between then and the end of the decade they turned out 128 locomotives. While not quite emulating Ford's famous offer of 'any colour you like as long as it's black', he did offer a very limited range, all based on this new design, but coming in three different sizes.

1st class	12½ x 16 inch cylinders	20,000lb loaded weight
2nd class	12 x 16 inch cylinders	23,000lb loaded weight
3rd class	10½ x 16 inch cylinders	20,000lb loaded weight

The Baldwin standard model was a very distinctive engine. It had a tall, domed firebox, with the drive wheels set behind it. There was an external frame, outside cylinders and long rods from the eccentrics, one to each cylinder, stretching all the way back to the footplate. The locomotives worked at what was, for that time, the comparatively high boiler pressure of 120psi. There was inevitably considerable rivalry between Norris and Baldwin, each offering their own version of the 4-2-0 locomotive. Supporters of the Norris claimed that their version gave better adhesive power, while the Baldwin had a better weight distribution and so caused less damage to the light track still in use.

Baldwin was a conservative designer. Having got a good design he saw no reason to alter it, and indeed saw the great advantages of standardisation – and began to adapt the works towards eventually using a system of interchangeable parts. Customers knew exactly what they would get with a Baldwin locomotive and most seemed to appreciate it. The chief engineer of the New Jersey Transportation Co., writing in 1838 recorded that the Baldwin could haul twenty 4-wheeled cars, each carrying twenty-six passengers at 20-25mph up grades of 'twenty-six feet per mile'. He went on to add;

'As to the simplicity of construction, small liability to get out of order, economy of repairs, and ease to the road, I full believe Mr. Baldwin's engines stand unrivalled. I consider the simplicity of the engine, the arrangement of the working parts and the distribution of the weight, far superior to any engine I have ever seen, either of American or English manufacture.'

Baldwin himself thought that his first class locomotive offered all the power that would ever be needed, yet one has only to look at the load it could pull and the speed, or rather lack of it, to realise that things would never just stop there. By the 1840s, he had to find ways of building more powerful engines, as did manufacturers and engineers throughout the railway world.

Just as Baldwin had inspected and adapted British designs, so too European engineers began to take an interest in what was happening on the other side of the Atlantic. As the railway system grew, the demand for engines and qualified mechanical engineers increased. Emil Kestler was born in Baden Baden in 1803 and went to study mechanical engineering at Karlsruhe. It was here in 1837 that he established an engineering works in partnership with Theodor Martiensen. They were well placed when local schemes were being developed. One of these was the Baden State Railway, the first section of which, between Mannheim and Heidelberg, was opened in September 1840. Kessler built his first locomotive *Bardenia* for the line in 1841. At the same time a state railway was also being developed in the neighbouring state of Würtemberg and the promoters inspected locomotives from all the leading European manufacturers – in Britain, France and Belgium – as well as America. They favoured the Norris engines and put in an order for locomotives to be built in Philadelphia, but at the same time they also ordered similar engines from Kessler.

The American engineers had inspected British locomotives and decided they could improve on some aspects of the design. Kessler did the same, though some of the differences between his and the standard Norris arrangement came from adding a mixture of different elements from British locomotives. The boiler was on the Stephenson model, with its distinctive Gothic dome at the top and he also used the Stephenson linkage. The engine had a plate iron inside frame and a longer boiler than the Norris engines. He was to continue to construct more locomotives and went on to create a new works in Stuttgart, an idea energetically promoted by the Würtemberg State Railway, in order to remove the need to import locomotives in the future. The days of British domination of world markets seemed to be coming to an end, but Britain was to find new markets in its overseas colonies in the latter part of the century. All railway companies, wherever they were based, were facing a new challenge. As more and more people travelled and more goods were sent by rail, there was an urgent need to provide more powerful engines.

Chapter Twelve

Speed and Power

Throughout the 1840s, railway development continued at an unprecedented pace and nowhere more so than in Britain where the process had begun. Major cities were linked by trunk routes, and many of the smaller companies were amalgamated to form a more cohesive pattern. The Midland Railway is the classic example. Under the leadership of the 'Railway King' George Hudson, the new company was approved by Parliament in 1844. The lines were centred on Derby. The Midland Counties ran from there to Nottingham and Leicester and joined the London & Birmingham via a branch to Rugby; the North Midland connected to Leeds; the Birmingham & Derby Junction is self-explanatory. Other lines were also eaten up over the years. Hudson was later to be convicted of fraudulent dealing in railway shares and imprisoned, but his basic idea of a system based on large companies capable of financing major developments was sound, whatever his personal failings.

The first five years of the 1840s were marked by a steady increase in lines that could reasonably be described as making economic sense. By 1845, 2,400 route miles had been completed, but in the next few years the country went through a period of wild investment in what came to be known as the 'railway mania' years. The success of the first trunk routes deluded investors into believing that all railways would be equally profitable: in 1845 a further 2816 miles were approved; the following year 4541 miles; and in 1847, 1295 miles. The popular magazine *Punch* satirised the situation by offering shares in the 'John o'Groats & Land's End Junction Railway with branches to Ben Lomond and Battersea.' Many of the companies approved in this period never laid a single rail, but nevertheless by the end of the decade well over 6,000 miles of route had been completed. The public were taking to rail travel, and a new type of journey was introduced when Thomas Cook ran the first excursion train from Leicester to a temperance meeting in Loughborough in 1841. The following year the young Queen Victoria gave the transport system official approbation when she and Prince Albert took the train from Paddington to Slough, the nearest station to Windsor Castle. In a letter of 14 June 1842, she wrote: 'We arrived here yesterday morning, having come by the railroad from Windsor, in half an hour, free from dust and crowd and heat, and I am quite charmed with it'. Albert it seems was slightly less enthralled. According to an account in the *Morning Post*, he was heard to say: 'Not quite so fast next time, Mr. Conductor, if you please.' Nevertheless, royal approval did a good deal to encourage the nervous to concede that travelling by train might be a good idea after all.

The system was now so widespread that passengers could no longer just turn up at their nearest station and look at the local timetable, as their routes might involve travel across lines owned by many different companies. It was to solve this problem that James Bradshaw issued the first of his famous *Railway Guides* in 1839. Rail travel was hugely important in the life of the country, and as the *Illustrated London News* noted in 1850, people were able to 'travel distances which their forefathers had neither time nor money to undertake'. Statistics are impressive. The following table from T.C.Baker and C.I.Savage, *An Economic History of Transport in Britain* 1959 tells the story of passenger bookings, numbers of journeys and miles covered, in 1842–3 and 1847–8.

	Year ending June 1843		Year ending 30 June 1848	
	Journeys	Miles	Journeys	Miles
1st class	4,576,540	118,990,040	7,190,779	180,380,695
2nd class	11,998,512	172,778,573	21,690,510	348,467,044
3rd class	6,891,844	86,148,050	29,083,782	378,167,196
Total	23,466,896	277,916,671	57,965,071	907,014,935

In just five years, both the numbers of passengers carried and the miles covered had more than doubled and by the end of the 1840s passenger mileage was reaching the 1,000 million miles a year mark. This has always been considered the more glamorous side of rail transport, but for the companies, freight continued to be equally important as a source of revenue. In the early 1840s coal was, as it had been from the start, a major part of the equation. In 1842 it was estimated that out of 5 million tons of goods carried by rail, 4 million was made up of coal. There was now, however, another big earner for the railways; carrying mail. The travelling post office was introduced as early as 1838.

Looking at the picture as a whole it is clear that demand for rail transport was increasing at an incredible rate, but that different types of journeys put different demands on the locomotives. Passengers were looking for ever speedier journeys; the Post Office wanted to see letters delivered as quickly as possible. For these services, the challenge facing locomotive engineers was to produce faster engines, but at the same time increase their tractive power in order to carry more and more passengers. With heavy goods such as coal, the rail companies wanted locomotives to be capable of hauling as big a load as possible; it was of little importance how long the journey of any particular train took. What mattered was getting a regular supply to the customer as economically as possible. Whether it was the need to carry greater loads or to move at greater speeds, or a combination of the two, it was clear that engineers would need to design more powerful locomotives. It was also becoming increasingly clear that a single class would not be equally suitable for every kind of traffic. It was also obvious that among the increasing number of engineers designing locomotives, not all their efforts were equally successful.

The Stephenson Patentees were among the most successful designs of their day, though they were constantly being changed and improved. The original designs had continuous outside frames supporting the axle boxes and inside frames between the cylinders and the firebox that provided some support for the crank axle on the inside cylinder engines. Later, the inside plates were brought forward of the crank axle. By 1850, the inside plate frames also ran from end to end. By 1841, however, Stephenson was already developing a major

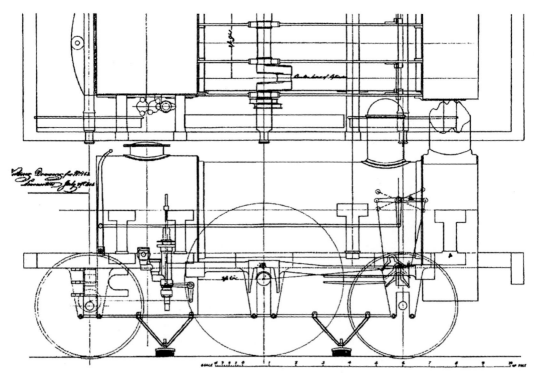

Working drawing for the Stephenson patentee *Provorny* of 1836.

improvement. Far more heat was being generated in the firebox than was being used to raise steam. As a result, the gases that reached the smokebox at the far end of the boiler were still so hot that the temperature could rise to nearly 300°C. He took what now seems the obvious and sensible step of increasing the length of the boiler to take up the excess heat by producing more steam. But changing one element in an engine will usually have an effect on other parts. He needed to ensure a good distribution of the extra weight without extending the wheelbase. His solution was to have the axles for all three pairs of wheels set in front of the firebox. Other major alterations also followed from this change.

The old system that had both outside sandwich frames and inside plate frames was replaced by one that had just inside plate frames. A recurrent problem on many early locomotives was the fracture of crank axles – as mentioned on p.113, *Fire Fly* was one of the early victims. Stephenson now decided to get rid of the problem altogether by using outside cylinders on the later long boiler engines. The change brought another benefit. The inside cylinders had always been positioned below the axle, so that if work needed to be done on the front axle boxes everything had to be dismantled before repairs could start. That was another problem automatically solved with outside cylinders. One surviving example of the new long boiler locomotives is *L'Aigle*, now preserved at the Cité du Train museum in France.

The engine was built at the Stephenson Newcastle works in 1846 for a new line between Avignon and Marseilles, on which work had started in 1843 and which carried its first

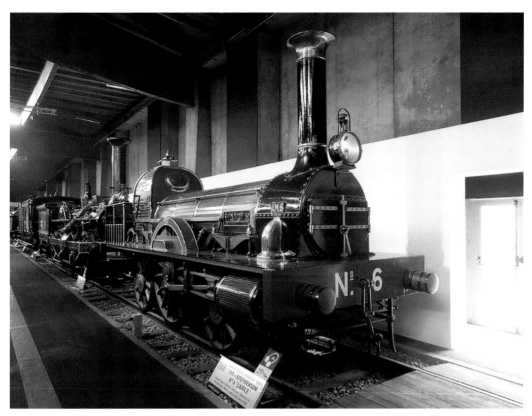

L'Aigle is the finest surviving example of a Stephenson long boiler locomotive, built in 1846 for the Marseille Avignon route and now preserved at the Cité du Train, Mulhouse, France.

passengers on part of the route in 1847, opening throughout two years later. It is interesting to note that even at this comparatively late date, continental railways were still turning to Britain for locomotives. It is a handsome engine in many ways, with its tall, brass-capped chimney and high haystack boiler. However, it seems less compact and less well-proportioned than the earlier Patentees. This is not surprising, as the boiler has been extended from the 8ft 6in found in, for example, *North Star*, to 12ft 6in, while still retaining the short wheelbase. The driving wheels are rather smaller than on *North Star* – 5ft 7½in compared with 7ft. It was not exactly an express locomotive, with typical running speeds of no more than 30mph. Attempts to run long boiler engines at higher speeds proved troublesome, due to severe oscillations – and on the Avignon-Marseilles route a speed limit of 60kph. was imposed. In spite of this, French railways ordered a large number of locomotives of this type, some of which were imported from Newcastle while others were manufactured in France under licence that involved payment of a royalty. The wheel arrangements covered the full range for three-axle engines from the typical 2-2-2 to 0-6-0 for goods engines.

These early years saw different engineers trying out different ideas about the best arrangement of everything from the firebox to the wheel arrangement. One of the few who put his ideas down on paper was Edward Bury, who set out his thoughts in the *Transactions of the Institution of Civil Engineers* in 1840. In it he argued the case for four-wheeled locomotives. Apart from the very obvious fact that it is cheaper to build small engines than it is to build larger ones, he reasoned that as a lighter engine required less power simply to move itself along, it would also be more economical to run. He also claimed that the engines were far safer and ran far more steadily than other locomotive types. He was so convinced of his own argument that he carried out an experiment. He partly cut through the front axle of his 2-2-0 Number 18 and set off down the line. Inevitably, with only an inch thickness of iron remaining, the axle broke. The engine, however, was able to continue on its journey, turn round and come back again, relying on the strong connection to the tender to keep it from collapsing. Quite what the footplate crew thought of this experiment is not recorded.

Bury's claim that because his locomotives were lighter they needed less power may have been true, but engine weight only represents a comparatively small percentage of the total weight that has to be moved. In practice, they were severely under-powered, with two or even three engines being regularly used on even quite modest trains. On one occasion, a goods train required a startling seven locomotives to draw a train of just forty-five loaded goods waggons. Bury continued building his four-wheelers for many years. One of these, built in 1848 in Liverpool at the Clarence Foundry, was officially simply Number Three but unofficially it was always known as 'Coppernob'. Now preserved at the National Railway Museum in York it is easy to see how it got its name. The domed firebox is encased in a gleaming copper sheath.

Stephenson was not the only engineer providing locomotives for the Liverpool & Manchester Railway. This Bury 2-2-0 was built for the line in 1835.

81a. Furness Railway 0-4-0 locomotive No3, 'Coppernob' was designed by Bury and is now preserved in the National Railway Museum, York. It is the oldest surviving inside cylinder locomotive.

If it did nothing else, it upheld Bury's claims of reliability. It remained in use right up to 1898, though for most of that time it was reduced to the rather humble role of shunter.

One of the companies who began manufacturing locomotives for Bury was Mather, Dixon & Co. of Liverpool. They began in the 1830s and one of the new men at the works at the time was William Buddicom, who was taken on as an engineering apprentice in 1831. He was not the likeliest candidate for a career in engineering. When he was born in 1794 his father was rector of Everton and had the boy educated at home, but his interest lay more with the practical than with the classical education of the day. By 1836 he had a new job as Resident Engineer on a section of the Liverpool & Manchester Railway that included the stationary engines at Edge Hill. It was there that he attracted the attention of one of the great civil engineers of the day, Joseph Locke, who had already established a role as one of the leading railway constructors of the age. He persuaded Buddicom to take up a new post as Resident Engineer on the Glasgow, Paisley, Kilmarnock & Ayr Railway, but before long he was moving on again with Locke's encouragement. His new job this time was as Locomotive Superintendent for the Grand Junction. One of his first actions was to improve efficiency by offering drivers a bonus if they worked on economising on fuel and oil use. It proved very successful. He then applied his mind to a problem that beset many locomotives of the day; the broken crank axle.

The company had another new recruit, Alexander Allan, who had previously worked for George Forrester & Co. of the Vauxhall Foundry in Liverpool. Together Buddicom and Allan began altering their existing engine stock, converting inside cylinder locomotives to outside cylinder. This type of engine became known as the 'Crewe' type and also sometimes as the 'Allan' type. Locke obviously rated Buddicom's talents very highly. Once again he asked him to join him on the latest venture for which he was the chief engineer, the line from Paris to Rouen. Although this was a French railway, there was a strong British presence. Apart from Locke and his assistants, the contractors were also British, William Mackenzie and Thomas Brassey, who brought with them a small army of British navvies. The latter were

The 2-2-2 Crewe locomotives were devised by William Buddicom and Alexander Allan. They were built with outside cylinders to overcome the many problems that had appeared when manufacturing engines with inside cylinders and cranked axles.

joined by workers from across Europe, which must have made communication interesting. Brassey later recorded that there were eleven languages spoken on site. Arthur Helps, in his biography of Brassey, explained the very basic means of communication used by the Brits:

'They pointed to the earth to be moved, or the waggon to be filled, said the word "d-n" emphatically, stamped their feet, and somehow or other instructions, thus conveyed, were generally comprehended by the foreigners.'

Life must have been equally complex for Buddicom when he arrived on the scene in 1841.

As work progressed there was an urgent need for locomotives and waggons to serve the contractors. Rather than import everything, a new works was established near Rouen under the direction of Buddicom and William Allcard. The latter had begun his working life as a pupil of George Stephenson, during the construction of the Liverpool & Manchester, and by the time of the opening, he was appointed one of two resident engineers. Like Buddicom, his fortunes became closely tied to those of Locke, following him first to the Grand Junction, then to France. So, once again, designs that had originated in Britain found their way across the Channel. One of these French built locomotives, the *St Pierre*, built at the Allcard, Buddicom factory at Les Chartreux has survived and is preserved at the Cité du Train at Mulhouse. Anyone who has a chance to visit this excellent museum will normally find it standing immediately in front of *L'Aigle*. It makes for an interesting comparison; the *St. Pierre* looks to be altogether better proportioned. The most striking features are the tall copper-sheathed steam dome set, quite unusually, immediately above the firebox and the large 5ft 7½in drive wheels. There are two safety valves, one immediately above the dome and the other on top of the boiler. Cylinders and boiler are both jacketed in teak cladding, held in place by brass bands.

The valve gear was devised in Crewe by Allan and used a straight linkage that raised the valve rods and dropped the eccentric link simultaneously. It is operated by a simple quadrant lever on the footplate. It was cheaper to make than the Stephenson gear and rather easier to use, as it was well balanced; the design was patented and Allen received a royalty for each engine on which it was used. The cylinders themselves are set at a $10°$ angle, with the horizontal valve chest set above the cylinders. The change from inside to outside cylinder required changes to the frame; the former sandwich frame was replaced by two separate inside and outside iron frames. Another Crewe locomotive of the same type *Columbine* was actually the first locomotive to be built at Crewe for the Grand Junction in 1845 and is part of the national collection and now on show at the Science Museum, London. Superficially all but identical to *St. Pierre*, it differs in having Stephenson linkage instead of the Allan straight linkage.

Crewe continued to turn out variations on the basic design, either as 2-2-2s or 2-4-0s, for about fifteen years with very few changes. Cylinder size was gradually increased and boiler pressure was raised from 75psi in the first models to 100psi in the 1850s and drive wheel size was also increased. In 1843, a new man came to take over as Locomotive Superintendent, Richard Trevithick's son, Francis. He worked with Allan to develop the Crewe engines.

St. Pierre was built in France by the company set up near Rouen by William Buddicom and William Allcard to serve the line being built between there and Paris. The most curious feature is the situation of the copper dome immediately above the firebox. Buddicom used the valve gear designed in Crewe by his former colleague Alexander Allan.

Together they produced a locomotive, Cornwall, with what was for the time immense drive wheels at 8ft 6in diameter. To accommodate such a high axle was a problem that was solved by moving the drive axle from its conventional position below the boiler to a point above the centre of a very low-slung boiler, which was designed with an indentation in the top to take the axle. The engine survives but has been much altered over the years. In its original form it was not a great success. He was later to design more conventional 2-2-2s with 7ft drive wheels, with the boiler above the axles.

The story of Crewe engines was one of steady improvement rather than spectacular change – with the exception of *Cornwall*, which was spectacular but not necessarily an improvement. Francis Trevithick described this process in his biography of his father. He took his lead from Joseph Locke who, in a report written at the end of 1839, wrote of 'the folly and expense of perpetually altering the engines for the sake of some trifling gain' and he argued the case for standardising parts:

Cornwall was Francis Trevithick's locomotive for the London & North Western Railway that was notable for the immense size of the drive wheels. This photo shows it after it was rebuilt in 1858' with the boiler in a conventional position instead of being beneath the drive axle as in the original.

'I lately found an engine standing idle for the want of a valve to the pump, a small piece of brass not more than 3lb. in weight, and although there are ten engines of the same class on the line (with two pumps to each engine), there was not one duplicate valve on the establishment.'

Trevithick recorded how the first outside cylinder engine had 12½-inch cylinders with 5ft diameter drive wheels and weighing 10 tons. It hauled ten carriages between Birmingham and Liverpool. By 1843, the trains had increased to fifteen coaches, boiler pressure had gone up from 50 to 60psi, drive wheels were 5ft 6in and three quarters of an inch had been added to the cylinder diameter. This locomotive would, it was claimed, take a train of sixteen coaches 'with the precision of clockwork' between Birmingham and Liverpool at a speed, including stoppages, of thirty miles an hour. The following year, a more powerful engine was designed for the Lancaster to Carlisle route that included the climb over Shap Fell, with a 1:75 gradient for five miles. The extra power needed to conquer this slope was provided by increasing all the factors: cylinders now up to 145/8in; drive wheels to 6ft; and boiler pressure to 75psi. As Trevithick wryly noted his father had used a cylinder of 14½in and steam at 100psi for *Catch-me-who-Can* in 1808, adding: 'Such was the slow progress of the locomotive engine'. However, he was understandably proud of the performance of the Crewe engines:

'One of these good little engines of 1845 gave special proof of efficiency. About the year 1846, on a rainy, blowing, Autumnal Saturday night, the writer was summoned, from nursing a influenza cold, to the railway station. Her Majesty, Prince Albert and the rest of the Royal family had unexpectedly arrived, and desired to be in London by ten the following morning. Continued rain had caused the line to be unsafe in places, except at comparatively slow speeds. Saturday night is proverbially a bad time for finding people wanted in a hurry. However, at six the next morning, in dim light and blinding rain, the Royal train was in readiness, and Her Majesty punctual to the minute when, after a little animated delay for the lady in waiting, a start was made, and the required speed of forty miles an hour steadily run, until a providential disobedience of orders by the pilot-engine man causes the steam to be instantly shut off, the brakes applied, and the speed reduced to one-half; fog signals exploded in close proximity to the danger; red flags were hurriedly unfurled, and in a moment the engine rolled as a ship in a storm through an alarmed group of a hundred navvies, who, thinking it a quiet day, had raised the rails and sleepers a foot above their bed of soft clay, that a thick layer of ballast might be shovelled under them. For a quarter of a mile did the precious freight pass safely over this bridge of rails supported by brickbats, the only injury being a bent driving axle and broken bearing-brasses, with which the engine kept time to the next relieving station, and then broke down.'

The somewhat bizarre wheel arrangement of *Cornwall* was due in part at least to the need to avoid infringing a patent that had been taken out in 1843 by Thomas Russell Crampton. Born in 1816 and privately educated, Crampton followed the conventional route into engineering, with an apprenticeship to a London engineer, John Hague. Once qualified he went to work for Marc Brunel and then moved on to assist Daniel Gooch, and was involved in the design of the first locomotives for the Great Western. It was during his time with the GWR that he came up with his idea. He was aware that having large drive wheels would result in higher speeds, but that with any conventional arrangement it would result in a high centre of gravity for the engine and inevitable instability. He solved the problem by placing the drive wheels behind the boiler. This meant that the boiler could be placed even lower than in conventional engines. He was not concerned with having a short wheelbase, so the locomotives mostly had two pairs of carrying wheels set well forward. The only disadvantage of the design was that there was very little weight bearing down on the drive wheels, so there was comparatively less adhesive force than in conventional engines. Nevertheless, Crampton engines with drive wheels up to 8ft in diameter both looked and were impressive.

The first two engines of this type were built for use on the Namur-Liège line in Belgium in 1846. This was also the year in which Crampton set up on his own as an engineer and the first British locomotive to use his design was built for the London & North Western Railway in 1848. The engine *Liverpool* was probably the most powerful of its day, recorded as travelling at a speed of 62mph with a load of 180 tons. However, the engine itself weighed in at 35 tons, and was widely considered to be likely to damage the tracks. Crampton presented his ideas to the Institution of Civil Engineers in 1849, but they were not well received by the members. He had better luck in France, where Crampton engines enjoyed a long and successful career. Altogether over three hundred Crampton locomotives were to be constructed, both in Britain and in continental Europe. Crampton continued to work as an engineer, but although

Crampton locomotives were popular in Europe. *Die Pfalz* was built by Maffei for the Bavarian Palatine Railway in 1853. This illustration shows a working replica now in the Nuremberg Transport Museum.

he produced no other outstanding designs for locomotives, he busied himself in other varied fields, from setting up a waterworks in Berlin to designing a hydraulic tunnelling machine. The search for more speed and power was not just an end in itself; it also developed from serious rivalries about how the system as a whole should develop.

One problem had become greater with the passing years, with the expansion of the Great Western broad gauge, up towards the Midlands. The Cheltenham & Great Western Railway was nominally independent, though its southern junction was at Swindon. The company soon ran out of money and the Great Western took over, completing the line as far as Gloucester in 1845. Up to this point, the GWR had been an entirely independent network, but now Gloucester found itself with two incompatible systems, one built to Stephenson's gauge, the other to Brunel's. With the Great Western and the various 'narrow gauge' companies competing to create new connections, Parliament stepped into the fight. The evils of a break in gauge were daily on display at Gloucester, where passengers and goods had to be shuffled between the two rival systems. In July 1845, a Gauge Commission was appointed to study the whole question and make recommendations. The three wise men who were given the job were an oddly assorted bunch. The first choice must have seemed obvious; Sir Frederick Smith, the former Chief Inspector of Railways. The other two caused many raised eyebrows: Peter Barlow, a professor of mathematics, described by Gooch unflatteringly as 'a fat old buffer' and George Biddell Airey, the Astronomer Royal, who was regarded by railwaymen as rather a bad joke when it came to the job in hand. The doubters were proved wrong; the trio did their job well.

The Commissioners called forty-eight witnesses in all, of whom most were in favour of the narrower gauge. Brunel, however, suggested that a trial should be held to see which produced the best results. Initially, he wanted to test the rivals against his engines on the equivalent of the whole of the London to Exeter line. This was rejected in favour of trials along two lengths of even track: London and Didcot for broad gauge; York and Darlington for the other. The Great Western was represented by a Fire Fly class engine *Ixion* and it achieved a commendable 60mph with an 80-ton train. The best a rival long-boiler 4-2-0 could manage was 53mph, while the other contender ran off the rails. It should have been a triumph for Brunel, but it turned out to be a disaster. The Commissioners made it clear that speed was not the only nor even the main criterion on which they would base their decision. They were concerned with the 'great evil' of the break of gauge, and with 1,900 miles of Stephenson gauge already built, they decided that 4ft 8½in was no longer the 'narrow gauge'. From now on it would be the standard gauge for the country. The broad gauge continued in use, but its days were numbered and there was little further development of broad gauge locomotives beyond the Iron Duke type of engine.

In one aspect of locomotive design, the Great Western differed markedly from other companies. Surprising as it seems today, most locomotives of the day were not fitted with any form of brake, relying either on a hand brake on the tender or in the guards van. Braking an inside cylinder locomotive was obviously going to be problematical as any sudden stopping of the drive wheels could damage the crank axle. If the hand brakes proved inefficient, the driver had to put his locomotive into reverse and hope for the best. Gooch introduced a new system on 4-4-0 tank engines in 1849, with a sledge brake bearing down on the rails between the pair of drive wheels. It certainly stopped the engine, but was also liable to throw it off the rails. No really efficient engine braking system was available until the introduction of air brakes, especially the Westinghouse brakes, in the 1860s.

It seemed that, in Britain at least, the way forward was very much seen as being tied to developing locomotives with huge driving wheels for fast running. Development continued for another two decades, culminating in the Singles designed by Patrick Stirling for the Great Northern Railway, arguably the most elegant of all nineteenth century locomotives. The Stirling Singles were also very efficient, one famously covering the 83 miles from Grantham to York at an average speed of 65½mph in 1895.

Most manufacturers aimed at finding a winning formula and sticking to it, creating a class of locomotives, with the obvious saving in costs at the works. One exception to this rule was John Chester Craven who joined the London, Brighton & South Coast Railway in 1847 as superintendent of locomotives and at once began improving and extending the locomotive works in Brighton. He firmly believed that establishing classes slowed progress. He preferred to build a locomotive, then maybe a second, but after that look for improvements and changes and start all over again with a fresh design. He remained at his post until 1870, by which time there were seventy-two different types of locomotive on the line, creating something of a maintenance nightmare. The directors suggested that it

John Chester Craven's locomotive No. 12 photographed at the Lover's Walk depot in Brighton on the London, Brighton & South Coast Railway. This is just one of over seventy types of locomotive he developed for the line. The engineer is seated in front with his family.

The London, Brighton & South Coast did not rely on locomotives from its own works. Among the most reliable stalwarts of the line were the 2-2-2s supplied by Sharp, Roberts and Company. Unlike Craven the company went on producing standard designs for many years with great success. The photograph shows a typical engine on the line, heading a passenger train.

would make sense to rationalise the position, by reducing the number of classes. Craven refused and offered his resignation; it was accepted.

One area of interest to locomotive engineers was fuel. The Liverpool and Manchester had stipulated the use of coke to avoid the nuisance caused by coal smoke. Other lines followed suit. Coke was efficient, but it was also expensive. Experiments on using coal were begun as early as 1836 and one popular solution was to use a mixture of the two fuels. The firebox designed by John Chanter was divided in two by a horizontal grate made of water tubes. The lower grate was fed with coal, the upper with coke and it seemed the smoke difficulty had been removed. But in 1836, the water-tube grate burst, injuring the footplate crew. The firebox was rebuilt with a vertical division, but the experiment was abandoned. In Britain, at least until the 1850s, coke continued to be the fuel of choice.

The railways of continental Europe were developing their own manufacturing and design facilities throughout the 1840s, even though they were still importing engines from Britain or building British designs under licence. However, new challenges were soon to require new solutions. The powerful Austro-Hungarian Empire had its capital in Vienna but its main seaport was on the Adriatic coast at Trieste. The Austrian government decided that it needed

This early postcard shows a section of the Semmering Railway and gives a good idea of the sort of problems faced by the engineers – and why it required especially powerful locomotives to operate the line.

a rail link between the two, but the line would have to cross the Alps via the Semmering Pass at an altitude of 936 metres. Trains were not required to go quite that high, as a tunnel was created below the summit at an altitude of 878 metres. Even so, the track had to twist and turn and the route out of Vienna had a 29km section with a gradient that constantly hovered around the 1:40 mark. There was considerable doubt whether any locomotive could manage such a climb; certainly none in existence at that time could have done so. There was talk of relying on fixed engines and cable haulage. A writer to a technical publication pointed out that this was exactly the scenario that had been played out at Rainhill; cable haulage versus locomotive. That had been settled by a trial, so why not have a Semmering Trial?

A successful locomotive had to ascend the pass with its train at a speed of 11.5kph and limitations were set that engines should not exceed 14 ton axle load though a very generous boiler pressure for the time was permitted at 120psi. No British companies offered up candidates, but four locomotives by four different European manufacturers were entered. However, there were inevitable British connections. The winning entry came from the company established in 1836 by Joseph Anton Maffei in Munich – a company that was to survive in various forms and was still to be at the forefront of locomotive development in the twentieth century. It was designed with the help of the English engineer Joseph Hall. It was unlike anything seen on rails before. There were four axles under the locomotive, the front two mounted on a bogie. All were connected via a mixture of conventional rods and chains. There were a further three axles under the tender, also connected to the drive axles, spreading the tractive effort over engine and tender. The wheels were small, just 3ft 6in diameter and the locomotive managed to haul its 132 ton train up the slope at a very creditable 18kph, well in excess of the competition target. The three other locomotives also managed to pass the test, but *Bavaria* was considered the most reliable. This turned out not to be entirely true in practice, as there were problems with the chain drive almost from the start and it was taken out of service.

Perhaps the most interesting of the other locomotives came from the John Cockerill Company, which, in spite of its name, was based in Belgium. The company was actually founded in 1799 by William Cockerill, who arrived from Britain to set up a company making textile machinery and from there it was a logical step to begin making steam engines to drive it. His son John took over the business and expanded it. He bought the former palace of the Prince Bishops of Liège at Seraing where he established the company headquarters and built a factory in the grounds. This was an immense concern, with its own blast furnaces, foundry and production factory with a workforce of 3,000. It was by far the most important manufacturing concern in Belgium but ran into serious financial difficulties in a major currency crisis. Cockerill travelled to Russia to raise funds, but contracted typhoid and died in Warsaw in 1840 before reaching home. The company was too important to be allowed to go under, so it was taken over by the state, while still retaining the Cockerill name. It was from this factory that the locomotive *Seraing* was sent to Semmering.

Seraing was an articulated locomotive, with a central firebox, and a boiler at each side. The appearance was of two locomotives that had backed into each other and become irretrievably stuck together. A set of four wheels set on a bogie beneath each of the boilers made it possible for this locomotive to have a large boiler capacity, a long overall wheelbase of 27ft, but still be capable of coping with the tight curves of the Semmering. The description of this engine probably sounds familiar; it could, of course, equally well describe the Double Fairlies built for the Ffestiniog Railway. In fact they appear to have been remarkably similar in many respects.

Neudstadt was built by the Wiener Neudstadt locomotive factory, south of Vienna, the largest locomotive and engineering works in the Austro-Hungarian Empire. It too had two 4-wheel bogies, but a single boiler. The fourth contender was designed by a Scotsman, John Haswell. Born in Glasgow, he received his early experience at the Fairfield shipyard on the Clyde, before leaving for Austria to help set up the repair works for the Wien–Raaber Railway. He became superintendent of the works, which

A silver medallion was struck to commemorate the opening of the Semmering Railway. One side contained this engraving of the double-ended locomotive *Seraing* built for the trials in 1851 by John Cokerill of Belgium.

soon began constructing locomotives and rolling stock as well as repairing them. Their locomotive *Vindobona* was a rather strange form of 0-8-0, with three axles conventionally placed under the boiler and the other, attached by a long connecting rod, under the tender.

The four locomotives were very much one-offs, designed to meet a specific set of extreme circumstances, but they proved that they could tackle conditions that had previously been considered impossible. The Semmering trial may not have had quite the same dramatic effect on locomotive development as its famous predecessor at Rainhill, but it did undoubtedly encourage engineers to look at new ways of constructing ever more powerful engines.

One problem that beset many early locomotives was unsteadiness on the line. Engineers had not really appreciated the fact that with pistons, crossheads and connecting rods all in motion, they would need to be balanced to prevent unwanted oscillations. It was a Frenchman, M. Le Chatelier, who set out the theory of balancing in a book published in 1849 that was to form the basis for a more scientific approach to solving the problem. Before that, attempts at balancing had been carried out, with varying degrees of success, on a more or less ad hoc basis.

In America, too, new ideas were being tried out, and there was a certain optimism in the air. A civil engineer writing in the *American Railroad Journal* in July 1836 declared that American

A very similar locomotive to the *Seraing* was developed in Britain by Robert Fairlie and first appeared here on the Ffestiniog Railway. The photograph shows one in action with a mixed train in the 1930s. Fairlies still run on this preserved line.

locomotives would be able to conquer the hills and mountains of the country, without any outside help from stationary engines and inclines. He was to prove correct, but to achieve that aim needed rather more power than was available in the early 1830s. The early locomotives, by Baldwin and Norris both used single drivers, but in different positions, Baldwin's behind the firebox as in the Crampton engines, Norris in front. The next rather obvious advance was made by Henry R. Campbell, the chief engineer for the Germantown Railroad, who combined the Norris and Baldwin ideas. He built an engine with four drive wheels, one axle in front and the other behind the firebox. The only problem with the engine was that there was no equalising beam for the two pairs of wheels. This was rectified in 1837 by Eastwick & Harrison of Philadelphia, with an 8-wheeled engine in which the drive axles were in a separate frame.

Baldwin was unimpressed. He was convinced that the engines would be unable to cope with the tight curves of so many American lines, and that one set of wheels was bound to slip when rounding the bends. His solution was to design a geared locomotive. A shaft placed between the two truck axles was connected by a crank to the drive wheel axle. Gears on this shaft meshed with cogs on the truck, with a suitable gear ratio, as the smaller carrying wheels had to move faster than the large drive wheels. It was not a success, and the experiment was abandoned. By 1842 he had a very different design to try out, which he patented that year. It was an unusual type of 0-6-0 engine. This locomotive had outside cylinders, set at an angle, with long connecting rods to the drive wheels at the rear. These drive wheels were then connected to the other wheels on a form of truck. These were held in a separate frame, and arrangements were made so that the two pairs of wheels could move independently of each other when going round bends. The coupling rods had ball and socket joints to allow for the necessary flexibility.

The new engine was tried out on the Central Railway of Georgia, where it was recorded that the 12-ton engine drew nineteen trucks, loaded with 750 bales of cotton, each weighing 450lb up a gradient of 36ft to the mile with ease. Railroad managers were soon writing in praise of the new design and orders began to flow: twelve engines in 1843; 22 in 1844; and twenty-seven in 1845. Baldwin did not rest on his laurels and was constantly looking for improvements and economies. In 1845 he began experimenting with using iron tubes instead of copper in boilers. He ran comparative tests between two locomotives on comparable runs and found little difference in performance. He was also quite ready to accept new ideas from others where they represented a clear improvement. American locomotives were almost entirely wood burners, which created a problem with sparks flying out of the chimney – hence the bulbous spark arresters on the chimney that were such a feature of all early American locomotives. When the company of French and Baird designed a far more efficient stack in 1845, Baldwin at once adopted it for all his locomotives.

Baldwin had been concentrating most of his efforts on constructing freight locomotives, where pulling power was the main criterion. In 1848 he was given a new challenge. The Vermont Central Railroad offered him $10,000 if he could build an express locomotive capable of maintaining speeds of 60mph. The locomotive was completed in 1849 and named *Governor Paine*, after the Vermont company's president. This time Baldwin went for a very different form of 8-wheeled engine. There was a pair of 6ft 6in drive wheels set behind the firebox, coupled to a smaller pair of wheels in front of it. The carrying wheels at the front were on a conventional bogie. The 17in diameter cylinders were placed in an unusual position in the centre of the frame. It met the criteria, and a Vermont official claimed to have recorded the engine as covering a mile in 43 seconds from a standing start, which was certainly a remarkable achievement for the time. The company also provided one unusual locomotive at this time for the Madison and Indianapolis Railroad, which included a 1:17 incline from the bank of the Ohio River at Madison. To conquer this slope, he designed an 8-wheeled rack and pinion engine.

One of the leading exponents of the 4-4-0 was Norris. Their locomotives were to typify the American pattern of engine, with the forward truck, the cowcatcher and the distinctive spark-arrester chimney. We have all seen variations on this basic type in scores of Hollywood westerns. But Norris did build other types as well. His grandest engine was the first 4-6-0, *Chesapeake*, built in 1847, a 22-ton engine with 46in drive wheels. Two years later he was to build an engine on a very different principle. In the 1840s, Robert L. Stevens visited Britain and was particularly impressed with Crampton's ideas. On his return he ordered an engine on a similar pattern from Norris. The first of the type was built in 1849 and others soon followed, the later versions having hugely impressive 96in drive wheels and a 6-2-0 wheel arrangement. They were undoubtedly fast, but they lacked tractive force and were notoriously difficult to start. By the middle of the 1850s, almost all had been converted into 4-4-0s. In later years, the problem of supplying extra tractive effort for express singles would be solved, but they were not destined to play a leading role in American locomotive development.

As the 1840s came to an end, the variety of locomotives on lines all over the railway world was remarkable. The number of builders also increased; some small and specialised, others, especially those run by the bigger companies, were developing into massive industrial units employing hundreds and even thousands of workers.

Chapter Thirteen

The Works

In the earliest days of the railways, when they were serving collieries, there was no need to establish special repair and maintenance shops. The mines already had their own facilities for looking after their steam pumping and winding engines. This changed with the arrival of the Stockton and Darlington Railway, and the company soon established its first works at Shildon. It set a pattern that was to be followed by other companies. The process began with hunting for a site. John Dixon, who surveyed the line in 1821, described the area that was chosen as being nothing more than 'a wet swampy field'. When the railway opened for business, there were four houses in various states of readiness, one of which was occupied by Timothy Hackworth as a temporary measure. He was later to move to a much grander house, now part of a railway museum complex. The works, such as they were, consisted of one, narrow building, divided between a joiner's shop and a blacksmith's shop with two hearths. There was also an engine shed, which remained roofless for years, which could hold two locomotives. Gradually, more cottages were built and the workforce grew from twenty to fifty men. Machine tools were almost non-existent, consisting of little more than hand operated lathes, and screw jacks for lifting parts for erection. According to an old workman, interviewed in 1872 for the *Northern Echo,* the place was so cold in winter that tallow from the candles froze as it dripped. The nature of the work ensured that if there was no heating, they were kept warm by their exertions. Wheels were always a problem, frequently cracking, and having to be laboriously hammered on and off the axles. For many years it remained no more than a repair shop, but Hackworth established his own Soho Works for building locomotives close by in 1833. Because of his official duties, he passed over the control to his brother, Thomas, and a local iron founder, Nicholas Downing. By 1840, Hackworth had resigned from the Stockton & Darlington and concentrated solely on Soho. It is interesting to see just how much had changed in a short time.

By the time Hackworth died in 1850, the works had developed into a major complex. The main range of buildings consisted of a foundry, with three cupola furnaces, a machine shop and a blacksmith's shop. There were separate buildings for stores and for the pattern makers and joiners workshops. Unlike the Cockerill works in France, the Soho foundry was not based on a blast furnace fed with iron ore, but on furnaces that were used to melt either pig iron or scrap iron. The wheel lathe was capable of turning wheels up to 10ft in diameter and a boring machine for cylinders up to 8ft diameter. The blacksmiths' shop had twenty-two hearths, with a fan blast to raise the temperature, and a separate furnace for wheel tyres. The works required skilled craftsmen of all kinds, from machinists to pattern makers.

As locomotives became more complex, so the need for accuracy in dimensions became more pressing. In casting, for example, everything depends on the skill of carpenters as much as on the foundry men. The process involves making a wooden version of the item, which is then packed round with special sand in the casting box. The pattern is then removed, leaving an exact impression behind that will then be filled with molten metal. Even an apparently simple object requires a high level of competence from the pattern maker. I have a pattern for a cog on the windowsill of my office. It is seven inches in diameter with thirteen teeth. To make it the carpenter had to turn the centre on a lathe, and then carve the identical curved teeth, which are fixed into the hub by perfect dovetail joints. One can easily imagine the skill needed to make some of the more complex parts of a locomotive. The Hackworth business went into decline and closed in 1883, but the original Shildon works developed and eventually became British Rail waggon works. Appropriately it was here that the replica of Hackworth's famous locomotive *Sans Pareil* was built for the celebration of the 150th anniversary of the Rainhill Trials.

The Stockton and Darlington was a modest railway compared with those that were to follow on after it, and bigger companies required far more extensive works. Initially, these were planned specifically for the repair of locomotives and rolling stock, but in many cases soon turned to manufacturing as well. Once the decision had been taken to establish a works, the next job was, as at Shildon, to find an appropriate site. In the case of one of the most famous of them all, the Great Western works at Swindon, we know exactly why the site was chosen, because Daniel Gooch wrote a long letter to Brunel setting out his reasons on 13 September 1840. It was also to be the engine depot, serving the whole line:

'According to your wish I give you my views of the best site for our principal engine establishment, and in doing so I have studied the convenience of the Great Western Railway only, but also think the same point is the only place adapted for the Cheltenham and Great Western. The point I refer to is the Junction at Swindon of the two lines.

'The only objection I see to Swindon is the bad supply of water. There is also an apparent inequality of distance or duty for the engines to work – but which is very much equalized when the circumstance attending it are taken into account. I find the actual distances are as 76½ to 41 and the gradients are for the short distance of 41 miles a rise of 318 feet or 7.75 feet per mile, and for the 76½ miles a rise of 292 feet or 3.8 feet per mile.

'Swindon being the point at which these gradients change, the different gradients necessarily require a different class of engine, requiring for the Bristol end a more powerful one than for the London end.

'That power can only be obtained conveniently by reducing the diameter of the Driving Wheels, therefore supposing we work between Swindon and Bristol with 6 feet wheels, and between Swindon and London with 7 feet wheels, there will actually be very little difference between the work required of the two engines when the additional gradients and curves, and the increased number of revolutions per mile which the small wheeled engine makes are taken into account…. A large station at Swindon would also enable us to keep our Bank engines for Wootton Bassett incline at Swindon instead of having a separate station for that purpose at the bottom of the incline, and in addition it would at any rate be necessary to have a considerable Station at Swindon to work the Cheltenham line, which would be saved if Swindon was our principal station.

'It also has the great advantage of being on the side of a canal [the Wilts & Berks, that was connected to the Kennet & Avon] communicating with the whole of England, and by which we could get coal and coke, I should think, at a moderate price. I am not sufficiently acquainted with the place to know how far we would be affected by the want of water, it might probably be collected in the neighbourhood, and as we have a great deal of side cutting they might be converted into reservoirs, and should even this fail us we have the canal. These reasons lead me to think Swindon by far the best point we have for a Central Engine Station. From the plans and sections there appear little or no difficulties with the nature of the ground for building upon and by placing the station somewhere as shown in the enclosed sketch, it might be made in every respect very complete. I have not thought of the Bristol & Exeter line in the arrangement, as it is quite possible to work it very well by engines kept at Bristol as long as they are fit for work … I am not aware of any difficulties connected with Swindon more than the water.'

The engine repair shed at Swindon from a lithograph by J. C. Bourne of 1843. The locomotive sits on a railed platform that can be moved up and down the length of the shed to a point opposite one of the empty bays, where the actual repairs will take place.

The letter is interesting not only in showing Gooch's logical thinking in selecting Swindon, but illuminates his thinking on locomotive design, with different engines to cope with the different terrain of the two sections. He was also thinking of banking engines at Wootton Bassett, where there was a section of just over a mile and a quarter at a 1:100 gradient; in a year book of 1848, however, it was noted that it was being worked 'without any extraordinary assistance'.

There was an urgent need to recruit skilled workers, but there was a problem. Swindon was a small market town, some distance from the works and with little or no suitable housing. The company decided that the only solution was to build houses and create a railway village; New Swindon. They would also need to be of a better quality than those in many of the new industrial towns that had grown up with the Industrial Revolution, if the company was going to attract skilled craftsmen and their families to move to the area. So the job of designing what would become New Swindon went not to a jobbing builder, but to the distinguished architect of Paddington Station, Matthew Digby Wyatt. The first houses to be built were on six streets, laid out in a regular grid, with a square at the centre. Each street was named after a destination reached by the railway, Bath, Bristol and so on. Like the works, they were built of local stone, much of it obtained from the excavation of Box tunnel. Unlike many Victorian

Swindon New Town was created for the Great Western workers and is seen here after refurbishment in the 1950s. It is in marked contrast to the huddled back-to-backs that were a feature of so many of Britain's industrial towns in the nineteenth century.

terraces in industrial towns, these have space, each with a small front garden, a courtyard at the back and facing a broad street. They had a minimum of two bedrooms each and a toilet for each house in the yard. Utilities were supplied by the company, who built their own gas works and pumped water from a well at Kemble. The fact that the houses are still there today, externally unchanged, is a mark of the quality of the building. The railway village would be extended over the years as the works grew, so that by the end of the 1840s, there were some two thousand men at work.

The company provided a fine range of facilities for the workforce and their families. They opened a school for the children and built a church. They encouraged the men to improve on their skills by building the Mechanics' Institute, opened in 1845 where they could take evening classes in appropriate subjects, such as engineering and mathematics, and there were classes for women, in basic reading and writing and domestic subjects. It was used for pleasure as well as more serious matters, with a lending library and activities such as drama. In 1844 they bought land that became a park for the use of the community. It is still there but now known as Faringdon Park. Perhaps the most remarkable provision was a health service. The hospital had eight medical officers, a consultant surgeon, three dentists, an ophthalmic surgeon, three physiotherapists and a chiropractor. There were Turkish and Russian baths, as well as more normal washing facilities, and at a later date swimming baths were added. It is no wonder that the Great Western inspired loyalty in the workforce, and that generations followed each other into the works.

The first buildings to be constructed at the works were: the main engine house for running locomotives, a massive structure 490ft by 70ft; a second rather smaller engine house for light repairs, 290ft by 140ft; an erecting shop for constructing new locomotives and major repairs; and a foundry. The light repair shop was very carefully planned. Locomotives could be run onto a traverser that travelled on rails down the centre of the shop. On either side were stalls, thirty-six in all, and the engine would be run off the traverser to take one of the available spaces.

In 1846, the company began building locomotives and in 1848 the works were extended to make Swindon the centre for all locomotive construction for the broad gauge. The first engine out of the works was built to a simple instruction from Brunel to Gooch to construct a 'colossal locomotive working with all speed'. It was intended to impress the Gauge Commissioners, and was completed in just thirteen weeks of hectic activity, the first of the 'Great Western' class. Although the singles were a great success, there was a fresh challenge in 1848. The atmospheric railway had been abandoned, and now the South Devon, with its severe gradients was to be worked by locomotives. Swindon built a new class of 4-4-0 'bogie' saddle tank locomotives, with coupled 6ft drive wheels. The works were to continue in use right up to 1964 and were to produce some of the most famous locomotives in railway history, including the first hundred miles an hour engine *City of Truro*. It was also to construct the very last locomotive to be built for British Rail, *Evening Star*.

As at Swindon, the company provided a wide range of facilities, including a school for the workers' children, supervised by a committee made up of directors' wives. Here too, there was a Mechanics Institution, bath houses and a health scheme. Gas and water were supplied, and, with an eye on future development, they established their own brickworks. One of the requirements was that the company should provide a church. Christ Church appeared a standard nineteenth century building, but if you rapped a pillar in the nave, instead of the dull thud of stone you got the ring of metal. The company found it more convenient and cheaper to cast the pillar in iron rather than employ a mason and expensive stone. Little now remains of the church apart from the tower.

The original site occupied 2½ acres and employed 161 men. A newspaper report of 1846 described the locomotive department in some detail:

'It presents the aspects of a Polytechnic Institution: all the vast implements of engineering science seem gathered together here. Planing machines of all forms and sizes fill up the centre, connected with endless straps to a power-transmitting drum; while on either side the lathes, punching, shearing and cutting machines … In the extreme wing is the brass foundry and brass work.

   'Not the least marvellous thing about this extensive establishment was the fact that the power which moved all the machinery throughout the buildings, covering thirty acres, was transmitted from one steam-engine of 20-horse power, worked on the Cornish or expansive principle. The arrangements secure the most perfect division of labour, and although six hundred men are employed, there was a total absence of bustle, hurry, or confusion. Each man like the machinery, seemed to fall naturally into its own place.'

Assembling the unit of firebox, boiler and smoke box at Swindon. Rivets are being heated in the hearth in the foreground, and two riveters are at work, hammering home rivets.

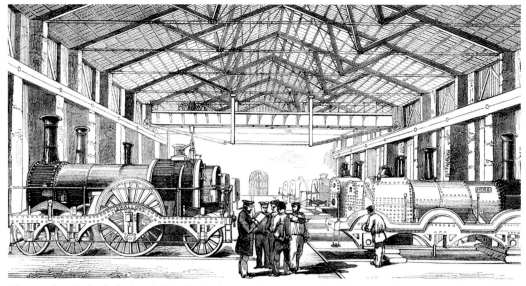

The erecting shed at Swindon. An Iron Duke class engine appears to have been completed on the left, while other engines in different states of completion can be seen on the right.

By 1847, the waggon department had been moved to allow the locomotive works to expand. That year there were 1,100 employed at the works and the number had gone up to 1,600 the following year, half of whom were employed in locomotive construction. That year it was recorded that they were turning out a new engine every Monday morning from 1 January.

The 1846 account records that the only source of power was a 20hp engine, suggesting that if the machine tools in use were indeed very numerous, they must also have been quite light. This was true of all the early locomotive works and a great deal of work was done by hand or by hand operated machines. The available materials were cast and wrought iron, copper, brass and wood. Steel was, at that time, only available in small quantities. The most efficient steel production in use by the late eighteenth century was crucible steel, a technique generally credited to Benjamin Huntsman, though it was remarkably similar to a steel-making method that had been used in many centuries in India, for making what was known as Wootz steel. The method involved heating very pure iron with carefully measured quantities of charcoal in crucibles, made of fireclay. A surviving example can still be seen at the scythe works at Abbeydale in Sheffield. It may have been effective but the quantities produced per firing were small. Steel was, however, essential for the works, not so much in construction as in the tool that was used throughout almost every part of the manufacturing process, the file. There was also a certain amount of steel used in manufacturing. Daniel Gooch, for example, patented a steel tyre to fit over the conventional iron tyre for locomotive wheels in 1840.

Much of the work was still done by hand rather than machine. Wrought iron sheets were limited in size, so that large objects, such as boilers, could only be built by joining several boilerplates together by riveting. The first stage in the process would be to bend the metal to the correct shape. It was essential that the cross section of a boiler should be as close to a perfect circle as possible, so that no uneven stresses should build up as it was heated. To join the plates together, holes had to be drilled round the edge of the plates and then lined up ready for riveting. The rivets themselves were like round-headed bolts, but without a screw thread. They would be heated to white heat in a brazier or small furnace then passed to the riveting team. One man would push a rivet though the aligned holes and hold the head in place with a heavy hammer. The man on the opposite side would then hammer his end, so that it spread out against the plate, holding the two pieces firmly together. Apart from being hard work, which required speed and precision, it was also incredibly noisy; deafness was a common complaint among boilermakers in later life. The boiler would be made up in short sections that were then butt-ended and joined together.

One of the problems in manufacture was wheel construction, and it sometimes seems there were as many answers as there were engineers. Before 1850, wheel hubs were almost entirely forged by hand. There were various types of spoke, round or square cross section and various methods of attaching them between the hub and the rim. The earliest reference to a lathe specifically designed for turning locomotive wheels appeared in an advert for Nasmyth, Gaskell & Co. in 1839, capable of turning wheels up to 7ft in diameter. Joseph Beattie of the London & South-Western Railway patented a lathe in 1841 that was capable of turning two wheels simultaneously.

Forging a connecting rod using a steam hammer at Swindon. Although the process was photographed in the twentieth century, the equipment and technique are identical to those in use a hundred years earlier.

Even more problematical was the forging of crank axles for inside cylinder locomotives. The axles had to be built up by forging wrought iron bars together to create the shaft, then forging on welded strips to form the throws. There were inevitable weak points, which helped to account for the large number of cracked and broken axles on early locomotives. The work was carried out either entirely by hand or by using a form of manually operated drop hammer, in which a heavy weight was hauled up by a team of men using pulleys and then allowed to fall back onto the iron on the anvil. Whichever method was used involved very hard physical labour. A better method appeared, not as a result of solving a problem in railway construction, but from shipbuilding, even though a famous railway engineer was involved.

Brunel had effectively proved that transatlantic travel by paddle steamer was both practically and economically viable with his pioneering, wooden-hulled ship *Great Western*. He now set about building a far larger vessel, but with an iron instead of a wooden hull. The hull of what would become the SS *Great Britain* was laid down in July 1839 and work began on designing an appropriate engine. Once again it would drive paddle wheels, but the crankshaft was simply too big for anyone to undertake the arduous task of forging it. The problem was presented to the manufacturing engineer, James Nasmyth. In his own words, the request 'set him a-thinking'. He realised that the most powerful hammers available were tilt hammers, which were pivoted at one end. But the gap between anvil and hammerhead was too small on all existing hammers to take the huge shaft. The answer came to him almost at once. The difficulty was removed if the hammer fell vertically between guides. All he needed was a power source to lift it, and he realised that this could be provided by steam and once the steam was cut off the hammer would fall under gravity. The speed with which he worked out the new machine is astonishing, as he himself wrote:

> 'In little more than half an hour, after receiving Mr. Humphries' letter narrating his unlooked-for difficulty, I had the whole contrivance in all its executant details, before me in a page of my Scheme Book.'

That Scheme Book survived and the sketch shows just what he had in mind, and exactly what would be produced, the Nasmyth steam hammer. It was later improved by using steam to power for the down stroke as well as for raising the head. The irony is that it was never used for Brunel's ship. Before work on the new engine had begun, Brunel had become aware of a new type of vessel, built by Francis Pettit Smith, powered by a screw propeller instead of paddle wheels. He at once threw out the old design and called for the ship to be redesigned as a screw-propelled vessel. This only required a simple, rotating shaft instead of a vast crank. But in solving the shipbuilding problem, Nasmyth had also provided the locomotive builders with a new and highly valuable tool.

The actual work of building a locomotive was, in these early days, very far from being organised in the way in which it would be in later years, with standard parts being made for assembly with a supervisor in overall control of quality. There was no smooth production line, but rather disparate groups of workmen, responsible for their particular part of the whole, perhaps consisting of a master craftsman and an apprentice, with one or more labourers.

Uniformity was made more difficult by the absence of standards. Screws were made, for example, to fit a particular job rather than to any fixed pattern. It was in1841 that Joseph Whitworth wrote a paper for the Institution of Civil Engineers in which he proposed setting a standard, with the use of a constant angle of 55 degrees and screws specified according to the number of turns per inch, but it was not until the 1860s that the Whitworth standard was widely accepted. The same lack of standardisation meant that it was the fitter's job to make different elements come together as accurately as possible. Edward J. Larkin and John G. Larkin in their book, *The Railway Workshops of Britain*, 1988 record the astonishing fact that 'centre-to-centre distances for connecting rods were not marked on Crewe drawings until 1859'. When a rod was fabricated, it had to be sent to the smithy to be adjusted to fit the actual distance between wheel centres.

   Lacking standardisation, individual measurements were taken with callipers, and adjustments made on the spot to ensure, for example, that a wheel fitted snugly onto its axis; sometimes this involved little more than a lot of lubricant and a certain amount of brute strength. The lack of standardisation also created difficulties when it came to repairs. An engine made by one manufacturer would have used screws and bolts made from dies at the original works, but if it went for repair somewhere else there was unlikely to be anything very similar available. Eli Whitney had opened his factory for making muskets in 1798 and by the early nineteenth century had established his system of manufacturing interchangeable parts. In his own words he intended 'to make the same parts of different guns, as the locks, for example, as much like

The Baldwin locomotive works in Philadelphia as illustrated in the nineteenth century catalogue of Baldwin locomotives.

each other as the successive impressions of a copper-plate engraving'. Locomotive manufacture in Britain was very far from reaching that state, but nor had it done so in Whitney's home country of America. As early as 1839 Baldwin had stressed the importance of standardisation of parts for each class of locomotive, but the most important step in achieving that goal was not taken until the 1860s, when standard gauges were introduced.

Unlike British companies, American railroads seldom established their own manufacturing works, but relied on the most important builders, notably Baldwin and Norris. The records for the latter show the size of the premises in the middle of the nineteenth century. There were ten three-storey brick buildings, containing the following workshops and offices: steam hammer shop; truck shop; tank shop; boiler shop; erecting shop; engine room; blacksmith; finishing; foundry and offices. These were served by twenty-four tracks linked by a central turntable. By this time, the construction progress was well ordered. Orders were confirmed by the office, after which detailed drawings were prepared and handed out to the appropriate departments who would manufacture the different parts. These were then brought to the erection shop and assembled in a set order, as described in a contemporary account:

'First, the boiler is placed and accurately levelled – the frame is set and fastened – the braces are set and fastened – the check and whistle stands are riveted fast – set the cylinder – then the rock arms and pedestals, the oiler flues put in – the driving boxes are put up and laid out for boring – the center pin set – the driver and the guides are set – pumps put up – next the reversing shafts – the footplate put on and fastened – the valve rod and valves – the steam pipes – the throttle valve – the dome – the safety valve – the feed and supply pipes – the wheels – the eccentric hooks – the connecting rods – the valves set – and the whole of the working part, being now about together, steam is raised, and after 'giving her a good blowing out' to get rid of dirt, etc., the cylinder heads are screwed on and the working of the new engine thoroughly tested. At these times the senior proprietor is always present.'

Norris did not limit themselves to their Philadelphia base. When Schenectady was getting its rail connections, two locals, Platt Potter and John Ellis, began to rally support for the idea of constructing a locomotive works in the town. They asked the Norris brothers to come and assess the situation, but only one brother made the trip from Philadelphia. In December 1847, Norris reported back that they estimated it would cost $50,000 'to purchase the ground, erect buildings and necessary tools and machinery'. The locals had only planned on raising $30,000 and were told: 'We certainly could with this amount make a start, but not with any advantage to the present prosperity of the works'. In the event Schenectady sold stock worth $40,000, $22,000 of which went on buildings, $17,800 on equipment and $1,000 for the land. The Norris family supplied $10,576 worth of tools and machinery. They also agreed to pay interest to the stockholders on the $40,000 over a period of eight years, at the end of which they would purchase the rest of the stock and become sole owners. So the final cost of setting up the works was very close to the figure of $50,000 that the Norris brothers had estimated in the first place, the equivalent of roughly $1.5 million at today's prices.

It was to prove a good investment in the long term. When the booklet *Growing with Schenectady*, from which the figures quoted above were taken, was published in 1972, the company was valued at $21 million. It did not fare as well in the short term. The first locomotive, *Lightning*, was completed in 1849, a fine and powerful engine, designed for speed. Alas it proved altogether too powerful and, at fifteen tons, too heavy for the flimsy track on which it was to run and had to be taken out of service before it wrecked the entire system. No further orders came in and the Norris family withdrew from the venture. It looked as if the whole enterprise was doomed, but locals gathered their resources together and relaunched the company in 1851, for what was to prove a successful venture. There are two interesting facets to this story. Firstly, it is valuable to have costings for setting up such a business and to see that well over half the capital was invested in machinery. Secondly, it is fascinating to find even at this late stage that some American railroad builders were still not producing lines that could take more than very light traffic. By contrast, Norris built the country's first 10-wheeled locomotive, the 4-6-0 *Chesapeake*, for the Philadelphia and Reading Railroad. Unlike *Lightning*, the 22-ton engine was a success, entering service in 1847 and remaining in use for another thirty years, though it was converted from wood burning to anthracite in 1862. However, in the long term, the Schenectady works were destined to outlast Norris; the latter closed in 1866.

By 1850, the United States had an extensive rail network in the east, but nothing had been built west of the Missouri River, and there was no through connection between the southern railways and those in the north. At least there was a network; no rails had yet been built in South America, Asia, Australasia or Africa, though that would soon change. Railways were a major part of a technological revolution that would transform life on every continent. In Britain, that change would be one of the themes of a Great Exhibition.

Chapter Fourteen

The Great Exhibition

When Richard Trevithick's little road locomotive went puffing its way up Camborne Hill, George III was on the British throne. The popular image of Georgian Britain is of elegant houses and Jane Austen heroines and it is easy to forget that it was also the age of the greatest change in the country's history since the departure of the Romans. We call it the Industrial Revolution. Fifty years later, Queen Victoria was the ruling monarch and the image has changed to gas-lit streets, hansom cabs and overstuffed parlours. By this time, the Industrial Revolution was nominally complete, in that the transformation from a society of craftsmen and women largely working in their own homes had given way to one dominated by mills and factories and the new industrial towns. Change continued, but as development of existing themes rather than dramatic changes in direction. The same process can be seen at work in the railway world, and particularly in the development of the locomotive.

It is easy to identify certain key elements that were to be vital to locomotive development. The starting point is evident; when Trevithick set the locomotive onto a railed track. From then on, a clear early development can be traced. Blenkinsop and Murray developed their engine for Middleton Colliery using the Trevithick patent as a starting point, and the success of their experiment encouraged other collieries to follow their lead. George Stephenson went to see the Middleton Colliery Railway, and used many of the locomotive design ideas that he saw there in building his own first locomotive. Stephenson contributed little that was either very new or of the first importance to locomotive development, but he did have the vision to see that railways could do far more than simply shift coal from the pithead to the nearest port or riverside staithes.

Once the Stockton & Darlington Railway had opened, the demands on locomotives to supply a very different system, one linking towns and cities, had to be met. The answer was found at Rainhill, with the success of Robert Stephenson's *Rocket*. Now key elements were in place that could be developed in later engines: the multi-tubular boiler, exhaust blast and cylinders moved from the vertical to, or close to, the horizontal. The way forward was now set, but there would be other key changes, not least the change from cast iron to rolled wrought iron rails that enabled engines to be built that were much heavier than the earliest models. Other developments had their own importance; the invention of valve gear that allowed for variable cut-off and the truck or bogie that helped locomotives to negotiate awkward tracks are good examples. But these can be seen as improvements rather than totally revolutionary ideas. So the story of the first fifty years is one of a few key moments, but also one of steady development and improvement. It is also the story of how this British innovation spread to other countries, where developments could follow different paths. 1851 is a good time to assess what had happened during that first half century and to see where engineers were looking for changes in the future. This was true of other industries as well as the railways and often there were essential links to be made. All these elements were to come together in the Great Exhibition.

The idea of the Great Exhibition did not appear overnight, nor was it, as is often thought, the brainchild of Prince Albert. The idea of fairs to promote all kinds of activities, including manufacture were not new in continental Europe, but were all but unknown in Britain. One of the earliest attempts to promote British manufacturing in this way was the work of the grandly named Society for the Encouragement of Arts, Manufacture and Commerce, founded in 1754 and granted a royal charter in 1847, after which it was more generally known simply as the Royal Society for Arts. It was Robert Stephenson who backed an Exhibition of the Products of National Industry in 1845, but it failed for lack of support from major industrialists. It attracted the interest, however, of Henry Cole, a man of considerably more talents and interests than his official role as Assistant Keeper at the Record Office might suggest. He had another life under a pseudonym, Felix Summerly, where he followed many different strands as both critic and publisher – *Felix Summerly's Home Treasury* published among other things Britain's first ever Christmas card. When the Society of Arts offered a prize for the best design of a tea service, it was won by Felix Summerly. He was soon elected to the Society and became a keen advocate for a major exhibition. He was able to enthuse the recently appointed President of the Society, Prince Albert and with royal patronage the exhibition began to take shape.

This was to be an exhibition on an unprecedented scale, and it would need to be housed in a suitably grand building, in every sense of the word. Hyde Park was the chosen site and an open competition was announced. The building committee was all but overwhelmed by entrants, 254 of them in all and none of them was even close to being satisfactory. The committee then decided to go to the man who was generally recognised as a genius unafraid of the big, daring idea. They commissioned Isambard Kingdom Brunel to design the exhibition hall. The result was a horror; a vast oblong brick building, topped by a huge iron dome. When the results were published in 1850 there was a huge public outcry. Not only was it immensely ugly, but it looked like a permanent structure, whereas the whole idea was that once the exhibition was over, the building would be removed and Hyde Park returned to the general public. It seemed very much as if the whole scheme had come to a dead end. That it did not was due to a meeting to discuss railway matters in the House of Commons.

Joseph Paxton had begun his working life as a gardener and it was in that role that he was taken on by the Duke of Devonshire to look after the grounds at Chatsworth. The Duke was a great enthusiast and was very keen on the current craze for exotics. To grow them he needed a hothouse and Paxton designed it, using an iron frame and immense areas of glass. It was so large that visitors could drive through the centre in their carriages and it was considered one of the wonders of the age. Paxton became famous and wealthy, and was soon interested in the developing world of railways, counting Robert Stephenson among his friends. He went to the House to visit a Member, Mr. Ellis, who was also Chairman of the Midland Railway. He was invited to hear a debate in the chamber of the Commons and afterwards they discussed the problems they were having with the new Parliament building. From there the conversation

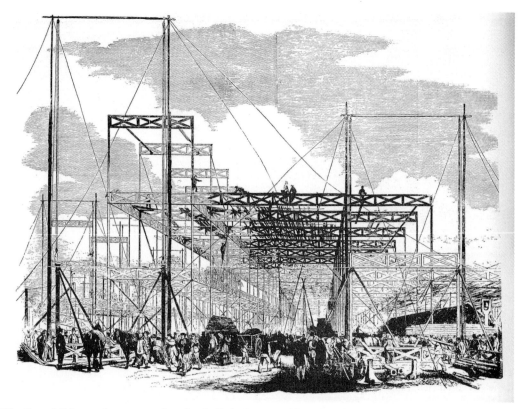

The Crystal Palace under construction; the similarity between this and modern construction methods is obvious.

turned to the other great building debate of the day. Ellis suggested that Paxton might like to try his hand at designing something appropriate and whisked him off to meet Henry Cole. Paxton agreed to give it a try, but had just two weeks to come up with a plan. As we all know, what he devised was akin to an overgrown hothouse, a grand structure of iron and glass that came to be known as the Crystal Palace.

The exhibition not only invited entries that demonstrated the latest available technology, but also encouraged inventors to come forward with new ideas and suggested improvements on old ones. It may not have been obvious to everyone at the time, but in many ways the most far-sighted exhibit of them all was the building itself. Constructed of iron modules, containing all the necessary structural elements, the entire structure consisted of 4,500 tons of ironwork and 293,655 panes of glass. It was completed in just twenty-two weeks. In many ways it was the precursor of the modern office block and the whole notion of constructing out of standard units. The range and variety of exhibits was extraordinary, over 100,000 of them entered by 13,937 different companies and individuals, arranged in thirty different categories. It is hardly surprising that some found it all a bit too much, including Charles Dickens: 'I find I am "used up" by the Exhibition. I don't say there's nothing in it: there's too much.' It covered the arts as well as industry and included sections devoted to different

This carving is part of a frieze running around the top of the Thomas Cook headquarters building in Leicester. It shows an excursion train with the completed Crystal Palace in the background.

countries from nearby France to faraway China. Section Five was 'Machines for direct use: including Carriages and Railway and Naval Mechanism'.

There are some 200 numbered items in the official catalogue devoted to railways and, like everything in the exhibition, showed great diversity. First on the list was what was described as a Great Western Railway 'ordinary engine'. This was the class of singles introduced in 1847 and the catalogue gave a few technical details; it weighed 32 tons ready for the road and could haul a 120-ton passenger train 'at an average speed of 60 miles per hour, upon easy gradients'. The 18-inch diameter cylinders had a stroke of 24 inches and drove 8-foot diameter wheels. 'The evaporation of the boiler, when in full work, is equal to 1,000 horse power.' This was impressive, but was not quite so much so as the London and North Western Railway Crampton engine *Liverpool*. This had 2,285 feet of heating surface, being 270 feet more than the largest broad gauge locomotive. It was 'rated at 1,140 horse power'. There was also a brief mention of Trevithick's *Cornwall*, but no technical details were given of that particular engine. There was also the Crampton engine *Folkestone*, built for the South East Railway Co. for service on the London to Paris line. One locomotive was on show outside the hall; the Great Western's *Lord of the Isles*, the last of the Iron Duke class to be built.

These were inevitably the glamorous starts of the railway section, but there were more workaday engines, just as important for the running of the system as the passenger expresses, and there were names that were to be famous for providing strong, sensible locomotives

The Crampton locomotive was one of the star attractions of the section devoted to 'locomotion'. The illustration appeared in the official catalogue.

Crampton locomotives appeared on many European railways in the years following the Great Exhibition. This locomotive was built for the French line, Compagnie de Chemin de Fer de l'Est, founded in 1853.

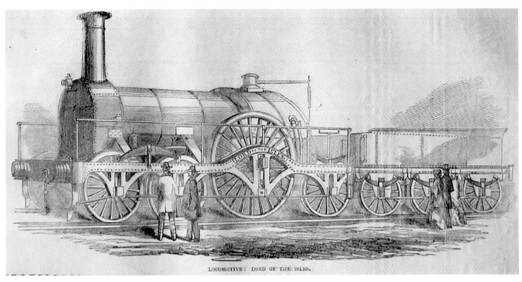

Lord of the Isles being admired at the Great Exhibition. The artist has made it seem even more impressive than it was as the drive wheels are 8ft diameter, not twice the height of the average visitor.

for a variety of mundane uses. Item 536, for example, was a typical 2-2-2 tank engine by Kitson, Thomson & Hewison. Other well-known names that appeared included Fairbairn and Hawthorne. In among these were ideas that were never likely to be of any practical importance. In spite of the failure of Brunel's atmospheric railway, the idea was still being promoted, together with systems based on compressed air.

Apart from the locomotives, there were exhibits featuring rolling stock, signalling and all kinds of new ideas to improve safety. Some were obviously sensible, others rather less so. Individuals brought forward their ideas, sometimes offering very different exhibits in quite different categories. W. MacKay of the Royal Artillery, for example, showed a 'model railway carriage with self-acting collision and atmospheric brakes' as well as a model of London showing how railways could be laid out in the streets. This was not quite as odd a combination as that offered by F. Lipscombe; a device for preventing vibrations in railway wheels so that they would run silently and a portable fountain for use in drawing rooms. Such oddities made up only a small proportion of the exhibits, many of which were there primarily because the companies showing them wanted to attract customers – though rules would not allow them to put prices on anything. So the Ebbw Vale iron works, for example, showed sections of every type of available rail that they could manufacture.

The exhibition attracted two very different types of visitor. There were the professionals, eager to see what was new in their particular field. One can easily imagine locomotive engineers taking a keen interest in what was on show in the machine tools section, while the tool manufacturers would want to see what the latest thinking was in the railway world and get an idea of what tools might be needed in the future. But by far the greatest number must have been the simply curious, anxious to see what marvels were on display. Between 1 May

This view shows the machinery hall at the Crystal Palace. Many of the machines on show were demonstrated at work, powered by a specially installed steam engine.

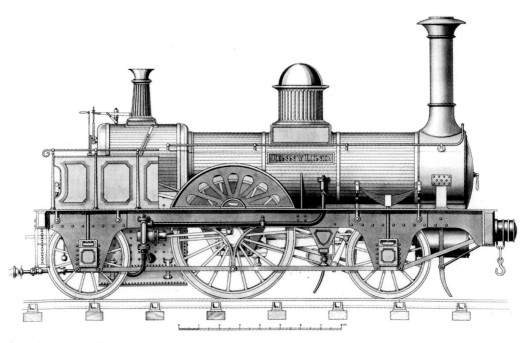

Jenny Lind was the first of the class to be built for the London, Brighton & South Coast Railway. An elegant engine, with its fluted dome and safety valve, it proved highly successful and altogether some seventy locomotives of this type were built.

1851 when the show opened and 15 October when it closed, an astonishing 6 million visitors came, an average of over 40,000 a day. Given that the population of London at that time was only 2½ million, many must have come from much further afield. That so many were able to visit was due in good measure to the fact that they could get there from all parts of the country, thanks to the railways.

Paxton appreciated the importance of attracting visitors from as wide an area as possible and he persuaded Thomas Cook to arrange special excursion trains from Yorkshire and the Midlands. Cook took to the idea with enthusiasm and even published his own paper, *Cook's Exhibition Herald and Excursion Advertiser*. His excursion trains carried 150,000 visitors to see the Crystal Place, and the final trip was probably the noisiest – 3,000 school children. It was such an important event in the company's development than when they came to build grand new offices in Leicester in 1894, the sculpted frieze at the top of the building included a carving showing a passenger train with the Crystal Palace behind it.

As well as showcasing what was considered best in railway technology, the Crystal Palace exhibition also highlighted the important role that the railways were then playing in British social life. It was the expansion of the network that had made that vast influx of visitors possible. By the time the Exhibition opened, Britain had some 6,000 miles of railway with another 1,000 miles under construction. Four years earlier, investment in railways had peaked at the point where it represented 7 per cent of the total national income, but now that the network was filling in that form of investment was in decline. However, with the proliferation of routes, there was now a real competitiveness between companies. And that would be one of the driving forces behind locomotive development.

Judging purely on the basis of the Great Exhibition, there was a general agreement among British locomotive engineers that the future for fast passenger trains lay with developing locomotives with just one pair of huge drive wheels, either in a 2-2-2 or 4-2-2 configuration. This was such a successful formula that the Great Western continued running Iron Duke class locomotives almost to the end of the nineteenth century.

Other makers had their own variations on the theme. John Gray's inside cylinder 2-2-2 locomotives had an outside frame for the carrying axles and inside plate frame for the boxes for the crank axle. Locomotives of this type became famous when E.B.Wilson & Co. of Leeds began manufacturing them for the Midland Railway in 1847. The first to appear was named *Jenny Lind* after the hugely popular Swedish soprano. The name stuck and became used for the whole class. They were very elegant engines and were particularly popular with the London, Brighton and South Coast Railway.

The advances had been immense, when one considers the satisfaction with which Trevithick had recorded the success of his Penydarren engine less than half a century earlier. He had taken a load of ten tons of iron, together with '60 or 70' people and 'it goes very easy 4 miles an hour, & is as tractable as a Horse'. Now at the Crystal Palace visitors could admire the Great Western train that could haul 120 tons at 60 miles an hour.

Many of the exhibits concerned safety, an area in which there had been many improvements over the first half-century. The first electric telegraph had been installed in 1838, enabling signal boxes to contact each other to relay information about train movements. This worked in conjunction with the block signalling system, by which a line was divided up between a series of 'blocks', and no more than one train at a time was allowed to enter the block, travelling in one direction. The system was first introduced on the Yarmouth and Norwich line in 1844. It was improved in the 1850s when signals and points were interlocked. Safety was increasingly important as train moved ever faster, but if things on the trackside were improving, communications on the train itself were still very primitive. *Lord of the Isles* was presented as the very latest thing in locomotive design, yet communication between guard and footplate crew was primitive. It was the work of the 'travelling porter', who was perched on a seat at the back of the tender, with no protection from the weather. It is hard to imagine that he would have been able to communicate anything at all, if the train was dashing along at 60mph in driving rain. If it seems like a none too subtle form of torture to make that unfortunate man sit out in the open like that in all weathers, one has to remember that the footplate crew received no better treatment. They too had little in the way of protection, though they did at least have the warmth from the firebox. It was generally believed by railway managers that keeping an open footplate ensured the driver and fireman always kept alert.

At the start of the 1850s, there was a great diversity of engine builders, ranging from the railway companies themselves to individual engineering companies. Many of the latter were also more general engineering firms, producing a wide range of products. William Fairbairn was one of the exhibitors at the Crystal Palace, and the history of the company is one of almost endless diversification. The founder was born in Scotland in 1789, but when the family moved to a farm near Newcastle upon Tyne, William got a job with the local colliery. During his time there he got to know George Stephenson, but later left mining to work as a millwright. Eventually, he was able to set up in business on his own in Manchester as a manufacturer of textile machinery. In the 1830s, he opened up a new business manufacturing paddle steamers, which soon outgrew the Manchester base and was moved to the Thames at Millwall. It was during this time that he first became actively involved with the world of railways. Robert Stephenson was working as chief engineer for the line to Holyhead, which involved crossing the Menai Straits. His plan was to produce a tubular wrought iron girder bridge, and he went to Fairbairn, simply because he was an experienced builder of iron ships. Fairbairn was able to demonstrate that the tubular girders wouldn't sag and buckle, by showing him an iron vessel, whose hull was only supported at either end. The bridge was opened in 1846 and Stephenson and Fairbairn took out a joint patent. By this time, Fairbairn had abandoned work in shipbuilding and concentrated on the Manchester works, which had now become William Fairbairn & Sons. It was there that they began manufacturing locomotives of the Bury type, mainly comparatively light engines for the Liverpool & Manchester Railway. But that was never the company's only output. They built a variety of other items, including steam cranes with a distinctive curved jib. One of these machines can still be seen at the dockside in Bristol.

The British scene in 1851 was one marked by a variety of manufacturers and their products. In America, on the other hand, there was remarkable agreement on what was best suited for that country's railroads, what came to be known as the 'American Standard'. This was the

4-4-0 locomotive, first introduced in the 1830s. The earliest examples were comparatively light, seldom more than 15 tons, with short boilers, low driving wheels and the carrying wheels on the front truck were placed quite close together. By the start of the 1850s, the engines had been refined. Boilers had been lengthened, horizontal cylinders were centred above the leading truck and for the first time drivers enjoyed the luxury of a proper cab. They were also much larger, now weighing up to twenty-five tons. Where the early versions had been quite plain, the new engines were quite ornate. Warning bells and whistles were of polished brass; the iron boiler plates highly polished and the cabin of varnished wood. Wheels were colourfully painted, and many locomotives featured elaborate murals on the tenders. These were the engines we have all seen in hundreds of Westerns. One of the great railway movies has to be Buster Keaton's *The General*. It is based on an actual event in the American Civil War, a raid by Confederates who managed to get away with two Unionist locomotives, one of which was *The General*, built in 1855. Keaton had to use a very similar locomotive for filming, but the original still survives in the Southern Museum of Civil War and Locomotive History in Kennesaw, Georgia.

The General was built by Rogers, Ketchum and Grosvenor. Like Fairbairn, Thomas Rogers had begun his manufacturing career making textile machinery at his works in New Jersey. In 1832, he was joined by two New York investors, Morris Ketchum and Jasper Grosvenor to form a company, specialising in manufacturing parts for locomotives. The first complete locomotive built there was assembled from parts shipped by Robert Stephenson, but by 1837 they had built their own first engine, a 4-2-0 *Sandusky*. It contained one innovative feature;

The locomotive *America* is a typical example of the standard American locomotive that was developed in the middle of the nineteenth century, with its 4-4-0 wheel arrangement, differing only in not having a bulbous spark arrester on the chimney. That is because it was built by the Grant Locomotive Works of New Jersey specifically for showing at the 1867 Paris Exhibition. The arrester was only needed in America because the vast majority of locomotives were wood burning.

the drive wheels were fitted with counterweights to balance out the forces created by the movement of the piston and piston rods. The company was to go on to manufacture more than a thousand locomotives over the years.

The American type dominated throughout the 1850s and well beyond, but they were not alone. There is an interesting survivor from 1851, now on show in the Smithsonian Institute. It was built by Seth Wilmarth of Boston and sent for trial to the Cumberland Valley Railroad. Construction of the line had begun in 1831 with the usual strap rails of the period. By 1849, the track was worn out and had to be replaced by T-rails and new locomotives were required. *Pioneer* was the first of the pair, joined by a sister locomotive, another *Jenny Lind*. It was a 2-2-2 locomotive of the type that had by then been considered unsuitable for American railroads. But it was very light, weighing just 12½ tons, less than half that of most American class engines of the time, and it had a very short wheelbase. It was ideal for the job of passenger traffic, since most trains consisted of nothing more than two coaches and a baggage car. It was a conventional tank engine, but had a most unconventional cab, with glazed windows, which looked like a gazebo on wheels. It gave good service for many years before finding its permanent home in the Smithsonian.

Although certain basic elements were in place, there were still innovations to come that would lead to a steady development in all aspects of locomotive power and performance. One of the most important changes in Britain in the 1850s was the change from coke to coal as the main fuel at considerable savings in cost, though it required changes in firebox design. The range of locomotives was increased by the use of steam injectors topping up the boiler while the engine was on the move. These and other changes were improvements rather than revolutionary changes. Perhaps the biggest change of all was not in the railway world itself but in metallurgy, in the manufacture of steel. It would make a great impact on railways as a whole.

As so often in the history of technology, changes were made more or less simultaneously by two men working in different places, in this case in America and Britain. William Kelly of Kentucky made sugar kettles from pig iron refined in a charcoal furnace. He was facing production problems, due to the steadily rising cost of charcoal. Then one day, he discovered that if he blew air over the molten iron, it burned off the carbon, even without the addition of charcoal. He managed to make the wrought iron he needed, but realised that if the right amount of carbon was kept in the metal, he would have produced steel. He began to build his converters, took out a patent in 1857 but before he had a chance to profit from his invention, he went bankrupt. A similar idea had been worked on at the same time in Britain and the man who had developed his system had to acknowledge that Kelly's patent gave him prior claim to the invention, and duly bought up the rights. His name was Henry Bessemer. The Bessemer converter became famous; the name of Kelly is all but forgotten.

Bessemer's tilting converter involved blowing a blast of air through the molten metal at very high temperature. One of the great virtues of the system was that a single converter could turn twenty-five tons of pig iron into steel in less than half an hour. It opened the way to the mass production of steel. There were teething problems, but the system was a huge success and steel became as readily available as wrought iron for the first time. The first and most obvious use was

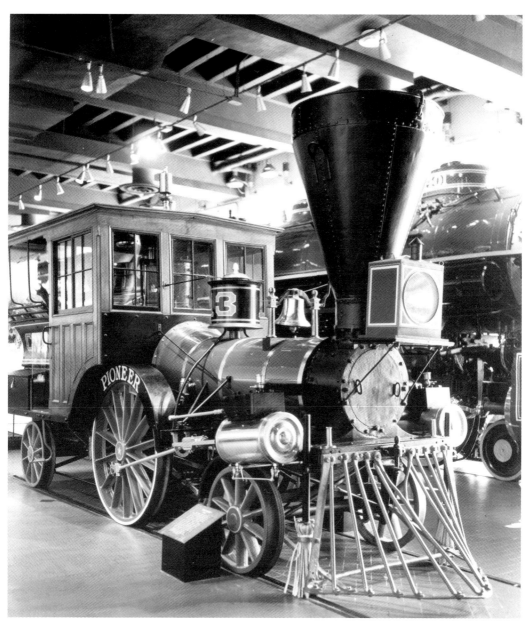

Pioneer was an exception to the general pattern of American locomotives, built as a 2-2-2. It is also unusual in being a very rare example of a locomotive of this period to have had an enclosed cab instead of an open footplate. It is now preserved at the Smithsonian in Washington DC.

for rails. Soon after the process had got under way in 1857, the Midland ordered mild steel rails from Ebbw Vale, the company who had exhibited their rail selection at the Crystal Palace. They tried them out on a particularly heavily worked section of track at Derby, which was carrying traffic of up to 500 trains a day and where they were having to replace wrought iron rails at three monthly intervals. The steel rails remained down for fifteen years. Such spectacular results were not obtained in general, but the steel rails were everywhere a vast improvement on the old system. It removed restraints on locomotive engineers, who could now build heavier and more powerful engines. The arrival of cheap steel also meant that it could now be used in locomotive construction as well and not just for components such as tyres and springs. The use of steel for boilers, worked by more efficient machine tools, enabled boiler pressures to be increased beyond the 120psi that had seemed the maximum that could be safely allowed with wrought iron. Steel frame plates allowed greater weights to be supported and so made it possible to manufacture more powerful engines, a process that was to reach a grand climax in the 1940s with the Union Pacific 'Big Boy'. There can be no better example of how far locomotives had come than to compare this locomotive, an articulated monster with four cylinders and a 4-8-8-4 wheel arrangement and modest *Pioneer*. Weight had increased from 12½ tons to 340 tons, and wheelbase from 22 feet to 72 feet. The 'Big Boy' was the giant of the steam age, but by the time the class was being built the end of steam was already in sight.

In 1831 Michael Faraday had demonstrated that by passing an electric current through a wire it was possible to make a magnet move, the basis for the electric motor. Most people who knew about the experiment were impressed, but uncertain what to do with it. When William Gladstone asked what was the use of electricity, Faraday gave him the sort of answer that was designed to gladden the heart of a politician: 'One day, Sir, you may tax it.' George Stephenson was rather more far-sighted and declared that one day electricity would power the world. It was not, however, until 1879 that Werner Von Siemens demonstrated the world's first electric locomotive at the Berlin Trade Exhibition. Electricity did not exactly take the world by storm even then, though in 1883 Magnus Volk got permission to open a 2ft 8½in gauge electric railway along the sea front at Brighton. When originally built, the power supply was a gas engine working a Siemens dynamo providing electricity at 40 amps and 20 volts. It is still there today, the oldest surviving working electric railway in the world. Electric traction was slow to make its impact, though it proved invaluable for the new underground railway systems being developed as well as for street tramcars.

It was not the only threat to steam. In 1892, Rudolf Diesel took out an English patent for an internal combustion engine in which heat generated by compression was used to ignite oil pumped into the combustion chamber. The first use of the diesel engine on the railways was in comparatively small railcars, but it was rapidly developed and began to show its merits. In Germany the State Railways introduced a two-car diesel service that became known as the Flying Hamburger. On the inter-city service between Hamburg and Berlin it notched up an average speed of over 77mph that could be compared with Britain's finest express service, the Cheltenham Flyer that only managed 71mph.

The two systems would eventually be united in the diesel-electric, in which the diesel engine powered a dynamo to provide the current for the electric motor. There were huge advantages in making the changes, not least the fact that the new engines did not take hours to prepare for work as steam was raised. It was evident to engineers that steam was on the way out, and in 1960 the very last mainline locomotive to be built in Britain was rolled out of the works at Swindon and named *Evening Star*.

The engineers of 1851 would have expected to see changes over the next century; after all, many of them had seen dramatic developments enough in their own lifetimes. Would they have foreseen the end of the steam railway network? That we can never know, but it is doubtful if they would have felt depressed by the thought of it. They were men of vision, always looking to find something new and better than anything that had gone before. They were also, above all, practical men, not much given to nostalgia. They would probably have been more surprised to find engines that, in practical terms of everyday transport, were completely out of date, not only still being run but actually being rescued from scrap yards and restored. The steam locomotive has not disappeared.

Today, many of us delight still in the world of steam railways. There is something almost magical about the idea that tons of metal can be moved at speed by nothing more than fire and water. We can see exactly how things work, because they depend on mechanical linkages and, as we travel behind a steam locomotive, the sound of the engine is itself a running commentary on the work it is being asked to perform. There are few, if any, mechanical devices that have inspired this level of love and fascination. We visit steam railways and find stations restored to represent an era that has long gone, with posters advertising products that haven't been made for half a century and staff wearing uniforms that are fifty years or more out of date. It is all too easy to forget that all this was once brand-new and the very latest thing in modernity.

If one looks back over history it is possible to realise just what an achievement it was to develop the steam locomotive. In the first century since Newcomen's engine first nodded its ponderous head over a mine shaft, the engine had developed from an atmospheric engine

In 1925, there was a cavalcade at Shildon to mark the centenary of the Stockton & Darlington. Lined up in the photograph are some of the key locomotives of the early years: a replica of *Rocket* heads the procession, followed by *North Star*, the Crewe engine *Columbine* and *Cornwall*.

Almost two centuries of progress: the replica of Trevithick's Penydarren locomotive is dwarfed by the Class 47/4 diesel, photographed together at Cardiff. The original pioneering engine weighed in at approximately five tons compared to the 120 tons of its diesel successor.

to a true steam engine, but it was still a monstrously large beam engine, rooted to the spot. To turn such an engine into a machine that could thunder across railed tracks at high speed was one of the greatest achievements of the nineteenth century. The pioneers who achieved this feat had no patterns to work from, no precedents to follow and very little in the way of theoretical background to draw on. Yet in just fifty years they transformed the locomotive from an unwieldy contraption, rumbling along at little more than walking speed, to an efficient engine that is easily recognised as having the essentials that would enable it to develop and thrive for another hundred years. It ranks as one of the great achievements not just of their own age but in the whole history of mankind.

Glossary

Articulated locomotive: A locomotive with two power units – cylinder, valve gear and drive wheels – that are contained within a single frame.

Banking engine: An extra locomotive added to a conventional train to allow it to overcome a steep slope or incline. Such engines are often permanently housed at the foot of an incline.

Bell crank: A lever that allows movement through 90 degrees.

Blast pipe: The pipe that carries the exhaust steam from the cylinder to the smokebox below the chimney. In escaping up the chimney to the atmosphere, it draws hot gases from the firebox through the boiler tubes, increasing the draught through the fire in the grate.

Connecting rod: The iron, or later steel, rod that connects the piston either to a crank on the wheel of an outside cylinder locomotive or to the crank axle of an inside cylinder engine. It is tapered, the 'little end' attached to the piston rod, the 'big end' to the crank.

Counterbalance: This usually takes the form of a weight attached to the wheels to correct for the forces that are created by converting linear motion into rotative motion, which, if uncorrected, results in a hammer blow effect of the wheels on the track.

Coupling rods: The rods that connect driving wheels, turned directly by the action of the piston rods, to extra driving wheels.

Crank axle: An axle connected to driving wheels in an inside cylinder locomotive. The crank enables the linear motion of the piston rod to be converted into rotation.

Crosshead: The link connecting the piston rod, which in early locomotives moved vertically to connect with cranks or gears. In later locomotives, it was shorter and ran between slide bars to keep the motion parallel to the axis of the cylinder.

Crown: The roof of the inner shell of the firebox.

Cut off: The point during the steam cycle when the valve closes off the admission of steam to the cylinder, allowing the steam to expand during the rest of the power stroke.

Dome: A raised, covered space at the top of the boiler, which is used to allow the regulator valve to be kept well above the water level of the boiler, to prevent water being carried over with the steam to the cylinders.

Drive Wheels: The wheels with a direct connection to the pistons that provide the driving force for the locomotive.

Eccentric: As the name suggests, this is a circular disc, the sheave, placed on an axle, but whose centre does not coincide with that of that axle. An eccentric rod attached to the sheave by a strap, which allows free rotation of the sheave, converts the eccentric motion into linear motion. This is used to provide backwards and forwards movement in the valve, covering and uncovering the different ports. A slip-eccentric is one that can rotate freely with the axle, until it engages with one or other of two 'dogs' that will provide either forward or reverse movement. A fixed-eccentric only allows movement in one particular direction.

Expansion link: Part of the valve gear, consisting of a curved, slotted arm. A separate member can slide, up or down the link and can be used both to reverse the engine and to allow the cut-off point to be adjusted.

Feed Pump: The system used before the invention of the steam injector to get fresh water into the boiler.

Firebox: The compartment set at one end of the boiler that holds the fire. It developed into a structure with two main parts, an inner and outer firebox, with a space in between and held rigidly together by stays. The space in between held boiling water to conserve the heat. Hot gases from the fire pass through tubes fixed into the plate that forms the back of the firebox. By the 1850s, the firebox also contained a brick arch, which was used when coal replaced coke as a fuel.

Frame: The main frame of a locomotive comes in a variety of different forms. Three types were commonly used in early locomotives. The sandwich frame consisted of a timber centre, with iron plates bolted on to either side; bar frames were formed from wrought iron bars, usually either circular or square in cross-section; plate frames were made of broad iron plates, usually stretching the full length of the locomotive.

Gauges: early locomotives were generally limited to just two gauges: the pressure gauge indicating steam pressure in the boiler, in early locomotives a column of mercury, and the water gauge that showed water levels in the boiler.

Hammer blow: A force exerted on the wheel caused by the forces generated by the action of the connecting rod and crank.

Horn plate: A plate fixed around the opening for the axle to reinforce the frame.

Lap: The amount by which the valve overlaps the steam admission ports of the cylinder when set in the mid-position.

Lead: The amount by which the steam admission port is open when the piston has stopped at the end of a stroke.

Piston rod: The rod that connects the piston to the crosshead.

Priming: This occurs when water is carried over with the steam from the boiler to the cylinders.

Regulator: A valve fitted to the top of the boiler, usually in the dome, which can be opened to allow steam to pass down the steam pipes to the cylinders. A mechanical linkage connects it to the footplate and a lever that the driver uses to adjust the amount of steam reaching the cylinders. In America it is known as the throttle.

Safety valve: A valve usually held shut by a spring but which is forced open if steam pressure increases beyond a preset level, allowing the excess steam to escape to the atmosphere.

Slide valve: The system used in early locomotives to control the movement of steam through the cylinders. As the name suggests, it slides over the ports in the cylinder to cover or open them.

Smokebox: A chamber at the end of the boiler, below the chimney that collects both the hot gases from the boiler flues and exhaust steam from the cylinders.

Stephenson valve gear: A form of valve gear developed at the Robert Stephenson works in Newcastle that allowed for both reversing the engine and changing the cut off.

Tank engine: A locomotive in which both coal and water are stored within the locomotive frame. The coal is kept in a bunker behind the footplate and the water by the boiler. The most common examples are the side tank, with rectangular tanks set either side of the boiler and saddle tanks, where the boiler is curved to fit snugly over the top of the boiler.

Throat plate: the portion of the firebox that connects it to the end of the boiler.

Tractive effort: The effort needed to move the locomotive from the starting position, usually measured in terms of cylinder, diameter, stroke and driving wheel size, but also affected by the weight of the locomotive.

Walschaert valve gear: A valve gear that, like the Stephenson gear, allowed for variable cut off. It was widely used in continental Europe, but only became common in Britain in the latter part of the nineteenth century.

Water gauge: A gauge on the footplate that indicates the level of water in the boiler.

Whyte's wheel arrangement: A notation system devised in America to show wheel arrangement, through numbers: the first number indicates the number of leading wheels, the second driving wheels and the third trailing wheels. In Europe there is a variation, based on counting axles instead of wheels.

Select Bibliography

The following are the most important documentary sources that have been used in researching this book.

BAILEY, Michael R., *Loco Motion, the World's Oldest Steam Locomotives*, The History Press , 2014

BAIRD, Matthew, et al, *Illustrated Catalogue of Locomotives: Baldwin Locomotive Works*, reissued as Gutenberg Project e-book, 2012

BURTON, Anthony, *Richard Trevithick*, Aurum, 2000

BURTON, Anthony, *The Rainhill Story*, BBC, 1980

KINERT, Reed, *Early American Steam Locomotives*, Dover, 1962

LARKIN, Edgar R. and John G., *The Railway Workshops of Britain*, Macmillan, 1988

REED, Brian, *150 Years of British Steam Locomotives*, 1975, David and Charles

ROLT, L.T.C., *George and Robert Stephenson*, 1960 Penguin

ROLT, L.T.C., *Isambard Kingdom Brunel*, Penguin, 1957

ROSE, David, *The Willing Servant: A History of the Steam Locomotive* Tempus, 2004

SNELL, J.B., *Mechanical Engineering: Railways*, Longman, 1971

SOLOMON, Brian, *The Heritage of American Steam Railroads*, Readers Digest, 2001

WHITE, John W., *American Locomotives: An Engineering History, 1830-1889*, Johns Hopkins University Press, 1968 (republished 1997)

WOOD, Nicholas, *A Practical Treatise on Rail-Roads*, Knight and Lacey, 1825

YOUNG, Robert, *Timothy Hackworth and the Locomotive*, David and Charles 1923, reprinted 1975

Index